THE
CENTER

THE
CENTER

··

*The Anatomy of Power
in Washington*

by Stewart Alsop

HODDER AND STOUGHTON

The lines by William Butler Yeats on page 351 from "The Second Coming" are reprinted by permission of Mr. M. B. Yeats and Macmillan and Co. Ltd. from *Collected Poems* by William Butler Yeats.

First printed in Great Britain 1968

SBN 340 04280 X

Reproduced from the original U.S. setting by arrangement with Harper and Row.

Printed in Great Britain for Hodder and Stoughton Limited, St. Paul's House, Warwick Lane, London, E.C.4 by Compton Printing Ltd, London & Aylesbury

CONTENTS

PREFACE

A rather equivocal and shapeless pudding.

When I had this book about half finished, I was driving west from Capitol Hill on Constitution Avenue in a taxi, when it suddenly came home to me rather forcibly that I really wasn't at all qualified to write a book about Washington.

I was passing the National Gallery on my left, and I noticed on my right an imposing building in vaguely classic style, flanked by two muscular rearing horses. What was it? I peered out of the taxi, and made out a sign over a doorway: "FEDERAL TRADE COMMISSION." I'd never set foot in the building, and I had only a very vague notion of what the Federal Trade Commission was supposed to do. For that matter, although Johnnie Walker, the director of the National Gallery, is an old friend, and I've been in the place many times, it occurred to me that I am not really at all qualified to write about the National Gallery.

It was a dreary, drizzly day, and it was rush hour. As the taxi made its way slowly up the avenue my gloom deepened.

There were a lot of buildings I had never been in, and I had hardly a clue to what went on inside them. The Smithsonian —Dillon Ripley, the secretary of the Smithsonian, was another old friend, but I know no more about the place than any tourist. The FBI—well, I'd been investigated by the Bureau several times, for writing what I wasn't supposed to write, but unlike millions of school-age children, I'd never even seen the famous pistol range or the exhibit that shows how John Dillinger got his comeuppance.

We passed the White House, and I cheered up a bit—I knew a good deal about the White House. Then there were the ugly World War I Navy "tempos" on the left. The first time I'd been in them was back in 1946, when I started reporting in Washington. I'd surprised the late Admiral Forrest Sherman, then Chief of Naval Operations, by asking him whether we really needed a navy, now that we had the bomb—I'll never forget the look of honest amazement on his face. Since then, the Navy high command has moved to the Pentagon, and I had never been back.

Then there was the Pan-American Union building—I'd never been in it—and another huge building I'd never really looked at before. It, too, had a sign: "CIVIL SERVICE COMMISSION." All I knew about the Civil Service Commission was that it was headed by a very smart man called John Macy, and that the Civil Service it administered was a bureaucratic disaster for which a great-uncle of mine was largely responsible.

And so it went. It was during that taxi ride that I realized I really couldn't possibly write the sort of book I had set out to write. When I started work on this book, I vaguely intended to do for Washington what John Gunther has done for several continents. The reader would be taken "inside" Washington and given all the essential facts about the place —about the Civil Service Commission, the FBI, the Federal

Trade Commission; about HUD and HEW and CAB and FAA and FCC and IRS; about how the District of Columbia is, and is not, governed; about what is worth seeing in Washington and what isn't; and even about Black Washington—which is almost two-thirds of the city, and which is as alien and mysterious to White Washington as Ulan Bator or Semipalatinsk—and how its inhabitants really live.

Maybe somebody, someday, will write such a book. This is not it. Now I understand why John Gunther has never written *Inside Washington,* although he at one time firmly intended to do so. There are just too many Washingtons to get inside of. And a good many of these Washingtons are interesting only to the people who inhabit them or are in some way involved in them. This book turned out to be only about the Washington that is inhabited by political journalists and the people they write about.

There are reporters in Washington who can tell you all about the Civil Service Commission or the Federal Trade Commission or HUD or CAB, and there are others who can tell you about Black Washington and about how the District is run. All the various Washingtons are covered by some members of the city's press corps of fifteen hundred reporters. But the Washington that is covered by a Washington columnist and political writer—which I have been for more than twenty years—is a tunnel-vision Washington.

The Washington which a political journalist sees with his tunnel vision is the American equivalent of the Moscow which Soviet politicians, diplomats, and *apparatchiks* call "The Center." Moscow is the true center of political power in the Soviet Union, and in the Soviet political empire beyond the borders of Russia. In the same way, Washington has now become this country's true center of political power. This book is about the inhabitants of the American "Center," and about the power they exercise.

Until rather recently, Washington was the true center of political power in this country only very rarely and intermittently. It was "The Center" during the Civil War, to be sure. But during the long prewar political doldrums, the era of the doughface Presidents, it was no true center of power. Nor was it in the decades between Abraham Lincoln and Theodore Roosevelt. The Washington Henry Adams knew, in that era of the robber barons and the conquest of the West, was a sideshow, sometimes fascinating, more often dull.

Theodore Roosevelt (the great-uncle who foisted Civil Service on the government) and Woodrow Wilson, who hated each other, together made Washington a genuine national capital, and the First War accelerated the process. There followed another era of the doldrums. Nobody would have thought of calling the sleepy, rather inconsequential Southern town that Washington was in Calvin Coolidge's day the center of anything very important. It was only during the depression and the New Deal that Washington again became, this time for good, the true center of American power.

This power shift largely explains the almost lunatic hatred which the rich and respectable, above all in the Wall Street financial community, felt for Franklin Roosevelt. The hatred was surely irrational in economic terms—in the New Deal era the rich got steadily richer. But power as well as money was at stake, and, more even than the loss of money, men instinctively resent, and bitterly resist, the loss of power.

The Wall Street financial community is still powerful, of course, and there are other major power centers in the United States. But the ultimate power lies in Washington. (This is one reason why Wall Street lawyers and financiers who have exercised power, Washington style, and then returned to Manhattan almost always feel a certain nostalgia:

having dealt in billions, the symbol of Washington's power, they find it hard to reconcile themselves again to mere millions.) Washington's power is economic and financial as well as political—it is Washington that must choose between easy money and hard money, between applying the brakes or the accelerator to the economy. But Washington's essential power is political. It is in Washington that the great domestic crises must be dealt with, and the great crises of foreign policy too, up to and including the ultimate choice between peace and war.

This centralization of power in Washington is no doubt a regrettable fact. But it is a fact. Washington is now permanently the center of the United States, as Moscow is Russia's center, or London England's. It is this, and only this, that makes Washington worth reading about. In this book, there are brief excursions outside The Center, but The Center—the complex political community which exercises power in Washington and which is the city's only reason for being—is the subject.

The Center is also the theme of this book, insofar as it has a theme. In his first volume of memoirs, *Winds of Change*, Harold Macmillan recalls a remark Winston Churchill made at one of his fortnightly luncheons with members of his shadow cabinet when he was leader of the opposition. A "rather equivocal and shapeless pudding" was served, which Churchill regarded with distaste. He called to the waiter: "Pray, take away this pudding, it has no theme." As Macmillan observes, this incident is "a warning to authors as well as to cooks." Unfortunately, this book is something of a pudding.

For power is like a pudding. It is formless, or rather it has so many forms that it is "equivocal and shapeless." Moreover, it is impossible to write about power without writing about the people who exercise it. As a result, this book is at

least as much about people as about power. And the people
who inhabit The Center, like Churchill's pudding, have no
theme.

Most of them have certain common characteristics. Most
of them are able people—a process of natural selection
winnows out the really incompetent and the really stupid, in
the top jobs. Most of them are ambitious, and most of them
enjoy the exercise of power. Otherwise they would not be
where they are, for power, rather than money, is Washington's measure of success. But the faces of the people who
exercise power in Washington are always changing, and it is
impossible for a cook to establish a theme when the ingredi-
ents of his recipe are constantly being altered. One thing is
wholly predictable: some of the people discussed in this
book will no longer be exercising power by the time the
book is published. Moreover, it would be wholly artificial to
try to find some single theme, some common denominator, as
between Lyndon Johnson and, say, Justice Potter Stewart; or
between Richard Helms and Everett Dirksen. They are not
only different men; they are different *kinds* of men. So the
book, it must be faced, is a pudding.

Even for a pudding-book, it is customary to express gratitude in a preface. I owe a debt of gratitude to my brother
Joseph Alsop, who made me a political journalist in the first
place. He had written a political column before the war with
Robert Kintner, who after the war left Washington for the
greener pastures of the broadcasting business. Casting about
for a new partner, my brother chose me—rather eccentri-
cally, since I'd never written a line for a newspaper—and we
worked together for twelve years. Later, when an ambitious
journalism student asked me how to get to be a columnist, I
gave the only possible reply: "Have a brother who already is
one." A good many of my brother's ideas rubbed off on me.
And although we disagree in some respects—notably on the

likelihood of anything resembling genuine victory for our side in Vietnam—I suspect that in the pages that follow he will recognize some unconscious plagiarisms, and some that aren't unconscious at all. In any case, this book owes a lot to him, and so do I.

I also owe a debt of gratitude to that ancient periodical, the *Saturday Evening Post*. I first began writing for the *Post* more than twenty years ago, and the number of articles and columns I have done for the magazine is positively mind-boggling by this time. I have occasionally plagiarized from myself, and from the *Post*, in this book, notably in the chapter on the Supreme Court—about which I knew next to nothing before the *Post* editors gave me a rather reluctant green light to write an article on the Court in 1967.

That is not the only reason I owe a debt of gratitude to the *Post*. In the days when Ben Hibbs was editor, the magazine editorially was well to my right, and nowadays, in some respects at least, the editors are rather to my left. But never during either regime have I felt the faintest breath of pressure to conform to any editorial line; the editors have always held to the rather old-fashioned view that the opinions expressed in a political article should be the writer's, not the editors'. This is why, despite its many vicissitudes, Ben Franklin's old periodical has always been a good magazine to write for.

And this suggests another way in which this has turned out to be a different sort of book from the one I had planned at first. It is not only a political journalist's book. It is a book by a political journalist called Stewart Alsop—and this fact has narrowed the tunnel vision of Washington more than I had anticipated.

Obviously, another political journalist would see another White House, another State Department, another Lyndon Johnson, another CIA, another Washington. It is possible to be factual about Washington, and in this book there are a good many facts which I have collected in more than twenty years of Washington reporting. But it is not really possible to be "objective" about Washington, for the word suggests that there are immutable truths about the place, and there are none. Each Washingtonian has his own favorite truths about Washington, which to other denizens of the city may not be truths at all. These are mine.

THE
CENTER

1

THE DRAMA OF CONFLICT

The sons-of-bitches are gaining on us.

....

It is best for a reporter to admit his bias. My bias is this: I like Washington. It is not only, after a couple of decades, my home town. It is also, in all the world, my favorite city.

There are lots of things wrong with Washington, of course. As everybody knows, the summers can be dreadful. There are no really first-class restaurants, and the parking lot operators practice legal highway robbery. Persons interested in theater, music, and the like are fed on very thin fare. The tax laws have encouraged real estate speculators to turn much of downtown Washington into a characterless mass of flat-faced, steel-glass-and-concrete office buildings.

There are other things that are more profoundly wrong with Washington. There is too much crime, and there are too many poor Negroes crowded into too small an area, which is, of course, one reason why there is too much crime. There are also things that are very wrong with the government of the

1

United States, which is Washington's only reason for existence. Even so, the bias is there: I like Washington.

I like Washington for small reasons, like May, or the
eleven o'clock rule, or the occasional whiff of the past. But I
like Washington for larger reasons, too.

The tourists come to Washington in April to see the
cherry blossoms, when Washington is often chilly and
blossomless. They ought to come in May. May is a lovely
month, but nowhere in the world lovelier than in Washington. Washington's May makes up for Washington's August,
which is saying a great deal.

As for the eleven o'clock rule, it is a lifesaver for anyone
who has to dine out a lot, and for most denizens of Political
Washington dining out is part of the job. The eleven o'clock
rule is a curious, un-American custom imposed by the fact
that Washington is filled with diplomats and other protocol-
conscious persons. The ranking guest leaves the house at
eleven—eleven-fifteen at the latest—which means that
everyone can get to bed sober and at a reasonable hour. And
because of the eleven o'clock rule, a sensible hostess serves
dinner within half an hour of the time the guests were
invited, without the eternal standing and guzzling which
precedes dinner in New York and most American cities. New
Yorkers who have lived long enough in Washington to become used to such amenities never again quite accustom
themselves to the barbarities of dining out in New York.

As for that whiff of the past, Washington is a young city,
of course, even by American standards. In 1800, when the
federal government moved from Philadelphia to the "Federal City" and Abigail Adams first hung her washing in the
East Room of the unfinished White House, Washington was
not a city at all, but a rather slovenly bad joke. But largely
because George Washington's dream of the Federal City
(modestly, he never called it Washington) as a busy indus-

trial center never came true, the smell of the past is strong in Washington.

It used to be strongest of all in the White House. As a very young man this reporter, as a rather distant Roosevelt relation, first attended family gatherings at Franklin Roosevelt's White House. (My father was always infuriated when the Alsops were identified in the newspapers as "Roosevelt kin." He felt that the Roosevelts ought to be identified as "Alsop kin.") In those days the big house was like some very old, very pleasant, slightly down-at-heel country mansion of a very rich family. The past was everywhere, in every crack in the plaster and creak in the staircase. Now there are no more cracks and no more creaks, and not much past either.

When the whole interior of the White House was hauled out, during Harry Truman's administration, so that the house consisted only of the outer walls, the past was hauled out with it. Mrs. John F. Kennedy did her brilliant best to refurbish and rearrange the house in such a way as to remind the visitor that it is an old house, with much history lived out in it. But it really isn't an old house any more, but a very new house with a commodious facsimile of what once was there built inside old walls. The house is not like a rich family's old mansion any more, but like the new house of a very rich man, filled with very expensive old furniture.

Was the gutting of the White House really necessary? Mr. Truman had no doubt that it was. I wrote to ask him about it and received this answer: "There was no question that the interior was in danger of imminent collapse and it was not possible to consider an archaeological restoration." Well, maybe so. But as John Kenneth Galbraith has pointed out, old houses always seem on the verge of disintegration, which is part of their charm, but they never do actually collapse.

The restorer-vandals have been at work on Capitol Hill, but they have not yet succeeded in excising the smell of the past—since the gutting of the White House it is stronger there than anywhere in Washington. Everyone who interests himself in such matters is aware of the horrors perpetrated by the nonarchitect, Architect of the Capitol George Stewart, and by his Congressional backers, notably that most admirable man, the late Speaker of the House Sam Rayburn. The chief horror is the extension of the east front of the Capitol. It is a faithful but meaningless replica of the old east front, in lifeless dull gray marble. As this is written, a drive is on similarly to desecrate the west front. But even if the vandals triumph, the smell of the past will still prevail in the interior of the old building.

It is conventional to admire the old Supreme Court Chamber, and like many conventions this is a sensible one. It takes very little imagination to see that semicircular, rather cozy room as it was when the Senate sat there, and to hear Webster thundering, or Calhoun defending "the South, the poor South," or Clay exercising the wily arts of compromise. But there are also odd corners, which are hardly known at all, and which are much as they were when Benjamin Latrobe, with Thomas Jefferson eagerly peering over his shoulder, began the building of the Capitol, even before the British in 1814 made a "most magnificent ruin" of the place, as Latrobe wrote to Jefferson.

There are plenty of other places in Washington where suddenly the past is present: in the corridors of the pre-Civil War Treasury Building, with the gilded pilasters topped by federal eagles; in the later Old State Department Building, with its open fireplaces and its endearing flounces and furbelows; in the Smithsonian Institution's red sandstone Norman castle; in the old houses of Georgetown. But for a real sense of the seamlessness of time's web, the place to go is Capitol Hill. In any case, the smell of the past is not hard to find in Washington for those who like it.

But the best thing about Washington is, quite simply, the people who live there. The people who live in Political Washington—in The Center—are involved in the business of governing the United States, or in the business of dealing with the rest of the world on behalf of the United States, or dealing with the United States on behalf of the rest of the world. In short, they are involved in politics, in its broadest dictionary sense—"the science and art of government . . . the theory or practice of managing the affairs of public policy."

It follows that those who find politics interesting find the people who live in Washington interesting. Mind you, Washington has its generous quota of bores. It is very easy to come across denizens of Political Washington who are only too happy to try out their latest speech on you, complete with gestures. Some of the women, who are in Washington only because they married Senator So-and-so or Secretary Such-and-such in their long-lost nubile youth, are boring quite beyond the bounds of belief. The vivid phrase "I felt as though I were being nibbled to death by a duck" was invented by a male Washingtonian subjected to the dinner-table conversation of such a rapaciously tedious female. But if you are interested in politics, it is not *necessary* to be bored in Washington.

Just as it is necessary to be interested in automobiles in Detroit, or movies in Hollywood, or insurance in Hartford, it is absolutely essential in Washington to be interested in politics. Culturally minded, nonpolitical persons tend to go mad if exposed to Washington for too long a period. Especially New Yorkers and especially ladies. But if you are interested in the political process, Washington is an interesting, even an exciting, place. There is drama in Washington—more drama, surely, than in making automobiles, or writing insurance, or even making movies.

Washington's drama is, curiously, a recent discovery for the rest of the country. Until recently, for example, the Washington novel, aside from such exotica as Henry Adams' *Democracy* and bits of Edith Wharton, hardly existed. Then Allen Drury wrote his *Advise and Consent*. Since then the bookstores have been flooded with Washington novels, in which generals unleash nuclear war, Senators commit sodomy, Presidents go mad, and beautiful hostesses leap relentlessly in and out of the beds of Very Important Persons. No doubt there is a certain amount of leaping in and out of bed among the town's movers and shakers, but far less than in the novels, for Political Washington is a rather moral town. The drama of Washington is of a different order.

It is of two kinds. First, and rarest, is the ceremonial drama, which can be unforgettable. A Presidential Inauguration is always moving, for it symbolizes the legitimate assumption of great power—and the transfer of power without risk of bloodshed is in itself a great, and historically novel, accomplishment. The Inauguration of John F. Kennedy was peculiarly moving, in part because it also symbolized the transfer of power from one generation to another. And surely no one who witnessed it will ever forget the ceremonial drama of the Kennedy funeral—the rearing riderless horse, the boots reversed in the stirrups, the drums beating to the tempo of the human heart.

But the drama of Washington lies more often in conflict than in ceremony. It is conflict that chiefly produces drama, and conflict is the stuff of which Washington is made—and always has been, back to the time when George Washington's two chief lieutenants become mortal enemies. When conflict concerns vital national issues, as in the case of Jefferson and Hamilton, the drama takes on grandeur. And although Washington has always had its share of squabbles based on personal ambition and petty rivalry, the basic conflict almost always revolves around issues of genuine importance—sometimes, of life-and-death importance. In today's Washington, for example, it is around such issues that the conflict between Lyndon Johnson and Robert Kennedy, as dramatic in its way as any conflict in Washington's history, revolves.

Anyone who has lived in Washington for a good many years can recall, out of the jumbled attic of memory, a few scenes that are still real and vivid after the passage of the years. I remember, for example, a dinner party in the spring of 1950 at my brother Joseph Alsop's Georgetown house. Dean Rusk, who was then the youthful Assistant Secretary of State for the Far East, was there. So was the Secretary of the Army, Frank Pace. So was George Kennan, then chief of the State Department's Policy Planning Staff. So were various other officials, as well as the accustomed assortment of politicians, private persons, and pretty girls.

It was a pleasant evening, and a relaxed party—the Berlin blockade had ended, and Senator Joe McCarthy had not yet become the Washington obsession he later became. The men were chatting over the brandy and cigars when Dean Rusk was called to the telephone. He returned gray-faced, and although the evening was still young, he said hasty goodbyes, murmuring that "something" had happened. Frank Pace was next, then George Kennan, then one or two lesser officials. No one was tactless enough to ask what the "something" was—that is contrary to the Washington ground rules—but it was obviously something pretty big.

It was. That was the evening that brought the first news of the North Korean attack on South Korea. In a properly written novel or movie script, somebody would have said something modeled on Lord Grey's famous curtain line: "The lights are going out all over Europe." Instead, everybody just muttered. But an adequate if wordless comment was made a few days later by George Kennan. At another party he was seen doing a little jig. The decision had just been made to commit American forces to the defense of South Korea. The jig was an expression of Kennan's delight. He was, and is, anything but a war hawk, but he knew better than most how steep a price the West would have to pay in time if the United States failed to meet Joseph Stalin's carefully calculated challenge in Korea.

Another small scene, which occurred not long after, and which was in some ways a direct sequel of the first (for Joe McCarthy was a product of the guilt and frustrations of the Korean War), frightened me more than it should have, as I can see in retrospect. It occurred on the floor of the Senate, during one of the debates that followed the McCarthy charge that there were large but constantly shifting numbers of Communists operating in the State Department. Mc-Carthy, with much advance beating of drums, presented his "evidence," in a long speech late in the evening, before a full Senate and crowded galleries. He had a lectern, piled high with documents on his various "cases." Any Senator, he said, who wanted to examine the evidence on his cases was at liberty to do so. Then he went into his familiar "I-have-in-my-hand" routine.

About halfway through the performance, Senator Herbert Lehman recognized one of McCarthy's "cases" and knew it was false. He rose, reminded the Senate of McCarthy's promise to let any Senator examine the evidence, and as he spoke he walked down the aisle and stood in front of McCarthy, with his hand out. The two men stared at each other, and McCarthy giggled his strange, rather terrifying little giggle. Lehman looked around the crowded Senate, obviously appealing for support. Not a man rose.

"Go back to your seat, old man," McCarthy growled at Lehman. The words do not appear in the *Congressional*

Record, but they were clearly audible in the press gallery. Once more, Lehman looked all around the chamber, appealing for support. He was met with silence and lowered eyes. Slowly, he turned and walked—or rather waddled, for he had a peculiar, ducklike way of walking—back to his seat.

"There goes the end of the Republic," I muttered to my wife, whom I had smuggled into the press gallery to see the show. It was a poor imitation of Lord Grey, but it did not seem exaggerated at the time. For at the time this triumph of the worst Senator who has ever sat in the Senate over one of the best did seem a decisive moment. The silence of the Senate that evening was a measure of the fear which McCarthy inspired in almost all politicians—an understandable fear, for McCarthy controlled absolutely something like a quarter of the votes in the big swing states, enough to make or break any politician. Thus old Senator Lehman's back, waddling off in retreat, seemed to symbolize the final defeat of decency and the triumph of the yahoos.

I was wrong, of course. McCarthy got his richly deserved comeuppance. The liberal intellectuals who despise President Johnson for his uncouth ways forget that the chief architect of McCarthy's destruction—other than McCarthy himself—was the young Democratic leader of the Senate. Surely one of Lyndon Johnson's more astonishing achievements as a Senate leader was the vote of every Democrat in the Senate, including the crustiest of the Southern conservatives, to censure McCarthy. (There was one absentee for reasons of health— John F. Kennedy of Massachusetts.) In any case, I was wrong, and in due time the country was cured of the strange McCarthy malignancy.

This suggests another reason why I like Washington. To the occasional visitor, and especially to the foreigner unaccustomed to our disorderly ways, Washington may seem an appalling capital for a great nation. And yet, over a period of years, Washington comes to seem an oddly reassuring place.

An elaborate, rather pointless, but curiously memorable tale which the late Frank Kent, a great newspaperman, used to tell, serves to suggest why. The story, which Kent claimed was true, was about an ancient and long since retired Maryland judge, who came to Baltimore once a year to see the sights and enjoy terrapin Maryland at the Baltimore Club. While in Baltimore he occupied the quarters of the chief judge—a previous chief judge had been his friend, and after his friend's death, he continued to use, as if by right, the quarters of his successors.

One day the current chief judge found it difficult to concentrate, because his aged colleague kept striding up and down, declaiming, "They're gaining on us, they're gaining on us all the time." At length, overcome by curiosity, the chief judge asked the obvious question: "Sir, you do me the honor to share my quarters. Do you mind telling me *who* is gaining on us?"

"Why, goddammit, Chief Judge," replied the ancient jurist, "the sons-of-bitches are gaining on us, of course. I counted twenty-six of them on Charles Street this morning."

In Washington the sons-of-bitches always seem to be gaining on us. Native yahoos or foreign enemies always seem to be on the verge of triumph. But the sons-of-bitches never quite catch up—which is why Washington comes to seem, in the long run, a reassuring place to live.

Frank Kent was also fond of instructing fledgling reporters (including this one, just after the Second War) on how to regard politicians: "The only way for an honest reporter to look at a politician is *down*." He was quite right—or, at least, an honest reporter has no business looking *up* to a politician. And yet, to be fair, the average Washington politician, though he may not inspire reverence, inspires a certain fingers-crossed confidence in the American political future.

The inhabitant of Washington—Political Washington, that is—has his nose rubbed hard and daily in the political realities. He is therefore no perfectionist. As Russell Baker has written:

The Washingtonian is too sophisticated to believe any more in solutions. . . . This makes him a professional and accounts for the glazed look which quickly betrays him in, say, a typical New York conversation about world problems after someone has announced that everything would turn out happily if only people would love one another.

The glazed look also betrays the Washingtonian when out-of-towners suggest that all politicians are crooks, thieves, or liars, and all civil servants and officeholders a bunch of lazy bureaucrats. The fact is that the level of ability at both ends of Pennsylvania Avenue is a good deal higher than the American citizenry deserves.

For a good many years, in company with such professionals as Louis Harris and Oliver Quayle, I have been going on polling expeditions to ring doorbells and ask questions of (to quote Mark Sullivan) "the great rancid American people." Public-opinion polling is fascinating in its way, and it makes good copy. But at the end of a long hard day of polling, it is sometimes tempting to succumb to the notion that the American people are a lot of ill-informed louts, filled to the eyeballs with misinformation and wrongheaded prejudice.

It is certainly true that most Americans are much less interested in the processes by which they are governed than in, say, baseball or their favorite television western. Political reporters and commentators are writing for 10 percent of the total population—and that is a generous estimate. And yet by some mysterious instinctive process most of the men the ill-informed citizenry choose to send to Washington are rather able men. Some are very able indeed. And very few are crooks or fools.

Joe McCarthy is the only politician or major public figure I ever really hated. I hated him not because he was a fool or a crook (he was not, at any rate, a fool) but because he came so close to destroying the American political system, as that scene with Herbert Lehman suggests. He did not play the game according to the rules.

The game, when played according to the rules, can be a rather uninspiring and even, on occasion, a rather sleazy game, with much mutual back-scratching or arm-twisting. But there it is—the system works, not very well, but better than any other. As Winston Churchill said: "Democracy is the worst form of government, except all those other forms that have been tried from time to time."

Democracy is also the most entertaining form of government. What seems to me the most striking characteristic of the Communist form of government is that it is so intolerably dull. As soon as you land in Moscow, or Bucharest, or Prague, or Budapest, or Sofia (but not Warsaw—Poles don't know how to be boring), you are engulfed in a great smog of tedium. Conflict, which is the chief ingredient of political drama, exists, all right, but it is concealed behind closed and locked doors. And everything that makes politics fun—the gossip, the jokes, the predictions about who is going to get whose job, the stories about some awful thing the President said to an amazed lady the other night, the head-counting before a major vote, the freewheeling argument on the issues—all this is wholly lacking.

It is good, too, to live in the midst of great events, to live in history—even as an onlooker, a mere provider of footnotes. And Washington is where most great events either begin or are molded and altered or end. In short, my bias is there: I like Washington. And at least the sons-of-bitches haven't quite caught up with us, not yet.

2

THE WASHINGTONS

The cities within the city.

••

The city of Washington is a city of 803,000 people and 71 square miles. (It was exactly 100 square miles before Congress, in 1846, rather absent-mindedly and without any serious debate, ceded Arlington County to Virginia.) In a human sense, Washington is not really a city at all—it is a series of cities-within-a-city. More than most big towns, it is a kind of amoeba-metropolis. It has divided itself into different cities, which have in turn divided within themselves.

In terms of population, The Center—Political Washington, directly concerned in the decisions and conflicts which shape the domestic government and the foreign and defense policies of the United States—is the smallest of all these cities-within-a-city.

The ordinary citizens of Moscow call their city, quite simply, Moskva. Moscow is The Center only to the members of the party and government *apparat*. Even in Russia, where the government (or the party, through the government)

14

decides such matters as the length of women's dresses and the production goal for ice skates, the members of the *apparat* are a small minority. In this country, despite the inexorable growth of government, the minority is smaller.

As this is written, there are 312,295 civilian government employees in and around the District of Columbia. There are 75,332 military, for a total of almost 400,000. All these people (many of them live in the suburbs, of course) are part of Government Washington. But only a very small proportion of them are truly inhabitants of The Center—of the Washington directly involved in the real business of governing the country and running its relations with the rest of the world.

If the tunnel-vision definition of The Center given in the Preface is accepted—"the Washington which is inhabited by political journalists and the people they write about"—The Center is really a very small place. Its population is in the rather low thousands.

The President and all the other members of the White House staff, above the cook-and-bottle-washer level, are of course inhabitants of The Center. So are all the policy-making officials and ranking Foreign Service Officers of the State Department. So are the Pentagon's two dozen or so policy-making civilian officials and three dozen or so general officers involved in nonhousekeeping chores. So are about fifteen or twenty of the leading movers and shakers in the CIA.

Add all the members of Congress and the Supreme Court (although a good many members of Congress hardly qualify under the above definition). Add all the members of the Cabinet and the four or five most important subordinate officials in the Treasury Department, Justice, and Interior, and perhaps two or three from Labor, Commerce, and Agriculture. Add the top men in the regulatory agencies and the Budget Bureau, and in such specialized agencies as the Atomic Energy Commission and the Council of Economic

Advisers. Add perhaps forty key foreign diplomats. Add a few hundred officials at the top of the Civil Service hierarchy, and throw in, for good measure, two or three hundred members of the press corps. Even if you add wives as well, the total population of The Center comes to not much more than five thousand or so.

Of the rest, the hundreds of thousands of government employees who are not a part of "the Washington that is inhabited by political journalists and the people they write about," the vast majority are in the Civil Service. This means, of course, that they have an unbreakable armlock on their jobs. Short of committing high crimes and misdemeanors in a very public way, there is hardly anything they can do to get themselves fired. This is one reason why almost everybody—including most intelligent members of the Civil Service—agrees that the Civil Service system is a disaster.

In 1945, after a seven-year stretch with the government, John Fischer wrote a witty article for *Harper's Magazine*, called "Let's Go Back to the Spoils System." "It can be argued in all seriousness," he wrote,

that Congress would do well to wipe out the Civil Service, hide, horns, and tallow, and go back to the old-fashioned spoils system. . . . The constant threat of a change in administration would help keep all government employees on their toes; they would never dare to sink into the smug mediocrity which now afflicts so many civil servants who are sure of indefinite tenure.

There have been various attempts to reform the system since Fischer wrote the above, but the article is in no way dated. Yet there is one very cogent argument against Fischer's proposal. The power of the Presidency is already enormous. A hire-and-fire power over the 2,951,083 civilians in federal employment would vastly augment that power. To illustrate the point, let those who very much dislike Richard Nixon imagine him as President presiding over a spoils system, and let those who very much dislike Lyndon Johnson imagine him doing the same thing. What Winston Churchill said of democracy, in short, is true of the Civil Service: it is a terrible system, but no one can think of a better one.

In fact, terrible as the system is, it produces some very competent people, especially in the thin upper level involved in the making of policy. The conservative Republican businessmen whom President Eisenhower brought into the government were uniformly surprised by the high quality of the men they found in the upper federal bureaucracy. The reaction of Secretary of the Treasury George Humphrey, the dominant figure of the first Eisenhower administration, was typical.

"I see everything through business eyes," he told me in an interview shortly after taking office. Through his "business eyes" he had always seen government as the enemy: "You've got to do something to bring this octopus the government has become back under control." But then he remarked, in a somewhat puzzled tone, that he had found in the Treasury "a pretty good setup." A good many of the top Treasury civil servants, he continued in a tone of considerable astonishment, "would be perfectly competent to take a big job in industry." Being a conservative Republican big businessman, Humphrey had clearly expected to find in government only incompetent drones with sinister leftish leanings. In amusing contrast, the Kennedy liberal intellectuals, conditioned since New Deal days to suppose that charges of waste, incompetence, and bureaucracy were mere Republican propaganda, were appalled by the bureaucratic sludge which they encountered in the government. Those appalled included the President himself. As Arthur Schlesinger has written:

Kennedy . . . was determined . . . to recover presidential control over the sprawling feudalism of government. This became a central theme of the administration and, in some respects, a central frustration. The presidential government, coming to Washington aglow with new ideas and a euphoric sense that it could not go wrong, promptly collided with the feudal barons of the permanent government, entrenched in their domains and fortified by their sense of proprietorship; and the permanent government, confronted by this invasion, began almost to function . . . as a resistance movement, scattering to the *maquis* in order to pick off the intruders. This was especially true in foreign affairs.

Kennedy himself was particularly frustrated by the State Department. Once in 1962, when I interviewed him for an article in the *Saturday Evening Post* on his "grand design," he mentioned another article I had written, which was then on the stands—"What's Wrong with the State Department?" "I read your piece," he said, and added that he thought it was "pretty good." But I had clearly not answered my own question to his satisfaction. "What's *really* wrong with the State Department?" he asked, with the familiar jabbing motion of the right index finger.

Then he volunteered a curious observation. Suppose you had a thousand people in a big room, he said, and they were all dressed exactly alike. If there were twenty FSOs—Foreign Service Officers—among them you could pick out the twenty from the rest right away. "There's something about them," he said.

He was not, of course, implying any lack of masculinity—he meant only that the State Department men, having lived their adult lives in the closed world of the Foreign Service, had developed special characteristics of their own. Kennedy had his favorites among the senior FSOs—he admired especially Llewellyn Thompson and Charles E. Bohlen, both former ambassadors to the Soviet Union—but he found it hard to communicate with most FSOs. So, for that matter, did Franklin Roosevelt. So does Lyndon B. Johnson.

Early in Kennedy's administration, former Secretary of State Dean Acheson proposed to Kennedy that he and former Secretary of Defense Robert Lovett be assigned a murderous task. They should be given joint authority to fire or retire a big proportion of the top-level State Department employees. This winnowing operation, Acheson acknowledged, might be unfair to a good many people, and would certainly make Lovett and himself the best-hated men in Washington. But in the end, Acheson told the President, the State Department would be rid of much deadwood. Probably unwisely, the President, on the advice of Secretary of State Rusk, refused Acheson's offer.

The fact is that *every* government department and agency is overstaffed to some degree—above all, the Defense Department, where the military bureaucracy is even sludgier than the civilian bureaucracy. But short of such not entirely serious proposals as John Fischer's, no one really knows what to do about it. And the fact remains that the system, for all its faults, manages to produce remarkably competent and hard-working professional public servants in the upper ranks.

The men at the top of the civil-servant heap are known as "Indians," in the Washington shorthand. The term originated in the Pentagon, in the pre-McNamara days when the Joint Chiefs of Staff really ran the Defense Department. Especially in the all-important budget sessions of the Joint Chiefs, each of the Chiefs was flanked by his "Indians," whose task it was to buttress and document the arguments of their Chief for more money for his service and less for the others. The term spread out from the Pentagon, so that any department head or major Presidential appointee is a Chief and his top-ranking civil servants are his Indians.

The Indians at the top of the Civil Service hierarchy, who are involved in the real business of governing the country and dealing with the world, are very powerful in a quiet way. They are the people who really run the government on a day-to-day basis, and they are an important part of The Center.

There are not many of them. At the very top, in Grade 18 (or GS-18, known as a "super-grade"), there are only 420 at this writing. There are 1,019 in the next grade down, GS-17. (The GS-18 civil servants earn $27,055 a year, and the GS-17s get $23,788 to $26,960.) Not all of these "policy-making" civil servants live in Washington, of course, and some of those who do have essentially routine, nonpolitical jobs. In short, only a few hundred of the more than 300,000 civil servants in the Washington area are really an active part of The Center.

The rest live lives of modest comfort and quiet routine, mostly in the suburbs, and they have hardly more to do with the crises and dramas of The Center than the citizens of Dubuque or Spokane. Their jobs are, by and large, like white-collar jobs in any big business—except that, because the sludge is even thicker in government than in business, the government white-collar jobs are apt to be even less exciting.

Diplomatic Washington is a part of The Center, but increasingly a separate part. It is increasingly separate partly because it has grown so big. In 1938 there were 18 foreign ambassadors in Washington and 5 ministers. Today there are 112 ambassadors and 2 ministers. The two ministers are from the nonexistent countries of Estonia and Latvia. The rank of minister is considered too lowly for the emissaries of such nations as Chad and the Central African Republic. The arrival of ambassadors from dozens of such newly created nations by no means entirely accounts for the vast expansion of the diplomatic corps. The embassies themselves have obeyed Parkinson's Law with almost as much enthusiasm as the U.S. Government.

The British Embassy, for example (which has always been the number-one embassy in Washington, whatever the protocol rank of the ambassador), has grown from thirty people in 1939 to more than six hundred today. This growth has had in turn an oddly insulating effect on the diplomatic corps. Before the Second War, and to a lesser extent even in the Truman and early Eisenhower years, a diplomat of middle rank from an important embassy, unless he was immensely unlikable or a born recluse (which diplomats are not supposed to be), was a full citizen of Political Washington. Washington was a cozy town then, and a reasonably well-liked diplomat was very much part of the scene—there was no other scene for him to be a part of.

Nowadays even a high-ranking diplomat is lost in the crowd, and a big embassy like the British Embassy has become more and more an inward-looking, self-contained world of its own. Most of the inhabitants of this small world have only the most casual contact with the natives, and those who make an effort to see citizens of the United States, and acquaint themselves with their strange tribal customs, are considered odd and are looked upon with a shade of suspicion.

There are exceptions. David Ormsby-Gore, now Lord Harlech, who was made British Ambassador at President Kennedy's request, was as influential as any but a handful of Kennedy's closest advisers, and thus the most effective British diplomat since Teddy Roosevelt's close friend, Cecil Spring-Rice. Harlech was very much an integral part of Kennedy's Washington. So, for different reasons, including a beautiful wife, was former French Ambassador Hervé Alphand. Their successors occupy no comparable position in their relations with the Johnson White House.

This suggests another reason for the increasing isolation of the Washington diplomatic corps. Bill Moyers once pointed out that Jack Kennedy, as the son of the Ambassador to the Court of St. James's, had commuted across the Atlantic dozens of times while still in his teens, whereas until he was a grown man Lyndon Johnson had "never crossed a body of water larger than the Pedernales River." By nature and instinct and background—at least until Vietnam engaged his obsessive attention—Lyndon Johnson looked inward, toward the mountains and the plains, while Jack Kennedy looked outward, toward the oceans.

Partly because he is not used to them, Johnson and foreigners do not ordinarily mix well together—former German Chancellor Erhard was about the only foreign dignitary who seemed to feel really comfortable in a Texas hat. The President tends to treat ambassadors rather as though they were Senators in his Majority Leader days. He has given a number of them, including Soviet Ambassador Dobrynin, the famous Johnson "treatment"—of which more later—and he has several times given a sort of collective treatment to five or six Latin-American ambassadors all at once, to their collective horror. Any diplomat, and especially any Latin-American diplomat, is instinctively suspicious of his colleagues, and fearful of uttering in their presence any but the most sterile platitudes. Johnson's mass sessions with the Latin Americans passed in stunned, suspicious silence on the part of the emissaries. These experiments in mass diplomacy have now been abandoned.

As this suggests, the subtleties of diplomacy are lost on Lyndon Johnson. An ambassador is not, after all, like a Senator; he is not his own man, but his government's man. This has frustrated the President's efforts to deal with the diplomats as he once dealt so brilliantly with his fellow Senators. As one result, the impact of the diplomatic corps on The Center is certainly less today than it was in Kennedy's day, and probably less than in Eisenhower's or Truman's or Franklin Roosevelt's day. Increasingly, the diplomatic corps is in The Center, but not of it. Increasingly, it is Diplomatic Washington, a separate little city of its own.

The august Supreme Court, at the apex of the "coequal" judicial branch of the government, is also in but not of Washington. Some Justices—Justice Felix Frankfurter before he died, Justice Arthur Goldberg before he resigned to go to the United Nations, Justice William O. Douglas—were or are very much part of Political Washington. But a man like Justice Douglas is a citizen of Political Washington despite the fact that he is on the Court, not because of it. The Supreme Court has rather the same effect on a man as great wealth: it hedges him off from his fellows, makes even the most bonhomous of men unapproachable. It is not correct to talk to an enormously rich man about the most interesting thing about him—his money. It is even less correct to talk to a Justice about his Court and the issues which confront it.

The press is very much part of the Washington political community—rather, some critics of the press suggest, as a flea is part of a dog. Reporters are in the same dependent position as the flea, but then the press is essential to the denizens of Political Washington, in a way that a flea is not essential to a dog. Even the press corps, as it has become larger, has tended to become more inward-looking. There are reporters who spend most of their time with other reporters, just as there are diplomats who hardly ever see nondiplomats.

But the press, the diplomatic corps, even the theoretically coequal judiciary are all essentially peripheral. They are attendant bodies, satellites shining in the reflected light of Washington's twin stars—the White House and the Hill.

That eccentric genius, Major L'Enfant, laid out his plan of Washington in such a way that all roads lead either to Capitol Hill or "The President's House." Ever since, either the Congress or the executive branch, over which the President rules, has dominated Washington. And ever since, the struggle for primacy and power between "the Hill" and "downtown" has been going on.

The inhabitants of the political community which comprises The Center have little contact with the other Washingtons into which the amoeba-metropolis is divided. There is, for example, only intermittent and occasional contact between Political Washington and Business Washington.

At the higher levels, of course, there is some intermingling. Lobbyists make up an important part of Business Washington, and it is their business to influence the political community in one way or another in favor of their clients. The lobbyists are always well represented at the "plate dinners"—from $25 to $500 a plate—which have become a major political fund-raising device. But, in fact, the registered lobbyists are both less effective and less powerful than most non-Washingtonians—including the lobbyists' clients —imagine.

Far more important than the registered lobbyists as a bridge between Business Washington and Political Washington are the lawyers. Nine out of ten Washington lawyers are involved in one way or another in dealing with the government on behalf of business. They are the in-and-outers—former government officials with close government ties (Dean Acheson, James Rowe, Paul Porter, Thomas Corcoran, Clark Clifford before he became Secretary of Defense, Henry Fowler before he became Secretary of the Treasury, Abe Fortas before he went to the Supreme Court, to cite a few conspicuous examples). The in-and-outers keep one foot in Business Washington and the other firmly planted in Political Washington. As the cases of Fowler and Fortas suggest, they may be citizens of Business Washington one day and of Political Washington the next.

The Metropolitan Club, which is the meeting place of the Washington Establishment (or, in the patois of the Negro intellectuals, the White Power Structure), also provides a bridge. At lunchtime it is common ground for Business and Political Washington. But with darkness the place becomes moribund, and the darkness also divides Business Washington from Political Washington.

Sometimes the ambitious wife of a Washington business-man will lead a successful raid on Political Washington, luring a few of its more conspicuous denizens to her parties by providing good food and free drink. The most successful raider in recent years has been Mrs. Morris Cafritz, whose late husband made a fortune in Washington real estate. But as a rule, and especially after dark, Business Washington and Political Washington are rigidly segregated.

Even more rigidly segregated are White Washington and Black Washington—which, with about two-thirds of the population, is now most of Washington. A few Negroes—a Thurgood Marshall, a George Weaver, a Carl Rowan—are inhabitants in good standing of the Washington political community, and many more are a part of the vast govern-ment bureaucracy of the Civil Service. But despite this overlapping most of White Washington goes about its busi-ness hardly aware that Black Washington exists. And when White Washington does become aware of Black Washing-ton, the awareness too often takes the form of fear.

The crime rate in Washington is appalling. More than 90 percent of the crimes are committed by Negroes—mostly against Negroes. But desperate Negroes have also invaded the white enclave in Northwest Washington sufficiently often that most white householders keep arms in their houses, and a good many houses are equipped with elabo-rate burglar alarms.

White Washingtonians very rarely venture into Black

Washington. Until rather recently, their only exposure to Black Washington was on drives north, when it was necessary to drive through Black Washington from the Northwest enclave in order to reach the Washington-Baltimore Expressway. Now most residents of the white enclave are spared even that brief exposure—the beltway system makes it easy to by-pass Black Washington entirely.

Some time ago, I asked a Negro reporter-acquaintance, Clarence Hunter of the Washington *Star,* to act as my guide on a tour of Black Washington. My notion was to have a good look at this unknown city, as a man might have his first look at Teheran or Bombay. Hunter showed me the Platinum Coast, and the two Gold Coasts, where the very richest Negroes live, up against Rock Creek Park, the Chinese Wall that divides the two Washingtons. He showed me the haunts of the "old-time aristocracy" in the neighborhood of Howard University. The "old-line aristocrats" are largely descended from pre–Civil War freed slaves, and some of them certainly have as much right to the title of aristocrat as any other American.

Descendants of William Costin, for example, have every right to look down their noses at the snootiest of Washington's ancestor-worshipers. William Costin was a free-born Negro of the early nineteenth century, and according to Washington's historian, Constance McLaughlin Green, his father was "a member of a distinguished Virginia family," while his mother was reputedly the child of Martha Washington's father, and thus George Washington's half-sister-in-law. The Syphaxes—there are nine of them in the D.C. telephone book—are probably descended from Bushrod Washington, and the lineage of other "old-line aristocrats" is hardly less exalted.

Clarence Hunter also led me on a guided tour of the Second Precinct, probably the slummiest of the ghetto slums. Places like the Second Precinct, of course, breed most of the crime which has frightened White Washington, and a lot of Black Washington too. For a white man, there is something genuinely frightening about the Second Precinct, even in broad daylight. Quite aside from pigmentation, extreme poverty is inherently frightening to the relatively prosperous. Even so, what surprised me about the Second Precinct was its resemblance to "fashionable Georgetown." Both were built before the Civil War, and with a bit of tarting up, the miserable shacks of the Second Precinct would sell in Georgetown for $60,000 or more.

But what surprised me most of all is how much most of Black Washington is like White Washington. I had expected something more strange and foreign, something odd and esoteric. Aside from the Black Muslim mosque, which no white man enters on pain of death, and a few such exotica as the signs advertising pigs' feet and chitterlings in the windows of cheap restaurants, there was really nothing very interesting or esoteric to write about.

Most of the inhabitants of Black Washington live very much like the inhabitants of White Washington; the houses they occupy look just like the houses occupied by people with similar incomes in White Washington. Perhaps there is more pink and pistachio, but that is the only readily visible difference. Most whites—especially white liberals who have never bothered to have a look for themselves—imagine the Negro ghettos as all seething misery and slummishness. This is simply not true; a great many Negroes live an essentially middle-class life according to wholly American (and therefore quite often false) values.

But there is an invisible difference between Black Washington and White Washington. This is the simple fact that most of White Washington is owned by White Washington, whereas most of Black Washington is also owned by White

Washington. Negroes own a few stores and restaurants, a bank, a few insurance companies, some automobile franchises, a good many funeral parlors. But most of the businesses and most of the real estate in Black Washington are owned by White Washington. This simple economic fact may help to produce bad trouble one day soon.

Bad trouble has been averted only narrowly so far—there have been at least three near-riots in recent years. The fact that Washington now has a Negro "mayor"—the able and appropriately named Walter Washington—and a Negro majority on the City Council may help to delay, or even avert, really bad trouble in the future (although there are times when the Southern Congressmen who control Washington's purse strings seem actually to want bad trouble). Meanwhile, some prosperous whites in the Northwest enclave are beginning to mutter about "getting out while the getting's good."

What the fearful whites fear more than riots or crime is a takeover of the city administration by Black Power extremists who would make life miserable, economically and in other ways, for the city's white minority. This is no doubt what Stokely Carmichael had in mind when in late 1967, on his return from a pilgrimage to Cuba, North Vietnam, and elsewhere, he announced his intention of taking up residence in Washington, and added: "This is *our* city, baby—and you better believe it." If the Negro majority began to make life miserable for the white minority, there would be, it must be admitted, a certain poetic justice.

For a very long time the white majority made life miserable for the city's Negro minority. Before the Civil War, of course, slaves were mere merchandise. Property taxes on slaves (as well as "all animals of the dog kind") made up a useful portion of the city's revenues. But Washington was considered a "good city" for freed Negroes, who congregated there in large numbers. In view of the pre–Civil War "black code," one can only imagine what a "bad city" must have been like.

At one point, after Nat Turner's bloody revolt in Virginia had thrown a scare into the ruling whites, the "black code" required a $1,000 bond from every freed Negro, signed by five white men, as a pledge of good behavior. The curfew ruled all Negroes off the streets after 10 P.M., and Negroes, while permitted to own and drive carts and other vehicles, were forbidden to own taverns or restaurants. "If they wish to live here," wrote a contemporary quoted by Constance McLaughlin Green, "let them become subordinates or laborers, as nature has designated."

For a brief time after the Civil War, Negroes—at least the tiny, educated upper class—were treated like human beings in Washington. Negro leaders like Frederick Douglass were respected by the white community, and Negroes were even included in the *Elite Register,* predecessor of today's *Green Book.* But that era passed quickly. In Franklin Roosevelt's day, and even after the war, Washington was a strictly segregated Southern city. As a Yankee newly arrived on the scene, in 1946 I invited a CIO official who was a Negro to lunch at a leading hotel. I was astonished and infuriated when we were politely shown the door.

From Thomas Jefferson's day to about 1950, Negroes made up a quarter to a third of Washington's population. Now that the situation is reversed, perhaps the white minority has some unconscious, vestigial, ancestral fear that whites will be treated as the Negro minority was once treated; that some future Stokely Carmichael will impose a ten o'clock curfew on whites and confine them to the more menial occupations. Much as it might delight a Carmichael, this seems unlikely to happen. The federal government is still firmly in white hands, and in the federal city federal power is omnipresent. This may be one reason why—as this is written—Washington has escaped a major Negro riot.

What could happen, and what may very well happen, is that Washington's white rich will be very heavily taxed to support Washington's black poor. The predictable result would be to accelerate the white flight to the suburbs. The city of Washington could one day be what Washington's public schools already are—more than 90 percent black.

Washington could become eventually a kind of black reservation surrounded by a fortress-ring of white suburbs, to which virtually the entire white working population would retreat after working hours. This is not at all what George Washington and Thomas Jefferson had in mind for the town, and it is not at all what John Kennedy and Lyndon Johnson had in mind either.

The relationship between the Presidency and the city has always been oddly proprietary, and even a relatively passive President—a Buchanan, a Coolidge, an Eisenhower—has always dominated the city, as its unchallenged Citizen Number One.

Thomas Jefferson, who more than any other man created the town, was consulted on every detail of running Washington. It was he, for example, who first ruled that houses in Washington should have a maximum height of four stories. (The limit is now 130 feet, and Jefferson can be thanked for the fact that Washington is not a jumbled maze of skyscrapers.) He was even consulted on whether the workmen could top the trees in the spring without danger to their later growth. In the Jefferson papers there is a curt reply to a query on this vital topic: "I think they may safely proceed, Th:J."

John F. Kennedy, with the important help of Mrs. Kennedy, saved Lafayette Square from total destruction by the insatiably land-hungry federal builders, and just about every

President in between has devoted a considerable portion of his time and effort to the federal city. Lyndon Johnson is no exception. "There are many things," he said early in his first term, "that I hope to accomplish during my allotted time in this office. But with all my heart, I hope that for generations to come these will be remembered as the years when Washington flowered into its finest age."

Those words were spoken at a time which now seems almost as distant as the Augustan era, the time of the Great Society and the National Consensus. Washington is an unhappy city these days, and Lyndon Johnson is preoccupied with other things than making Washington flower into its finest age. But the history of today's Washington will certainly be dominated by the tall, oddly ungainly figure of Lyndon Baines Johnson.

3

THE CENTER OF THE CENTER

This strange, proud, cruel, sentimental, insecure, naive, and bitterly driven man.

The geographical center of Washington—the point at which Major L'Enfant's "magnificent avenues" converge—is Capitol Hill. But the real center of political Washington is, of course, the White House. The White House is the center of The Center.

Residents of Political Washington remember past events in terms of Presidential administrations. ("No, we sold the house in 1948—it was the same year Harry Truman was elected." "She got married in 1959—it was late in the second Eisenhower administration, after Chris Herter took over as Secretary of State.") The President, even so passive and benign a President as Eisenhower, utterly dominates Political Washington. Lyndon Johnson is never passive and not always benign, and no President, not even Franklin Roosevelt, has dominated the town in quite the same way Johnson has.

Oxford dons have a way of dismissing a subject that

bores them by remarking that it is "not a topic." To most of the country, Lyndon Johnson is not a topic, to judge by the way books about him sell, or by the newsstand sales of magazines with his face on the cover. When the excellent book he wrote with Robert Novak, *Lyndon Johnson: The Exercise of Power,* failed to make the best-seller lists, Rowland Evans remarked that "we should have called the book 'Between Two Kennedys.'" But though he may bore the rest of the country, Lyndon Johnson most definitely is a topic in Washington. Except for the Vietnamese war, real estate, and the weather, no topic is more endlessly discussed.

Whenever two or three journalists are gathered together in one place, one of them is sure to ask: "Have you heard the latest Johnson story?" The Johnson stories, some of which are at least partly true, usually reflect the President's well-known earthiness, and are thus usually unprintable. The President's equally well-known passion for concealment, for camouflage and indirection, is such that "Lyndonology," the art or science of divining what Johnson is really up to, has joined "Kremlinology" in the political lexicon.

Lyndon Johnson is, in fact, a remarkably interesting human being, if only because he is so totally unlike any other human being. A peculiar little episode that occurred very soon after he became President seems to me to convey the flavor of oddness, of singularity, which marks the Johnson style. This small episode occurred on Sunday, November 24, only two days after President Kennedy's murder.

The Johnsons had not yet moved out of their big, characterless Spring Valley house. On that Sunday evening, the new President summoned a former Senate aide, Horace Busby, who lived nearby, to come and keep him company. Busby, a quiet-mannered, square-faced Texan, found the new President in his bedroom, getting a massage. For an hour or so, Busby and the President talked, and then, at about ten, the masseur left, and Mrs. Johnson came into the room, greeted Busby pleasantly, and got into bed. The President reached up and put out the lights, and Busby rose to go.

"Now, Buzz, don't you leave me," the President said. "I want you to stay right there till I go to sleep."

Busby obediently settled back into a chair, and silence fell in the darkened bedroom. Then Mrs. Johnson sat bolt upright in the bed.

"Lyndon," she said, "I just can't stand it."

"Bird," said the President, "what can't you stand?"

"Eleven more months of this, Lyndon," said Mrs. Johnson. "I just can't stand it."

"Bird," said the President, "you're just gonna have to stand it. And besides, it's not eleven months. That's to election. It's fourteen months to Inauguration."

Mrs. Johnson lay back in the bed. Then Horace Busby spoke up: "You're both wrong. It isn't eleven months and it isn't fourteen months. It's nine long years, and you're both just gonna have to stand it."

Again silence reigned, for a minute or so. Then Mrs. Johnson repeated, this time with a note of anguish: "Lyndon, I just can't stand it." The President grunted. A few minutes more, and Horace Busby thought he heard a soft snuffling. He removed his shoes and started to tiptoe out of the room. He had just reached the door, when he heard the familiar voice:

"Buzz . . . Buzz . . . You still there?"

Later, and then later again, Busby tried to leave, only to be stopped in mid-passage by the President's "Buzz . . . Buzz . . ." It was after two o'clock when at last he made good his escape.

Whether Horace Busby's prediction will turn out to be accurate remains to be seen. But this small episode is worth recalling, for it serves to suggest that President Johnson is after all a human being too, subject to human strains—and

as the days since President Kennedy's murder have length-
ened into months and years, and the little war in Vietnam
has become a large and cruel war, the strain has hardly
lessened. But the episode serves also as a reminder that
Lyndon Johnson is a very special sort of human being, with
a very special sort of personal style. Who else but Lyndon
Johnson would have ordered a friend to stay in his bedroom
until he went to sleep, in perfect confidence that his order
would be unquestioningly obeyed? Who else, indeed, would
have *wanted* another man in his bedroom with himself and
his wife?

A man is rarely puzzling or mysterious to himself, and one
suspects that it has hardly ever occurred to Lyndon Johnson
that his way of doing things may appear strange or odd to
other people. In 1966 during a campaign speech in Des
Moines, Iowa, the President remarked rather plaintively: "A
President is not a Rock of Gibraltar. He is just a plain,
simple human being."

The statement was received politely by the Iowans, but
among the reporters at the press table there were ill-muffled
snickers. No doubt President Johnson really does see himself
as "just a plain, simple human being." But nobody else does
—neither his friends nor his enemies.

There is no way of knowing whether the verdict of history
will finally rank Lyndon Johnson among the handful of
Presidents who have been tragic failures (which seems possible); the handful who have been truly great Presidents
(which also seems possible); or the majority who have done
as well as they knew how, and perhaps a bit better (which
seems rather probable). But one thing is certain: Lyndon
Johnson is the *least* "plain and simple" of all the thirty-five
Presidents who have occupied the White House. He is, in
fact, a very strange and unusual human being—egregious,
eccentric, totally idiosyncratic.

He is an intelligent man—a very intelligent man indeed—

a fact which his idiosyncratic personal style tends to conceal. One good judge, who knows the President and all his chief subordinates well, guessed that in an IQ test the President would rank above all department or agency heads except Robert McNamara, then Secretary of Defense. But even his intelligence is of an odd and unusual sort. It has something in common with the intelligence of Sherlock Holmes. When the faithful Dr. Watson exclaimed in surprise at a display by Holmes of total ignorance of some well-known fact, Holmes explained that his brain was like an attic. Space was limited, and he kept in his head only things that were useful to him in his profession.

When Johnson, in World War II, made a nine-month foray into the Pacific as a Navy lieutenant, his fellow officers were amazed at the gaps in his knowledge. The names of the great movie goddesses of the time, for example, meant absolutely nothing to him. Similarly, when he inherited the Presidency, he at first appalled his foreign policy experts by using Iran and Iraq, and Indonesia and Indochina, interchangeably. Until he became President, those places had not been useful to him in his profession, and there had been no room for them in his mental attic.

But like Holmes, where facts are important to him, his ability to grasp and retain them is prodigious. An ex-aide remembers him in his Senate days reading a book for information necessary in an upcoming debate (he has never been known to read a book simply for pleasure or even for general knowledge). While the issue was to the fore, the Johnson aide recalls, Johnson could quote whole pages from the book. After the debate was over, he could not even recall the book's title—it had been discarded to make room for something else in his mental attic.

His rare press conferences provide one measure of the quality of his intelligence. He recalls without hesitation the names of even very minor appointees, and he loves to cite reams of statistics—often meaningless statistics, since the number of "major bills" passed does not really measure the effectiveness of a legislative session, any more than the number of times the President has called for " unconditional" negotiations with the North Vietnamese is a true measure of the earnestness of his desire for peace. But the President prefers facts, even facts that really do not mean anything much, to theory.

His press conferences are revealing in another way. A transcript of a Johnson press conference makes a very striking contrast to a Kennedy or an Eisenhower transcript. Almost as much as Eisenhower, Kennedy used to become utterly lost in the tangled thickets of his own syntax. His sentences, like Eisenhower's, wandered uncertainly like wounded snakes, and quite often they were never finished at all. Almost without exception, Johnson's sentences parse. They are for the most part simple declarative statements, with a beginning, a middle, and an end.

A press conference is a critical moment for any high official. One indiscretion can haunt him forever after ("I shall not turn my back on Alger Hiss"). To use correct grammar in such circumstances requires intelligence. But it is also, one suspects, a measure of Lyndon Johnson's instinctive caution with what he clearly regards as his enemy—the press.

This is one reason why Johnson's televised press conferences have been singularly ineffective politically, as compared with Kennedy's or Eisenhower's. (A poll in December, 1966, in the Washington *Star*, rating various public figures as "TV performers," rated both Kennedy and Eisenhower very high, while poor Johnson came out at the bottom of the list, with 25 percent calling him "poor" and almost 40 percent rating him "terrible.") Kennedy and Eisenhower, less cautious than Johnson, spoke naturally, spontaneously, in the way that one man talks to other men. Johnson's sentences parse, but the net impression is one of artificiality, of cautious constraint; and the sense of direct communication which Kennedy and Eisenhower both established with the national television audience is disastrously lacking in Johnson's case—or was, until November 17, 1967.

On that day, Johnson astonished Political Washington when he suddenly began to talk at his press conference the way he talks when he is exercising his famous powers of persuasion before a small audience of fellow politicians. He wore for the first time a lapel microphone, which allowed him to move around freely, gesturing with his long arms, and this seems to have had a psychologically liberating effect. In any case, for the first time, a Johnson press conference was not what all previous Johnson press conferences had been—a bore. What made them boring was the same extreme caution—the wariness, the innate suspicion—that causes the President's sentences to parse when he speaks in public.

This caution is deeply a part of the man. "Lyndon's as cautious as an old coyote," an old friend, the late Tim McInerny, once remarked. Johnson's coyote caution is aroused above all by the fear that he might "lose his options," to use his own phrase—that he might be committed, fenced in. This horror of commitment extends to the details of his living, to when he will eat, to where he will go.

Logistical planning for a Johnson trip is a nightmare. When a President moves from one place to another, he is trailed by a vast retinue. About seven hundred people—press, security officers, aides, attendant politicians—usually accompany him, and quite often more than that. This retinue travels in a fleet of airplanes. There is Air Force One for the President, with Air Force One A standing by just in case something should go wrong with Air Force One. There are a souped-up Convair and a two-engined Jetstar in case the President should take it into his head to land somewhere—the LBJ Ranch, for example—with a short landing strip. There is a press plane, a Boeing 727, usually. And of course the bubble-top Presidential car, with the Presidential seal emblazoned on it, is sent on ahead, and all sorts of other elaborate prior arrangements are made to ensure the President's comfort and safety, and to cater to his retinue. Presidential travel is, in short, logistically complicated in the extreme. But it is immensely further complicated by a President who stubbornly insists on his right to change his mind up to and after the last minute—and who very often does just that.

The results of this mind-changing are, in the language of the Pentagon, contraproductive. If the President at the last moment decides, for example, to go to Omaha instead of attending a Governors' Conference in Los Angeles, the Los Angeles politicos are thoroughly miffed, while the President speaks to embarrassingly thin audiences in Omaha because the local Democrats have not had enough time to summon the faithful.

Any husband who has ever felt restless because his wife has committed him to a dinner party weeks in advance will have some faint glimmering of the President's hatred of being precommitted. But what is a mild resistance in most people becomes in the President a phobia. In this way as in so many ways, Lyndon Johnson is larger than life.

Most people have their small vanities—they think they are better-looking than they are, or they find it surprising that their friends age so much more rapidly than they do. The President's vanities are not small; they are colossal. Mark Twain once wrote a paragraph about his old friend Andrew Carnegie which calls Lyndon Johnson to mind:

If I were going to describe him in a phrase, I think I should call him the Human Being Unconcealed. He is just like the rest of the human race but with this difference, that the rest of the race tries to conceal what they are and succeed, whereas Andrew tries to conceal what he is but doesn't succeed. . . . He is an astonishing man . . . in his juvenile delight in trivialities which feed his vanity.

Both the "unconcealed" and the "juvenile" qualities that Twain perceived in Carnegie are very visibly present in Johnson. Lyndon Johnson seems perennially dissatisfied with himself as he is, and he is constantly trying to pretty up his surface. The trouble is that the prettying-up process takes place in the full view of a vast audience. For years he has fought a losing battle with the press photographers, using every means to get them to take pictures of him from the left side only, since he is oddly convinced that his left side is his handsome side. Anybody but Johnson would have known in advance that the photographers would vie with each other to get pictures of his right side—preferably in the act of stroking his long nose or pulling his ear.

For a time he wore contact lenses when he appeared on television. The contact lenses fooled nobody, and because they hurt, they made him irritable and out of sorts. There was also a period when he insisted on having not one, but two, teleprompters—his idea was that shifting from one to the other would make him look spontaneous when he spoke. Again, they fooled nobody, and instead of spontaneous, the teleprompters made him look sneaky, as his dark, rarely blinking eyes shifted from one to the other. Former White House aide Jack Valenti performed his last service to the President when he persuaded him to dispense with the teleprompters.

"There's one thing the President just can't get through his head," says another ex-aide (there are so many former Johnson aides that they constitute one of Washington's biggest alumni associations). "A public relations gimmick is useful when it conceals a blemish. But it is worse than useless when both the gimmick and the blemish are perfectly visible to the naked eye."

It is always when he tries to be what he isn't that Lyndon Johnson is at his worst. Remarkably shrewd and longheaded in most ways, when he himself—Lyndon Baines Johnson, son of Samuel Ealy Johnson and Rebekah Baines Johnson—is involved, he loses judgment and perspective. Only Lyndon Johnson would have failed to realize that those contact lenses, with which he tried to improve his "image," were not only painful but also as bad for the Johnson image as they could possibly be.

Again and again, in matters much larger than the wearing of contact lenses or the use of teleprompters, the President's curious blind spot where he himself is involved has led him to do the right thing in the wrong way. He cannot resist throwing up a smoke screen, which is supposed to conceal what he is really up to. But the smoke screen either leads the onlookers to suppose that he is doing something he ought not to be doing, or it soon rolls away, leaving the President as "the human being unconcealed."

To judge by results, President Johnson probably did the right thing when he intervened in the Dominican Republic in the spring of 1965. But he threw up so vast a smoke screen of internally contradictory verbiage, and he sent so unnecessarily vast an army (23,000 men) into the little island to do the job, that he made himself look like an old-style imperialist. It was, in fact, the Dominican intervention that first began the alienation of the liberal-intellectual-academic community, which the war in Vietnam has made almost total.

Johnson's decision to intervene with American combat

troops in Vietnam was certainly the key decision of his years in the White House. Whether it was the right decision must be left to history. But the thing was unquestionably done in the worst possible way.

Marines were first committed in the area of Danang in March, 1965. Instead of taking to the television screen to explain and defend his decision to send in the Marines, the President simply pretended he had not done so. Robert McCloskey, a State Department press officer, was the first official to acknowledge that U.S. troops were in combat in Vietnam. When the President heard what McCloskey had said, he was furious, and the White House promptly announced that there had been "no change" in the U.S. mission in Vietnam. But this smoke screen inevitably soon rolled away. In a few months the number of U.S. troops in the little country was climbing rapidly past the 100,000 mark.

Perhaps the President was trying to fool himself more than he was trying to fool others. He agreed to commit U.S. combat troops to Vietnam only after agonizing indecision. His major civilian advisers—Secretary of State Rusk, Secretary of Defense McNamara, Special Aide McGeorge Bundy —had been inherited from John F. Kennedy. They all told him the same thing: he had no choice but to intervene unless he wished to stand by and permit a total Communist victory in Vietnam. His military advisers—the Joint Chiefs of Staff —had also been inherited from Kennedy, and they all told him the same thing.

There was something else he had inherited from Kennedy —a very large American commitment in Vietnam. When John Kennedy died, there were sixteen thousand American troops in the little country; by the time the President had to make his decision in 1965, there were more than twenty thousand. If President Johnson had chosen to disregard the advice of all his Kennedy-inherited advisers and permit

South Vietnam to go down the drain, he would have had to stage a miniature American Dunkirk.

It is not at all difficult—certainly not for a politician as experienced and as suspicious as Lyndon Johnson—to imagine what his political enemies would have made of a President who "chickened," who "welshed" on the commitments made by his courageous young predecessor and who accepted the most humiliating defeat in American history. On several occasions, President Kennedy had warned of the dire consequences of permitting the capture of South Vietnam by the Communists. In March, 1963, for example, he had warned that the result might be "having the Communists control all of Southeast Asia with the inevitable effect that this would have on the security of India and, therefore, really beginning to run perhaps all the way toward the Middle East."

Add the fact that Johnson, along with such men as McNamara, Rusk, and Bundy (who are by no means fools), genuinely believed that a Communist victory in Vietnam would be disastrous to the national interests of the United States. It is then not very difficult to see why he made his agonized decision to commit combat troops to Vietnam. But the net result of the way he went about it was to make it seem that the President had got the United States into a major ground war in Asia by devious and oblique means. It is hard to imagine a worse way to get into a war.

When he was Majority Leader of the Senate, Lyndon Johnson very often managed to have his cake and eat it too. Thus he managed to be the chief architect of two major civil rights bills and at the same time the "Southern candidate" in 1960. When John Kennedy chose him for his Vice Presidential candidate, mainly in order to appease the South, Johnson managed to run both for the Vice Presidency and for his old Senate seat—a no-lose proposition. In his management of foreign affairs, especially in his management of the Vietnam war, the President often seems to be trying for no-lose propositions. Alas, in some situations there are none.

His intelligence, his vanity, his fear and hatred of being fenced in, these are qualities on which virtually all those who know him agree. There are others. Lyndon Johnson is a very moody man. He has many ups and downs, but his moods are hard to measure; as one of his ex-aides has said, "He has high ups in his downs, and deep downs in his ups."

The President's moods may vary from towering rage to sentimental affection, from euphoria to pitiful sadness, within the course of a single day. But he also has weeks-long ups and downs, which could be charted, on very wiggly lines, like the chart of a fluctuating stock market. At the time of the Dominican intervention, he had an up. Reporters who covered the White House at the time still recall in awe the frenetic ebullience which Johnson then displayed, in his lopes about the White House lawn and his virtually nonstop press conferences.

After he had his gallstone operation in early October, 1965, he had what is sometimes called in the White House "the long down" (he also had a long down after his heart attack, a decade earlier). "That scar hurt," says one White House inmate. "It hurt like hell, and Lyndon Johnson isn't the sort of man who lives with pain silently. A lot of other people got hurt before the scar stopped hurting."

Between bursts of irritation, he seemed listless and sad for weeks after his operation, and his old urge to manage everything and everybody in sight seemed strangely stilled. The New York blackout in November, curiously enough, provided the first glimpse of the old Johnson. He was driving a car about the ranch (he drives fast, and without a mere mortal's regard for roads) when the news came. Instantly he reached for the car telephone to call Secretary of Defense McNamara. From six that evening until the early hours of the morning, he was on the telephone, first in the car, then at the ranch house, giving orders, arranging for substitute power sources. He kept insisting to McNamara that emergency power must be found for the elevators. "People panic in elevators," he said. This may have been a reflection of his own claustrophobia; to a man who hates to be trapped by a speaking engagement or even a meal hour, the thought of being trapped in an elevator must be horrible. At any rate those around him were deeply relieved by this reappearance of the old Johnson. Some of them had feared that he might be sliding into a prolonged depression.

The passion for running things is another of those Johnsonian characteristics that are so marked that they make him seem larger than life. On the ranch he even manages the love lives of his animals, deciding which bull is to be mated with which cow. He will insist that a car packed with his guests' luggage be repacked to his specifications, though the improvement is discernible to no one but himself.

This passion for detail has led one of the President's ex-aides to compare working for him to driving in a New York taxicab: "The driver zigs and zags and steps on the gas to get through an opening with an inch to spare, and then slams on the brakes and throws you up against the front seat. But of course because of the traffic and the lights you can only go so fast anyway, and when you get there you realize you'd have gotten there quicker if you had walked."

At least in his up moods, the President seems to have a need for constant physical movement. At other times, when he is sad, or when it suits his purposes to seem to be sad, he displays an Oriental calm, sitting back in his chair, his feet up, speaking slowly and so softly as to be almost inaudible. It was in this mood that he liked to hint that he might not run again: "There's no law to prevent me going back to the ranch, to put my feet up on the porch railings, and watch the Pedernales roll by." From 1964 on, he threw out such hints like confetti, but except for ABC's William Lawrence and a surprising number of intuitive ladies, hardly anybody took them seriously.

Those who know him well differ about the reality of the President's moods. Some think they are perfectly real, that he is a deeply emotional man, while his nonadmirers (who include several who know him pretty well) think Lyndon Johnson's whole life is a long series of turns or acts. One visitor to his office recalls a telephonic display of the famous Presidential wrath. The President chatted pleasantly for a few minutes, then glanced at a note on his desk, lifted a telephone, and gave the nameless victim on the other end of the line a blistering tongue-lashing. Then Johnson put down the telephone and pleasantly resumed the conversation.

"You know," recalls his visitor, "whoever it was on the other end of the telephone must have been worried about another heart attack, the President sounded so angry. But I doubt if his blood pressure went up a single notch."

Whether or not Johnson's moodiness is largely play-acting, this is certainly a man who can maintain an iron grip on himself. He proved this in his years in the Vice Presidency, which he himself has described as "miserable." From time to time he would "break out of his cell with a helluva yell" (notably when he gave the Rebel yell in the Taj Mahal), but at least in public he endured the powerless obscurity of the Vice Presidency stoically. Similarly, when the President is faced with a big decision, he displays an iron self-control.

"He's almost supernaturally calm," says one aide. "His voice is down to a whisper, and there are long silences. Everybody has to speak to go on the record. There's a sense of pressure, of being at the bottom of a tank."

Everybody who has ever worked for Lyndon Johnson is at least to some extent obsessed by the man. All his ex-aides have their own favorite theories about what makes him tick. One who worked for him for many years has a curious psychological theory about him: "He's a strangely tactile man. He wants to *feel* everything, to have actual physical contact in order to know everything." The aide believes that this theory explains the President's occasional, almost compulsive vulgarity, which provides the material for most of the "Johnson stories."

Unlike Kennedy, who was indeed a hero to his valets, Johnson has never inspired a blind hero worship in any of his aides. The attitude of most of them is a curious mixture of irritation and admiration: "He just can't stand success, but he's good in adversity, you've got to admit that. He'll fly into a temper about a door that slams or a memo that's late, but when the bullets are really flying about those big ears of his, he can be magnificent."

Is he a likable man? The President himself once received a rather brutal response to that question. After his downward slide in the polls began, he complained to former Secretary of State Dean Acheson, an old friend, that although he tried every day to do the right thing, the voters did not seem to like him.

"You're not a very likable man," replied Acheson, who is much given to excessive candor. Then Acheson went on to say that likability is not an essential characteristic in a President; what was important, he said, was getting the job done, and the President was good at that. The flaw in this Achesonian theory is that a President who loses his popularity soon also loses his national authority.

Lyndon Johnson can be likable, although in a rather overwhelming way; he tells good stories, and he is an accomplished, if rather cruel, mimic. (He used to entertain reporters with imitations of Adlai Stevenson, among others.) When he is relaxed and at his best, especially on the ranch, his oddly childish pleasure in his own possessions has a kind of boyish charm. When he was in the Senate, he had authentic friends—Earle Clements, Richard Russell, Robert Kerr, Hubert Humphrey, several others. But even then, his friends were almost all political friends. In the nature of things, a President is hedged off from other human beings, this one more than most. As President, Lyndon Johnson has few authentic personal friends, if any.

Instead of friends he has "advisers" and "staff"; the President himself makes a sharp distinction between the two categories. And this distinction helps explain one of the most striking phenomena of the Johnson administration.

As this is written, no less than five Johnson Cabinet members are Kennedy men, and Robert McNamara undoubtedly would have stayed with the President through November, 1968, if he had been sufficiently urged. By way of contrast, every major Roosevelt appointee was out of office within a matter of months after Harry Truman inherited the Presidency. This has almost always been the case when a Vice President became President.

A Cabinet member has a large independent empire of his own, and he is physically separated from the President. He is thus, in the President's mind, in the "adviser" category, and this in part explains the longevity of the Kennedy men in the Johnson Cabinet. An adviser is someone who is expected to exercise independent judgment, and whose advice is to be listened to with respect, though it may be accepted rather rarely.

Also in the adviser category are a number of men most of whom have been in and out of the government for years, but who are not members of the President's official family. Of these the most important are probably Justice Abe Fortas, who advised the President on his personal affairs before he went to the Supreme Court (he advised him, after Kennedy's assassination, to sell all his personal holdings, but the President unwisely resisted that advice); Clark Clifford, before he became Secretary of Defense; and former Secretary of State Acheson. Businessman Don Cook, and lawyer and New York Democratic National Committeeman Edwin Weisl, both of whom were close to Johnson in the Senate years, are also advisers. So are former aides like Jack Valenti and Horace Busby—but not Bill Moyers, the manner of whose departure Lyndon Johnson resented. So are a number of old New Dealers whom Johnson knew as a young Congressman —men like James Rowe, Tommy Corcoran, and Ben Cohen.

One of those who appears on most lists of the Johnsonian "inner circle" deprecates the influence of the nonofficial advisers: "He uses us more as a sounding board than anything else. He talks a lot more than he listens. A man who is identified in the press as a 'Presidential adviser' is not likely to deny his own importance, but in fact we're a lot less influential than we've been made to seem."

The President's attitude toward those whom he puts in the "staff" category is totally different from his attitude toward "advisers." It always has been, back to the early Capitol days. And this difference in attitude helps to explain the striking contrast between the remarkable stability of the Johnson Cabinet and the total instability of the Johnson White House staff.

A few months after he took office, the President seemed to have achieved a successful melding of Kennedy men and Johnson men in the White House. But by now all the Kennedy men have left, without exception, Richard Goodwin and McGeorge Bundy being the last to go. What is more striking is that all the Johnson men of that early period have also left the White House—Walter Jenkins, Horace Busby,

George Reedy, Jack Valenti, and the last to go, Bill Moyers. In short, not a single major Kennedy man or Johnson man has survived from the period between the Kennedy assassination and Johnson's election in 1964.

Again by way of contrast, all but one of the men who joined John Kennedy in the White House after his 1960 election were still there on the day he was murdered. The exception was Walt Rostow. Why the contrast?

There were, of course, all sorts of perfectly understandable reasons for the mass exodus from the Johnson White House. The Kennedy men had come to the White House to work for John Kennedy, not Lyndon Johnson, and it is hard to imagine two more different men. As for the Johnson men, Walter Jenkins (one of the ablest of the lot) had a nervous breakdown. George Reedy suffered from hammertoes, and Horace Busby, Jack Valenti, and Bill Moyers all had a natural desire to better themselves financially. But the story does not end there.

The fact of the matter is that it takes a very special sort of man to work for Lyndon Johnson in the "staff" category. The President's attitude toward his staff is that of a stern, if sometimes sentimental, Victorian paterfamilias toward his children. They are to be seen but not heard—or not more than absolutely necessary. They are to be at the beck and call of Daddy at all times and all places, and, above all, Daddy *always* knows best.

Lyndon Johnson made a real effort to treat the Kennedy men he inherited with a special reserve and respect. But the habits of a lifetime are not to be broken. "He'd not only tell you when to eat and where to eat," said one Kennedy man after he had escaped the Johnson White House, "he'd tell you *what* to eat."

The Presidential White House routine is very odd—inevitably, Johnson being Johnson—and this puts an added

strain on his staff. The President works a two-day day, and
he expects his aides also to crowd two working days into one
twenty-four-hour period.

The first of the President's daily two days begins at breakfast time, around eight or a bit later, when the President
holds a levee, after the manner of the French kings. Marvin
Watson, the Texas businessman who is currently the President's Man Friday and chief White House administrator,
always attends the levee. While the President munches his
breakfast, he collects the President's "night reading," asks
questions when necessary about the scribbled orders, dis-
cusses upcoming appointments and the business of the day.

Watson is occasionally the only courtier at the levee to
begin with, but others appear as the morning wears on.
Sometimes there is an attendant lord from outside the White
House—a publisher, an important politician, some mover
and shaker who has been invited to breakfast with the
President. Occasionally one of these visiting firemen is dis-
concerted not only to be received by the President in bed,
but to find Mrs. Johnson in bed with the President. Richard
Nixon is one of those who have, to their own surprise, found
themselves breakfasting *à trois* with the Johnsons.

As the President's long morning in his bedroom continues
—often he does not descend to his office until ten-thirty or
eleven—and the President dresses by stages, other members
of the staff are often summoned to the bedroom.

When domestic matters are to the fore, Joseph Califano
may be invited up to the bedroom (but not before nine-
thirty—Califano works so late that his only chance to see his
wife and children is in the morning, and he therefore gets to
his office well after nine, very late by White House standards). Harry McPherson and Douglass Cater, speech writers,
idea men, and maids of all work, attend the bedroom rallies
less frequently, usually when some speech-writing chore is

to be attended to. Walt Rostow, foreign policy specialist and one of two resident White House intellectuals (the other is John Roche), also attends occasionally.

After the President has disposed of his breakfast, and sometimes before, the telephone is kept constantly busy. The telephone is, in fact, in a mechanical sense, the President's chief instrument of power. It is also an outlet for the President's sometimes frenetic restlessness. He uses it almost compulsively, and will sometimes call the same man again and again. (Once when I was interviewing Robert McNamara, he received five calls from the President within the space of half an hour.) When the President, fully dressed at last, descends to his oval office, the telephoning continues, interspersed with appointments. Sometimes it goes right on, without any break for lunch, until three or three-thirty.

Like just about everything else about him, Lyndon Johnson's attitude toward food is very strange. He can go for hours on end without the slightest twinge of hunger. He rarely eats lunch before two-thirty, and he quite often goes without any lunch at all. He himself has expressed the curious theory that his stomach, which is large, stores up food the way a camel's hump stores up water. A more credible theory is that the soft drinks which he consumes seriatim throughout the day still his hunger pangs.

Except when some such function as a state banquet commits him to a preordained hour, the President eats when *he* wants to eat—no later and no sooner. His late hours induce a certain faintness and queasiness in those accustomed to answer the call of hunger at the same hour every day. After a couple of two-thirty or three o'clock lunches at the White House, Dean Acheson invoked the privilege of an elder statesman and refused a Presidential luncheon invitation. He was accustomed, he told the President, to lunching at precisely one, after precisely one martini. He would come to the White House at any time the President wanted, and stay as long as he wanted, but lunch—no thanks.

At three-thirty or four the President returns to his bedroom, gets into his pajamas, and gets into bed. His second daily day begins when he wakes up, after an hour or more of sound sleep. He wakes up refreshed, with what Jack Valenti called his "extra glands" fairly pumping out adrenalin. He expects his aides to display a similar vigor. Some escape by seven-thirty, but others may find themselves co-opted by the President, and they may be lucky to get home at midnight. Again, they must be prepared to go without food until the President feels the urge. Sometimes Johnson does not eat until eleven. At one moment of crisis early in his Presidency, he and a number of aides sat down to dinner at one in the morning.

After the last exhausted aide has left, the President goes to his bedroom again, and starts on his night reading, which consists of intelligence reports, memoranda, suggestions for future action from White House staff men or from department and agency heads. He reads fast (although not as fast as President Kennedy), and every night he gets through a big pile of night reading. On the papers he scribbles cryptic notes and orders—"No" or "More" or "See me" or "Good idea." Often the President does not go to sleep before two in the morning or later. Sometimes, especially when there is a major air operation over North Vietnam, he will stay up virtually all night until he hears the results of the operation.

As the President's eating habits suggest, the Kennedys' French chef, René Verdon, had good reason to leave the White House; a serious chef can hardly be expected to rustle up a meal at any hour of the day or night, especially for an employer who prefers deer meat sausages and tapioca to

French dishes. The President's other habits suggest why so many of his aides have followed René Verdon out of the White House.

After a day spent with Johnson campaigning in Iowa in 1966, Iowa's Governor Hughes complained that he felt "like a bangle on a horse's tail." Anyone who spends much time with Lyndon Johnson is likely to feel the same way. One of the President's long-time aides who has now left the White House has explained his departure this way:

"There are two kinds of people—those who like action for the sake of action and prestige for the sake of prestige, and those who can't stand running around in circles at a furious pace for no purpose. The second kind have left the White House."

There is certainly a retrospective bitterness in this remark, since, although Lyndon Johnson unquestionably runs at a furious pace, it is rarely "for no purpose." But it is extraordinary how much time and effort the President will devote to some project which would hardly have attracted the attention of John Kennedy, and which his aides would never even have mentioned to Dwight Eisenhower.

This obsessive attention to detail makes working for Lyndon Johnson, even at a distance, hard work. Working directly under the President, in the White House, within easy reach of his long arm, is the hardest sort of work there is, and to those who dislike feeling like a bangle on any horse's tail, it is frustrating and irritating work. This is why only a certain kind of man can work for Lyndon Johnson, and why nobody—literally nobody—seems to be able to work for him in the "staff" category indefinitely. Even to a George Reedy or a Bill Moyers or a Jack Valenti, the urge to escape becomes in time insuperable.

This is not to suggest that the Johnson staff men are mere

varlets and whoreson knaves, cringing under the Presidential lash. They are, for the most part, able men, and some are very able. They are also men with strongly marked individual characteristics.

Marvin Watson is an intensely parochial Texas businessman. He once remarked to another aide that he had never owned anything foreign in his life—not so much as a tie or a shirt, let alone an automobile. Foreigners, he said, just couldn't make things as well as they were made in America. It is not impossible to imagine Lyndon Johnson saying something of the sort himself in his younger days; when he was a young man, "abroad" was strictly *terra incognita* to Johnson. As this suggests, Watson is a sort of human mirror of one part of Lyndon Johnson—the parochial, Texan part. Watson is also, like his boss, a cautious and suspicious man.

Watson undoubtedly hastened the departure of certain White House aides—notably McGeorge Bundy—when he instituted a system of surveillance. Under the Watson system anyone who telephoned any White House inmate was required to give his name to the operators, who kept a list of callers and reported them to Watson. White House aides were also supposed to write a memorandum about what was said during any contact, no matter how casual, during or after business hours, with reporters. The Watson system has since been abandoned, but the fact that it was ordered with the expectation of pleasing Paterfamilias Johnson, and presumably with his approval, suggests some of the pressures involved in acting as a bangle on the tail of this Presidential horse.

Joseph Califano, the President's chief domestic affairs man, is a very able, very hard-driving, very ambitious man, who has built up a staff of first-rate younger men under him. Califano was co-opted by the President from McNamara, and he is a McNamara-ish sort of man—brisk, competent, knowing where the levers of power are, and capable of using them confidently.

Walt Rostow, who succeeded McGeorge Bundy as the President's chief foreign affairs man in the White House, is an ex-MIT professor, highly articulate—his critics find him *too* articulate—and highly intelligent. Rostow originally came to the White House as Bundy's deputy under Kennedy, then shifted to the State Department's Policy Planning Council, and returned to the White House when Bundy left. He is thus the only major Kennedy aide to have left the White House during the Kennedy era, and the only former Kennedy man now working in the White House.

Some of his fellow ex-Kennedy men like to make fun of Rostow, picturing him as Dr. Pangloss to Johnson's Candide, assuring the President that "everything's for the best in this best of all possible worlds," as disaster succeeds disaster. It is true that Rostow is one of nature's optimists, and true also that his cheerful prognoses about the course of the Vietnamese war have quite frequently been found wanting. But in this respect he is by no means alone. And according to all accounts he has done a very competent job—in a surprisingly monosyllabic and understated style—of acting as a conduit for the President in the field of foreign policy.

Harry McPherson, a Texan, and Douglass Cater, an Alabamian, who do speech-writing and other literary chores, are both Southern-style liberal intellectuals. Cater is former Washington editor of the liberal magazine *The Reporter*, and McPherson, a poetry lover and a witty man, is a very different sort of Texan from Marvin Watson—or Lyndon Johnson. George Christian, the press secretary, is a self-effacing fellow, who follows orders—which may be the only kind of press secretary who can survive under Lyndon Johnson.

These are the principal Johnson aides as these words are written. They are likely not to be the principal Johnson aides as these words are published, for the old joke about cooks—"She was a good cook as cooks go, and as cooks go, she went"—clearly applies to aides of President Johnson. (But not to cooks, other than French chefs. The President's cook, Zephyr Wright, has been with him for more than twenty years.)

There is, finally, one element of complete stability in Lyndon Johnson's exceedingly unstable personal entourage —Mrs. Johnson. Lady Bird Johnson, a woman of great charm and intelligence, plays a vital White House role, and plays it brilliantly. Even those who intensely dislike her husband find it impossible to dislike her. Her chief function is to act as a sort of balance wheel for her moody husband. There are some Lyndonologists who believe that his moods get out of hand only when she is away—she was not in the White House, for example, during the Dominican crisis, and when she returned, the freewheeling, nonstop press conferences, the plethora of Presidential television appearances and official pronouncements, suddenly ceased.

"You know what would scare me more than if LBJ had a heart attack?" one White House correspondent has remarked. "If Lady Bird had a heart attack. Then Lyndon would *really* come unstuck."

The moody President has badly needed a balance wheel, especially since May, 1966. That was the month when his long slide in the polls began. Before that month he had never once scored under 60 percent in his "job ratings." Before that month he used to carry the polls about with him in his coat pocket like talismans and fish them out to show almost any visitor to his office—James Callaghan, for example, when he was British Foreign Minister. The President no longer carries the polls in his pockets.

"There's never been a President happier in the Presidency," Hubert Humphrey said to me in the spring of 1965, when Lyndon Johnson was still riding high. "The reason is that the President knows both what to do and how to do it."

It is very unlikely that Hubert Humphrey—or anyone else —would say the same thing today. For Lyndon Johnson more and more resembles the Ancient Mariner:

> "God save thee, ancient Mariner!
> From the fiends, that plague thee thus!—
> Why look'st thou so?" "With my cross-bow
> I shot the Albatross!"

Johnson's Albatross is, of course, the war in Vietnam, which has plagued him more and more fiendishly since he committed U.S. combat troops there, in his devious-seeming fashion, and thus shot his Albatross. In the spring of 1965, Lyndon Johnson was indeed happy in the Presidency, and with his great 1964 electoral victory under his belt and the remarkable legislative record he was then extracting from Congress, he did indeed seem to be a President "who knows both what to do and how to do it."

In those days (which are not really very long ago) the President had won, not the affection, but at least the grudging admiration of the liberal intellectuals. Now all is changed. The President's standing in the polls has collapsed, and the Johnson "consensus" has collapsed with it. Vietnam has utterly alienated the liberal intellectuals. They instinctively disliked Johnson to begin with, but Vietnam has given them an excuse to hate him.

The hatred has gone so far that a good many intellectuals professed to see artistic merit in *MacBird!*, a tasteless and inept parody of Shakespeare, whose real merit in intellectual eyes is that it portrays the President as a buffoon and the murderer of John Kennedy. The liberal intellectuals are, of course, a small minority ("How many eggheads are there?"), but their influence is far greater than their numbers, and they have hurt Johnson badly, especially with the young.

Perhaps the time will come when Lyndon Johnson's Albatross will "fall like lead into the sea," and some honorable way out of the Vietnamese man-trap will be found. But as this is written, the Albatross is still fastened firmly about Lyndon Johnson's neck. It must be even more galling to him than to other men.

He is wholly unprepared, by temperament or by previous experience, for the situation in which he finds himself. He is in his every instinct a compromiser. His formula has always been something for everybody—"one for the rat, one for the mole, one for the badger"—and it worked admirably in his Senate days. There was nothing in his previous political experience to prepare him for a Ho Chi Minh, who is not interested in compromise, who flatly refuses to "reason together," who says, in effect, "First you accept my conditions and then we'll talk." This is not a matter of a vote traded for a committee assignment. It is war to the knife and no quarter asked.

Lyndon Johnson is also wholly unprepared by temperament for the course his liberal-intellectual critics wish to take, although they never put it in quite such terms: capitulation in Vietnam, if possible politely disguised. Lyndon Johnson is a product of his place and his times—of rural Texas and the period between the wars—and he is uncompromisingly square as regards flag and country. "We will fight in Vietnam," he has told many audiences, "until our American soldiers can proudly come marching home"—a phrase which carries echoes of 1918 when Lyndon Johnson was a young boy. "We're not gonna duck our tail and run out of Vietnam," he says again and again, and he means it.

Defeat of the United States in war is simply inconceivable to Lyndon Johnson, however the defeat might be disguised. And something else is even more inconceivable: the failure and humiliation of Lyndon Johnson, son of Samuel Ealy and Rebekah Baines Johnson, and President of the United States.

In an interview in 1958 Lyndon Johnson described to me his experiences as president of his high school "debate team" in his boyhood:

"We won sixty-five of sixty-six debates, only lost the last one. We won the city and the county championship, but we lost the state, by a vote of the judges of three to two. We were on the wrong side—we had the affirmative of 'Resolved, that the jury system be abolished.' I was so disappointed I went right into the bathroom and was sick."

There was not a flicker of a smile on his face as he recalled that long-ago moment when, in the horror and pain of failure, he vomited in the bathroom.

"We shall prevail," he says in his speeches about Vietnam, "we shall *succeed*." Failure is genuinely horrible to this man, and the thought of leading his country, as its President, to its first real defeat in war must be horrible beyond imagining.

"Are we being fair to Lyndon?" This is a question constantly debated wherever Washington's journalists are gathered. Being unfair to Lyndon Johnson is a very tempting exercise, because he is a man so capable of unfairness to others. But it certainly is true that the press has been unfair —sometimes bitterly unfair—to President Johnson. Above all, there is a tendency among all commentators, left and right, to overlook the terrible dilemma he faced in Vietnam, and which he inherited from John F. Kennedy. It was Kennedy, not Johnson, who committed American prestige so deeply in Vietnam that it would have been virtually impossible for any President to fail to honor the commitment.

Lyndon Johnson is not a man who invites sympathy. And yet it is difficult, at this point in his amazing career, not to feel something like pity for this strange, proud, cruel, sentimental, insecure, naïve, and bitterly driven man.

4

A BACKWARD GLANCE

Scarce any better than a swamp.

The history of Washington starts with a flaming row, which involved both real estate and the bureaucratic pecking order. This was a highly appropriate beginning. There have been flaming rows in Washington ever since, and Washington has always been preoccupied with real estate and the pecking order.

The story of the row is both a bit funny and a bit sad, like the story of many Washington rows. In 1791 President Washington and his Secretary of State, Thomas Jefferson,

NOTE: This chapter is an attempt to give some flavor of the city's past. For those seriously interested in Washington's history, *Washington: Village and Capital, 1800–1878* and *Washington: Capital City, 1878–1950* by Constance McLaughlin Green (Princeton University Press, 1963) are highly recommended. *Thomas Jefferson and the National Capital,* a collection of letters to and from Jefferson, edited by Saul K. Padover, and published by the U.S. Government Printing Office in 1946, is wonderfully rewarding. Another government publication, *Washington, City and Capital,* written under the auspices of the Federal Writers' Project of the WPA and printed in 1937, is also very useful. So is *The National Capitol* by George C. Hazelton, Jr., pub-

62

hired a talented Frenchman and Revolutionary War veteran, Major Pierre Charles L'Enfant, to make a plan for the new capital of the Republic. At the same time, they appointed three local landowners to act as commissioners of the ten-mile-square tract of federal land, with vague powers to oversee and direct Major L'Enfant.

From the beginning, L'Enfant quarreled with the commissioners and disregarded their instructions. To judge from his correspondence with Jefferson, L'Enfant must have been a kind of Charles de Gaulle of his day—brilliant, vain, stubborn, and impossible to deal with. His letters to Jefferson are one long wail of complaint about everything from the weather—another subject which has long preoccupied Washington—to the alleged unreasonableness of the commissioners.

Things came to a head when one commissioner, Daniel Carroll, decided to build a house on some empty land he owned in the new federal territory. L'Enfant loudly objected. The location of the house, he said, was where he planned to put a street—obviously, L'Enfant wanted to put Carroll in his proper place in the pecking order. Carroll nevertheless proceeded with the building of his house. What happened next is related in a furious letter from the commissioners to President Washington, in November, 1791:

lished in 1897, and still the chief source book of the Capitol guides. *Jeffersonian America*, the reminiscences of Sir Augustus John Foster, Bart., a snobbish but perceptive British diplomat during Jefferson's Presidency, is vivid and readable. *Democracy*, by Henry Adams, was the first and is still the best Washington novel, and the reader will be surprised to find how much the Washington of Henry Adams had in common with the Washington of today. Other useful source books are *White House Profile* by Bess Furman, *The Story of Capitol Hill* by Paul Herron, *Washington Wife* by Mary Ellen Slayden. *The American Past*, by Roger Butterfield, a pictorial history of the United States and the best book of its kind, has a lot of Washington in it. I also found useful a long article from which I cribbed freely—"That's Politics for You," *Saturday Evening Post*, October, 1952, by Joseph and Stewart Alsop, mostly the former.

We are sorry to be under the disagreeable necessity of mentioning to you an occurance which must wound your feelings. On meeting here today, we were to our great astonishment informed that, Majr. L'Enfant, without any authority from us, & without even having submitted to our consideration, has proceeded to demolish Mr. Carroll's house.

Washington wrote to Jefferson, and asked him to handle the matter. It would be "a serious misfortune," he wrote, to lose L'Enfant's services, but "at the same time *he must know* [Washington's italics] there is a line beyond which he will not be suffered to go."

The headstrong Frenchman insisted on going beyond that line. He wrote to the President that he "had as much right to pull down a house as to cut down a tree," and to Jefferson he made it abundantly clear that he had no intention of paying any heed to the "*commissionaires*," as he called the commissioners. With great reluctance—for they recognized his talent—Washington and Jefferson decided to fire L'Enfant. On February 27, 1792, while L'Enfant's design was still wholly on paper, Jefferson coolly informed the Frenchman that "your services must be at an end."

There is a sad little postscript to the story, in the form of a long and rather pathetic letter from L'Enfant to Jefferson nine years later, after Jefferson had moved into the new White House as the third President. L'Enfant had waited those long years, disconsolately and in increasing poverty, in the vain hope of being reinstated. In L'Enfant's peculiar English, the letter asks for "a Compensation for Services and for Injuries experienced at the hands of the Jealousers of the reputation and of the fortune which the planning and the Execution of the City of Washington promise me."

L'Enfant died in 1825, bitter and impoverished, and he had to wait for nearly a century for his "Compensation," such as it was. For all those years, his name was almost forgotten, and his plan consistently violated. Then, in the administration of Theodore Roosevelt, the L'Enfant Plan was revived and partly executed, and the fiery major's corpse was grandly reinterred in Arlington Cemetery.

L'Enfant and the men who fired him, George Washington and Thomas Jefferson, stand *in loco parentis* to the federal city. L'Enfant, of course, gave the city its shape, choosing the location of the Capitol, the White House, and the principal streets. Washington chose the site, certainly in part because it was conveniently close to Mount Vernon.

Washington also invented the real estate deal by which the city was to be built and paid for. In 1791, in his first year as President, at Suter's Tavern in Georgetown, he met with the landowners of the ten-mile-square tract of land which he had chosen for the capital. He proposed that the landowners sell the government any land needed for public buildings or avenues, at $66.66 an acre. The rest of the land would be divided into lots and sold, the proceeds to go half to the government, half to the landowners. Some of the landowners insisted that they should get more, but in fact it was a fine deal for them. The city lots sold for about ten times the price per acre of plantation land. They thus made a profit of 1000 percent—a rate of gain which even the more avaricious of Washington's contemporary real estate speculators would consider respectable.

Washington had big hopes for the city named after him. The Potomac Canal system, he firmly believed, would make Washington a major port and stimulate manufacturing, transforming the swampland he had selected as the national capital into a great industrial metropolis. These expectations, fortunately, came to nothing. The federal city has remained essentially a one-industry town. The industry is politics, which employs a smokeless fuel, and Washington has thus been spared the defacing effects of industrialization. But although Washington's scheme for selling off the federal land was much less immediately successful than he had hoped, real estate has remained the city's second industry. After sex and politics, real estate is still one of the city's three main subjects of conversation, and most of the big indigenous fortunes have been made in land and buildings.

But if Washington put the federal city on the map, and L'Enfant gave it its physical shape, Jefferson gave the city its character. The Jefferson letters reveal Jefferson's extraordinary—indeed, his obsessive—interest in the town. As the first Secretary of State in 1791, he was far more involved in overseeing the founding of the city than in foreign affairs. Throughout his two terms as President he was constantly breathing down the necks of Benjamin Latrobe, William Thornton, and the other architects of the Capitol and the White House, and involving himself in such matters as the planting of trees—the "Jefferson poplars," planted under his direction along Pennsylvania Avenue, lasted almost until the Civil War. And long after he had retired to Monticello, although he never set foot in the town again, he continued to interest himself in the affairs of the rather grubby village that Washington then was.

In fact, Jefferson's influence almost certainly accounts for the fact that Washington has remained on the site the first President chose for it. The most vivid picture of the Washington of the Jeffersonian era is to be found in the memoirs of Sir Augustus John Foster, Bart., who served first as Secretary of the British Delegation in 1805–1807, and then as Minister in 1811 and 1812, when this country's second and last war with Britain interrupted his career. Sir Augustus blamed Jefferson for the fact that the seat of government of the United States remained in what he called "this discouraging waste."

"The Congress removed to Washington at the commencement of this century," Foster wrote, "and much inconvenience was experienced by everybody on this occasion: the change from such a large and agreeable town as Philadelphia to what was then scarce any better than a swamp having been difficult to digest, particularly for members of the diplomatic corps."

There were, to be sure, minor compensations: "Excellent snipe shooting and even partridge shooting was to be had on each side of the main avenue and even close under the wall of the Capitol." But there was no other civilized entertainment of any kind—"no clubs established and no theatres in the place except for rope dancers." There were "no streets in the place, and the few scattered habitations are designated by the number of buildings, six, seven, or twenty in a group, to which they belong."

Thus the "more respectable deputies" wanted to "vote for returning to Philadelphia or to some other location where a good sized town has already been formed." But Jefferson always stood in the way of this sensible inclination:

Mr. Jefferson in particular used all his influence to prevent the removal, giving as a reason the danger that might ensue to the Union if a door were again to be opened to disputes among the different states on a subject so interesting as selecting a spot for the seat of government. . . . Nevertheless . . . the fact was that his power was founded on the court he paid to the Democratical party, and he could not have appeared in a great town, as he did in Washington, without attendants . . . or in yarn stockings and slippers when he received company. Neither could he have had the members of the legislature so dependent upon him . . . for the little amusement and relief which they could obtain after public business. His house . . . being in fact almost necessary to them unless they chose to live like bears, brutalized and stupefied as one of the Federalists who did not frequent the

Great House once confessed to me that he felt from hearing nothing but politics from morning to night and from continual confinement to his Senatorial duties with scarcely any relaxation whatsoever.

Relaxation is more easy to come by in today's Washington, but plenty of its inhabitants—especially the wives of politicians and journalists—still on occasion feel "brutalized and stupefied from hearing nothing but politics from morning to night." In any case, Jefferson certainly deserves most of the credit—or blame—for retaining the capital in a place "scarce any better than a swamp," although long after he had retired to Monticello, and especially after the burning of the Capitol and the White House by the British, there were repeated attempts to move the capital elsewhere. Even as late as 1871, Constance McLaughlin Green records, Washingtonians were still afraid that Congress might ruin the real estate market by voting to put the federal city in some other, more central and more salubrious place.

Foster's memoirs serve as a reminder of a fact often overlooked by the Society of the Cincinnati, the Daughters of the American Revolution, and other ancestor-worshipers— that this country had its origins in a revolution. At least for the adherents of the "Democratical party" the revolution was social as well as national. "Manners," Foster noted, were "rather despised as a mark of effeminacy by the majority, who seem to glory in being only thought men of bold strong minds and good sound judgment." Jefferson received the aristocratic Foster wearing "yarn stockings and slippers down at heel" for essentially the same reason that Nikita Khrushchev refused to wear evening dress when he was received at Dwight Eisenhower's White House. A tuxedo is to a devout, old-line Communist a symbol of capitalism; and Jefferson's down-at-heel slippers and casual manners were similarly symbolic, of an anti-aristocratic and revolutionary democracy.

The manners of the Americans in those days could indeed be casual in the extreme, especially among members of the "Democratical party." Foster, who greatly preferred the aristocratic Federalists, tells of one Democrat, a tavern-keeper and member of Congress,

who committed an act of great impropriety in my house when I gave a ball for the Queen's birthday. When the drawing rooms being left empty on the company going to supper, he thought poor fellow that he was alone and unobserved, but two stray Federal Members . . . espied his attitude and the joke was too good to be lost so they had it all in the papers and all over the states in prose and verse ringing the changes on "the Extinction of the British Fire."

The problem which the tavern-keeper sought to solve so boldly is another problem still to be met in Washington, especially at the large, pompous embassy parties.

The President, then as now, was the undoubted social leader of Washington, not only because he was Chief Magistrate, but because he had much the best house in town. To be sure, the White House was not, to begin with, a very good house. It had been on the verge of collapse less than five years after it was finished. Benjamin Latrobe, the architect and Surveyor of Public Buildings, reported to Jefferson in 1804 that

the Roof & gutters were so leaky as to render it necessary to take off all the Slating; to take up the Gutters and to give them much more current . . . To strengthen & tie together the roof which, having spread, has forced out the Walls;—to put up the Stair case . . . and sink a Well for the purpose of procuring good Water, of which the House was in absolute Want.

Latrobe estimated the cost of putting the house in shape at $10,740.43, which was a lot of money in those days.

The way the President ran "the President's house" depended on the man, and on his politics. Jefferson and Jackson, for example, were ostentatiously democratic, whereas James Monroe, in the earlier tradition of Washington and the first Adams, was positively regal. He was determined, Monroe announced, to place the social and diplomatic life of the White House "upon a footing of form and ceremony." In Constance McLaughlin Green's history of the city, a contemporary of Monroe's is quoted on the resulting horrors of dining at the White House.

The ordeal began at five-thirty, when guests were led, "indian file," into the East Room (where Abigail Adams had hung out her washing only a few years before), to find the President sitting in regal splendor, alone in the center of the room. His guests solemnly and wordlessly shook his hand, and then took their places in chairs lined up against the wall, where they "sat in a row in solemn state. . . . Not a whisper broke upon the ear to interrupt the silence of the place, and everyone looked as if the next moment would be his last."

It must have been horrible. But Monroe made up for his stuffiness by his excellent taste in French plate and furniture. Some of the best things in the White House today owe their presence there to his discerning eye.

A President is both the Chief of State, and thus the social equal of any sovereign, and an elected politician, and thus dependent on the fickle favor of the people. In their tenure of the White House, the Presidents, up through John F. Kennedy and Lyndon Johnson, have been part monarch and part democratic politician, the mixture depending on the man. Dwight D. Eisenhower, for example, strongly inclined to the monarchical manner of the Washington-Monroe tradition. At White House dinner parties, the President and Mrs. Eisenhower customarily sat side by side, on the theory that it gave the commonalty pleasure to be able to feast its eyes simultaneously on *both* the President and his First Lady.

There was a strong flavor of a royal court about John Kennedy's White House too, albeit a gay and unstuffy court. Lyndon Johnson's White House is a nice mixture of the monarchical—members of the White House press corps maliciously refer to the President as "His Majesty"—and the Jefferson-Jackson "Democratical" tradition.

In this as in so many other ways, the muddy, streetless settlement which Jefferson helped to create was the legitimate progenitor of the Washington of today, as the child is father of the man. It is odd how constantly certain themes repeat themselves. One is the powerful female influence on the town. The female influence ended the Presidential ambitions of three men—Alexander Hamilton, John C. Calhoun, and Samuel J. Tilden—and saved one President—Andrew Johnson—from impeachment.

Before the election of 1800 Hamilton publicly and most indiscreetly confessed that he had paid blackmail in an attempt to conceal an "amorous connection" with a Philadelphia lady, one Mrs. Reynolds. The admission began the process of his political destruction, which was physically completed in 1804, when Hamilton was already a political has-been, and when Aaron Burr's bullet ended his life on the wooded heights of Weehawken.

Calhoun's ambitions were stultified by a snobbish wife. Andrew Jackson had appointed an old army pal, Major John Eaton, as Secretary of War. Eaton's wife, the beautiful Peggy, was "no better than she should be"—it was even rumored that Eaton had been her lover while her first husband, who died a mysterious death at sea, was still alive. Peggy was roundly denounced by the pastor of the Second

Presbyterian Church, and the ladies of the Cabinet, led by the strong-minded wife of Vice President John C. Calhoun, ostracized her.

Jackson, whose own wife had been calumniated as his "paramoor" during the vicious 1828 campaign, was furious. He called the Cabinet into session and lectured the members angrily, insisting on the virtue of the lovely Peggy. But Mrs. Calhoun was adamant, and the other ladies of the Cabinet stood fast with her. Then, on a morning horseback ride, Jackson's Secretary of State, the astute Martin Van Buren, known as "the Red Fox of Kinderhook," put forward a modest proposal. Why not solve the problem by firing the whole Cabinet and getting a new one?

Jackson did precisely that, and Van Buren lost his job, along with the rest of the Cabinet. But Van Buren became Jackson's trusted adviser and protégé, and when Jackson ran for his second term, in 1832, Calhoun, Jackson's logical successor, was cast into outer darkness, and Van Buren replaced him as Vice President. In 1837—thanks to the snobbish Mrs. Calhoun and the notorious Peggy—the Red Fox of Kinderhook succeeded to the Presidency, while Calhoun, furious in disappointment, took so blindly adamant a stand on the slavery issue that he helped to bring on the Civil War.

The savior of Andrew Johnson was winsome Vinnie Ream, a schoolgirl-sculptress, who was only sixteen when she sought, and obtained, permission to sculpt the head of President Abraham Lincoln from life. In 1868, after the President's assassination, Vinnie, nineteen years old by this time, was working away to complete a memorial statue of the murdered President, in a cozy little studio in the Capitol. Her warm friend, admirer, and protector, Senator E. G. Ross of Kansas, had obtained for her both the commission to complete the statue and the Capitol studio.

Senator Ross was a Republican, but not a radical Republican like Thaddeus Stevens, leader of the move to impeach Andrew Johnson, and the most merciless and vindictive politician the United States has produced. Stevens and the other ruling radicals passed the word that Senator Ross had better vote for impeachment if pretty Vinnie wanted to keep her studio and her commission. But Ross, bravely encouraged by Vinnie, refused to bow to this blackmail, and Vinnie lost her studio and her commission, while the impeachment of Andrew Johnson failed by one vote.

The story had a happy ending for Vinnie Ream. Uncharacteristically, the radicals relented and restored her commission and even her studio in the Capitol. In 1871 Vinnie's statue of Lincoln was duly unveiled and placed in the rotunda of the Capitol, where it is still a favorite with tourists.

It was not a favorite with Mark Twain, who wrote that in passing through the rotunda

you could not help seeing Mr. Lincoln, as petrified by a young lady artist for $10,000—and you might take his marble emancipation proclamation which he holds out in his hand and contemplates, for a folded napkin; and you might conceive from his expression and his attitude that he is finding fault with the washing. Which is not the case. Nobody knows what is the matter with him; but everybody feels for him.

Despite Mark Twain's waspishness, Vinnie became a successful sculptress. She opened a prosperous studio on Farragut Square, where her statue of Admiral Farragut, a favorite target for pigeons, still stands. And in the end she married, not the noble Senator, but one Engineer Lieutenant Hoxie, and lived happily ever after.

But the ending was happy also for the United States. For the defiant vote of her "protector," Senator Ross, provided the one-vote margin which defeated the attempt by the radicals to destroy the power of the Presidency and substitute government by a Congressional clique. If Ross had knuckled under, and the attempt to impeach President Johnson had succeeded, the balanced American political system, which on the whole has worked miraculously and mysteriously well, would certainly have been undermined and might have been destroyed.

The lady who kept Samuel J. Tilden out of the White House was Kate Chase Sprague, a redheaded beauty. Tilden not only wanted to be President; he was duly and legally elected to that office, when, thanks in large part to the beautiful Kate, the Presidency was flagrantly stolen from him.

Kate Chase Sprague is almost wholly forgotten now, but in her time she was a major political figure. She never got to the White House, though not for want of trying, but she dominated Washington socially as it has been dominated by only a few First Ladies, like Dolley Madison and Jacqueline Kennedy. Kate was a woman of truly astonishing arrogance, and she was only twenty-two when she demonstrated her consummate mastery of the art of one-upmanship, which has always been sedulously practiced in Washington.

She was the daughter and official hostess of Abraham Lincoln's first Secretary of the Treasury, Salmon P. Chase. As such, she was invited to the President's first dinner party for his Cabinet.

"I shall be glad to see you at any time," said Mrs. Lincoln in kindly tones to the young girl, as the guests took their leave.

"Mrs. Lincoln," said Kate, "I shall be glad to have *you* call on *me* at any time."

Kate's father was appointed Chief Justice of the United States, but that was not good enough for Kate; she wanted to preside over the White House as her father's hostess. To that end, she persuaded him to switch to the Democratic Party, and at the 1868 Democratic Convention Chief Justice Salmon P. Chase was a promising dark horse. Kate herself circulated through the convention hall, charming the delegates with her beauty and wheedling votes from them, but Chase's official manager was the Governor of New York, Horatio Seymour.

Another big wheel at the convention was Samuel J. Tilden, a rich and very able corporation lawyer, who always looked as though he had just swallowed a persimmon. Tilden was strongly anti-Chase, and he cut the ground out from under the Chase candidacy by engineering the draft nomination of Chase's manager, Horatio Seymour. Thus Kate's Presidential aspirations for her father were ended, and Kate conceived an undying hatred for Samuel J. Tilden.

She had her revenge eight years later, when Tilden had become a Presidential candidate himself. By this time, Kate had married Senator William Sprague of Rhode Island, an immensely rich, immensely dull textile manufacturer. Kate soon abandoned as hopeless any Presidential ambitions for Sprague, and chose, both as her lover and as her next Presidential aspirant, Senator Roscoe Conkling of New York.

Conkling is also almost wholly forgotten now, but he also was a major political figure in his time. He was immensely vain—he was especially proud of his athletic figure, and in order to preserve it, he had a habit when walking of pulling in his belly and expanding his chest. As a result, Conkling's way of walking was a "turkey-cock strut," as Senator James G. Blaine ("of the state of Maine") pointed out in public, thus initiating a lifelong feud with Conkling.

Conkling must have been able as well as vain. For a time he dominated the Senate as it has been dominated by only a handful of men, like Henry Clay, or Nelson Rockefeller's grandfather, Senator Aldrich of Rhode Island, or Senator Lyndon B. Johnson in our own time. Conkling was the original of "Senator Ratcliffe" in Henry Adams' *roman à clef*, *Democracy*, and Kate Chase Sprague is "Mrs. Lightfoot Lee" in the same novel. Anyone wishing to enjoy the full, ripe flavor of Washington life in the post-Civil War period should read the novel.

In 1876 Samuel Tilden, who had by then broken the Tweed Ring and served as Governor of New York, won the Democratic Presidential nomination without serious opposition. He went on to win the election with a plurality of 250,000 votes over the Republican candidate, Rutherford Hayes, and a majority in the electoral college of 196 to 173. But Union troops were still in the South, and carpetbagger Republican election boards in Florida and Louisiana voided some fourteen thousand votes for Tilden, enough to give the twelve electoral votes of those states to Hayes. Thus Hayes was given a thoroughly phony majority of one in the electoral college.

A great uproar quite naturally ensued, and Congress created an Electoral Commission of five Senators, five Representatives and five Justices of the Supreme Court to choose between Hayes and Tilden. The Commission was divided along party lines, eight Republicans to seven Democrats. Conkling, who had himself hungered mightily for the Republican nomination, hated Hayes like poison. He had enough influence to swing over at least two of the eight Republican votes on the Commission to Tilden, the rightful winner, and he planned to do so, and thus enjoy his revenge on Hayes.

But the lovely Kate hated Tilden even more than Conkling hated Hayes, and she badgered her paramour, storming and fretting until her hatred of Tilden prevailed over his hatred of Hayes. So in the end the eight Republi-

cans on the Commission voted solidly against the seven
Democrats, and the stolen election was confirmed for Hayes.
Thus Tilden paid with the Presidency for his mistake in
frustrating the indomitable Kate in 1868.

There was one good result. Hayes, in a gesture of appease-
ment to the Democrats and the South, withdrew the Union
forces from the Southern states, and so ended the hateful
Reconstruction era. Otherwise the story of Kate Chase
Sprague, unlike the story of Vinnie Ream, ends sadly.

Her protégé and lover, Roscoe Conkling, carried on endless feuds with his fellow Republicans—notably with President Hayes over Civil Service reform (Conkling called it
"snivel service reform")—and he had almost wrecked the
Republican Party by the time he died of overexposure in the
Great Blizzard of 1888. As for poor Kate, she lost all her
money and grew old and ugly. As an old woman, she rang
the doorbells of the rich, to peddle milk and eggs and
chickens produced on a run-down place her father had
bought in the days when Kate dominated the Washington
social scene. Thus the arrogant beauty who had snubbed the
President's wife got her comeuppance.

The female influence in Washington always has been, and
still is, oblique, like Kate Chase Sprague's or Vinnie Ream's
or Peggy Eaton's. When the Nineteenth Amendment was
ratified in 1920, there were masculine fears that the ladies,
being a majority of the population, might take over the
Congress, or even the White House. In fact, no female politician, not even the durable Margaret Chase Smith of Maine,
has ever achieved a really important position of influence in
Congress. The women who have occupied high appointive
posts have generally performed an essentially decorative
function, as visible evidence of the tender regard for the
female vote of the administration in power. Washington is
still, despite the Nineteenth Amendment, run by men (like

every other city in the country, contrary to the old myth about the United States being a matriarchy). And there are still women in Washington who share the sentiment expressed by Peggy Eaton in her old age: "God help the woman who must live in Washington."

Yet the oblique power of the "women who must live in Washington" is very real all the same. One reason may be the female habit of outliving males, which seems to be even more marked in Washington than elsewhere. In the post-World War II era, Mrs. Nicholas Longworth, Mrs. Robert Woods Bliss, Mrs. Robert Bacon, Mrs. Borden Harriman, and Mrs. Truxtun Beale were all Washington hostesses who were so respected and influential (and who laid such good tables) that their invitations were royal commands. All were widows in their seventies and eighties.

Another example of the longevity of the Washington female is found in the list of dignitaries invited to attend the laying of the cornerstone of the Washington Monument. Alexander Hamilton was killed by Aaron Burr in 1804, and James and Dolley Madison left the White House in 1817. The cornerstone of the Washington Monument was laid in 1847, and the ceremony was attended by *both* Mrs. Hamilton and Mrs. Madison, both long widowed by that time. Old Dolley, who kept a house in Lafayette Square opposite the White House (from which she had fled in 1814 with a Stuart portrait of Washington and the family silver), was famous for her splendid New Year's Day parties. From 1817 to 1849, when she died at eighty-one, she was the town's most popular hostess.

The Washington hostess has always performed an essential function in bringing together in one place the men who run (or, far more often, think they run) the country. Dining out is regarded as part of the job by most inhabitants of Political Washington—politicians, upper bureaucrats, diplomats, journalists, and the like—and hostesses, pretty, witty, or merely rich, are essential to the process of dining out.

The main purpose of dining out is to talk, not to eat, which is doubtless one reason why Henry James called Washington "the city of conversation." The conversation at Washington dinner parties can be as boring as the conversation at dinner parties in Grosse Point or even Manhattan, above all to those uninterested in politics, the city's single industry. But Washington has produced some good talk in the past, and on occasion still does.

Some researcher with a sense of humor ought to undertake an anthology of Washington wit—especially the well-phrased political insult, which has been a Washington specialty ever since the days of John Randolph of Roanoke. Randolph, a brilliant, elongated Viriginia aristocrat, had been rendered sterile by a mysterious disease which left him with a hairless face, a high, childish voice, and bitterness in his heart. He was perhaps the best hater American politics has produced—better even than old Thad Stevens—and his pet hate (among many) was Henry Clay. Andrew Jackson, also a good hater, called Clay "the Judas of the West," but Randolph was far more devastating: "He shines and stinks, like rotten mackerel by moonlight."

There is a macabre and lunatic quality in this insult which has never been surpassed. (Some authorities claim that the insult was addressed, not to Clay but to Edward Livingston, but Clay seems a more likely target.) Randolph did almost as well in replying to an enemy who remarked of him during a Congressional debate, "Thank God that this father of lies can never be the father of liars."

"Sir," Randolph responded, "you pride yourself on an animal faculty in which the Negro is fully your equal and the jackass infinitely your superior."

Randolph's pet hate, Henry Clay, was himself no slouch at repartee. His best counterthrust was inspired by a particularly pompous and tedious member of the House, who in the course of a debate declared to Clay, "You, sir, speak for the moment. I speak for posterity."

"You are right, sir," said Clay. "And apparently you are determined to speak until the arrival of your audience."

In our own day, Alice Roosevelt Longworth has probably displayed the greatest mastery of the dying art of political insult. Two remarks about Thomas E. Dewey which have been attributed to her (incorrectly, she modestly insists) are appropriately devastating: "He looks like the little man on the wedding cake" and "You have to know Dewey *really* well in order to dislike him thoroughly."

Her description of Czolgosz, whose murder of McKinley elevated her father to the Presidency, as "the founder of the family fortunes" has the faintly macabre quality of good Washington wit. So does her warning about politicians with the tonsorial habits of an Arthur Vandenberg or a Douglas MacArthur, both of whom combed their hair so as to conceal their bald spots: "Never trust a man who parts his hair under his left armpit."

Mrs. Longworth's husband, Nicholas Longworth, Speaker of the House, and a very dark horse Presidential candidate in 1928, was also witty. Perhaps his most crushing riposte was directed at a presumptuous Congressman who passed his hand over Longworth's bald head and remarked, "Feels just like my wife's bottom."

Longworth passed his own hand over his own head, and then said thoughtfully: "By golly, it does, doesn't it?"

In any anthology of the art of the political insult another Speaker of the House would certainly have pride of place. Thomas B. Reed of Maine was Speaker in the Harrison, Cleveland, and McKinley administrations. "Czar" Reed, a plump, moon-faced, brilliantly able man, also a dark-horse Presidential aspirant, was responsible for the best definition of a statesman: "A successful politician who is dead." Here is a small selection of other Reedisms:

To a pious politician who used the old cliché that he "would rather be right than President": "The gentleman need not worry—he will never be either."

To the youthful Theodore Roosevelt, of his self-righteousness: "If there is one thing more than another for which I admire you, it is your original discovery of the Ten Commandments."

When the chaplain prayed unctuously that the Speaker would conduct the affairs of the House according to the will of God and without regard to partisan politics: "I never heard a more preposterous prayer addressed to the Throne of Grace."

In reply to the fatuous speech of a political opponent: "The gentleman never opens his mouth without subtracting from the sum total of human knowledge."

There have been recent times when political humor has been suspect as somehow subversive, notably during the McCarthy period and the Eisenhower administration. John Kennedy made humor respectable again, but political humor is now left largely to such brilliant specialists as Art Buchwald and Russell Baker, and the art of the really devastating riposte, in the manner of Randolph of Roanoke or Czar Reed, is almost a lost art.

Another lost art, alas, seems to be the ability to design and erect reasonably pleasing public buildings—not that there has ever been a period in Washington's history when that art was thoroughly mastered. From the time when L'Enfant designed a totally imaginary capital city, "magnificent enough to grace a great nation," Washington has been as preoccupied with its appearance as a young girl; and some of the things that have been said about the city's appearance would produce a traumatic shock in any young girl.

Sir Augustus John Foster's description of the place as "this discouraging waste" and "scarce any better than a swamp" typified the reaction of most foreign visitors. Oddly enough, Mrs. Trollope, whose snotty book on the *Domestic Manners of the Americans*, published in 1832, infuriated the entire country, liked Washington: "I was delighted with the whole aspect of Washington; light, cheerful and airy, it reminded me of our fashionable watering places." One suspects that on her visit Mrs. Trollope was peculiarly lucky in the weather.

Harriet Martineau, another British literary lady, who visited America a few years later, gave a vivid if not very complimentary picture of the city in the late eighteen-thirties.

The city itself is unlike any other that ever was seen, straggling out hither and thither, with a small house or two a quarter of a mile from any other; so that in making calls "in the city" we had to cross ditches and stiles, and walk alternately on grass and pavements, and strike across a field to reach a street. . . . Then there was the society, singularly compounded from the largest variety of elements; foreign ambassadors, the American government, members of Congress, from Clay and Webster down to Davy Crockett, Benton from Missouri, and Cuthbert, with the freshest Irish brogue, from Georgia; flippant young belles; pious wives dutifully attending their husbands, and groaning over the frivolities of the place; grave judges, saucy travellers, pert newspaper reporters, melancholy Indian chiefs, and timid New England Ladies, trembling on the verge of the vortex; all this was wholly unlike anything that is to be seen in any other city in the world; for all these are mixed up together in daily intercourse like the higher circle of a little village, and there is nothing else.

Another visiting British writer, Captain Frederick Marryat, who came to Washington about the same time, wrote:

Everybody knows that Washington has a Capitol, but the misfortune is that the Capitol wants a city. There it stands, reminding you of a general without an army, only surrounded by a parcel of ragged little boys, for such is the appearance of the dirty, straggling, ill-built houses which lie at the foot of it.

Visiting America and writing unpleasant things about the country has always been a considerable industry among the British literary, but never more so than in the pre-Civil War period. Until Rudyard Kipling came along, Charles Dickens was probably the champion America-denigrator. He wrote a famous passage about Washington in 1842, in which he said that the city consisted of "spacious avenues that began in nothing and lead nowhere; streets a mile long that only want houses, roads, and inhabitants; public buildings that need only a public to be complete; and ornaments of great thoroughfares which need only thoroughfares to ornament." Washington, he decided, was a "monument raised to a deceased project." He was convinced that the "project"—L'Enfant's ambitious plan for that city "magnificent enough to grace a great nation"—would never be revived, and for a good many decades he was right.

Native critics of the place were equally caustic. President Madison, who liked society almost as much as his wife Dolley, complained that when Congress was not in session the city was "a solitude." Washington Irving called it a "desert city" during the Congressional recess. Until rather recently, Washington was indeed a desert city after Congress had gone home, especially in the hot summer months, when the President and the diplomatic corps would also flee the town. Nowadays Congress stays on through the early autumn at least, and air-conditioning makes the summer more supportable.

Also until rather recently, foreign diplomats disliked being assigned to Washington, not only because it was a diplomatic backwater, but because the town was so hot, ugly, and uncomfortable. Constance McLaughlin Green tells in her admirable history of the city how Napoleon III's Minister to the United States, Prévost-Paradol, shot himself in Georgetown, during the height of a heat wave. The real reason was his despair at the outbreak of the disastrous Franco-Prussian War, but it was widely assumed that "the excessive heat had unhinged his mind"—a very natural assumption, as anyone who has spent a summer in Georgetown without benefit of air-conditioning will surely agree.

Washington seems to have come in for especially harsh criticism in the post-Civil War period. A Senator in the seventies called Washington "the ugliest city in the whole country," and Horace Greeley summed up the general reaction to the town: "The rents are high, the food is bad, the dust is disgusting, the mud is deep, and the morals are deplorable." Another contemporary Senator complained of "the infinite, abominable nuisance of cows, and horses, and sheep and goats, running through all the streets of the city, and whenever we appropriate money to set up a shade tree, there comes along a cow or a horse or a goat, and tears it down the next day, and then we appropriate again."

The cows and other livestock have gone, and so have the dust and the mud. But the "excessive heat" is still very much a part of the Washington scene, and no one will maintain that L'Enfant's old dream has been wholly realized even yet. Washington is a museum of American taste in public architecture, a great deal of it execrable. The invaluable WPA guide to Washington is particularly caustic about the post-Civil War period of Washington architecture.

"The vast disrupture of the war," writes the anonymous but highly articulate author of this section of the book,

followed by our expanding industrialism and the conquest of the West, was accompanied by a collapse in taste that gave rise in turn to a fearful and wonderful architecture. Within the brief span of a few decades it passed through numerous influences— Victorian, Gothic, Romanesque, neoclassic, Egyptian, and possibly a combination of all these—without apparent anguish, unless we count our own. It left . . . a great architectural backwash of ill-conceived forms devoid alike of rhyme or reason.

The writer points to the Smithsonian Institution, which was started in 1847, "as a kind of forerunner of the architecture to come," and to the National Museum, the Old State Department Building next to the White House, and the Library of Congress as horrible examples of post-Civil War architecture. Beauty lies in the eyes of the beholder, of course, and in the eyes of this beholder, these nineteenth-century horrors elicit a kind of affectionate pleasure, especially the Old State Department Building.

It is easy to see why Henry Adams called the building an "architectural infant asylum," and why the architect Charles F. McKim, asked what he thought of it, replied: "Bring me an ax." Still, this architectural oddity with its endless profusion of strictly nonfunctional balusters, balustrades and balconies pleasingly recalls a simpler time.

In the years immediately after the Second World War, when James F. Byrnes was Secretary of State, and I first started reporting in Washington, the State Department was still housed in the old building, and some of the senior officers still had fires in their fireplaces. There was a human dimension about the State Department then, a sense of personal contact, which is utterly lacking in the vast and hideous monument to bureaucracy which now houses the department. Ever since the department moved out of the old building, it has become bigger and bigger, and the making of foreign policy has become sludgier and sludgier. There are those who maintain that the only way to reverse the process of progressive sludgification is to cut the department back to its size in James Byrnes' day, and move back into the old building.

Time tames the ugliness of most buildings, even the ugliest—the Smithsonian Institution, a Norman castle in red sandstone, is another example of this rule. The big, conventionally classic buildings of the Beaux Arts period after the turn of the century seem not unpleasing by now, in a placid, conventional way, and the buildings of the Federal Triangle, built in the nineteen-twenties, are at least tolerable by this time. The Capitol is perhaps the best example of all of the mellowing influence of time. Here is the anonymous WPA author on the Capitol:

The interior, taken by and large, is lamentably bad; the exterior is not above question and criticism; yet, viewed as a whole, the Capitol dominates the architecture of Washington like a kind of grand dowager—rich in meretricious possessions, yet secure and queenly in her superb setting.

There are also structures in Washington which even the most captious find pleasing—notably the White House and the Washington Monument. The most displeasing public buildings (in the eye of this beholder) are those built since World War II, all of which are ugly, and some of which, like the curiously vulgar New House Office Building, are very ugly indeed. Perhaps time's mellowing effect will cause future generations to view even this heavy-handed horror with affection, but it seems unlikely.

The best view of Washington is from an airplane, flying low, in summer, on a clear day. Despite the horrors, Washington from the air is a handsome city. A chief reason is the custom of planting trees, which Jefferson started, and which was revived by "Boss" Sheperd, a now forgotten local political figure who was much criticized for his extravagance in planting six thousand shade trees. Washington has been a sort of urban forest ever since, and thanks to the trees, and to federal money, and to the passage of time, Washington is certainly no longer "the ugliest city in the whole country." In fact, it is probably the third handsomest (after San Francisco and Manhattan). On a fine spring day the city even deserves the adjective "beautiful."

Since George Washington's old dream of making the federal city a great center of trade and industry died its fortunate death, more than a century ago, Washington's only big business has been the business of government. That business has enjoyed an enviable growth rate, especially since the turn of the century. A few figures tell the story. In 1800, when the U.S. Government moved to Washington from Philadelphia, the Washington bureaucracy consisted of about 130 clerks. At the end of John Quincy Adams' administration, there were 301 government employees; at the end of the Civil War 7,000; 7,800 by 1880; 26,000 by 1901; 166,000 in Washington by 1940; and today government employees in Washington or the Washington area number 312,295, not counting the Central Intelligence Agency and the National Security Agency.

At least since the Chesapeake and Ohio Canal project collapsed, there has never been any doubt at all that the federal government has been the city's only real reason for being. Government means politics, and politics means conflict. Conflict, in turn, leads to violence, and violence in one form or another is also a recurrent Washington theme.

In American politics there is a tradition of verbal violence, as the examples of Washington wit cited earlier clearly suggest. Especially in the early days of the Republic, verbal violence often invited physical violence. Burr, for example, challenged Hamilton on the basis of a newspaper report of the "despicable opinion which General Hamilton has expressed of Mr. Burr." Henry Clay, finally goaded beyond endurance, challenged John Randolph because of Randolph's description of a temporary political alliance between Clay

and John Quincy Adams as "the combination, hitherto un-
heard of, between Blifil and Black George, between Puritan
and blackleg." The only casualty was the long white great-
coat or wraprascal which Randolph habitually wore—it
suffered a single bullet wound.

Dueling was standard practice in pre-Civil War days.
Commodore Stephen Decatur, hero of the war on the Bar-
bary pirates, for example, was killed by his former superior
officer, Commodore James Barron, when Decatur refused to
apologize for what Barron considered a slander on his name.
President Jackson fought several duels, and carried a dueling bullet in his chest, and another in his arm, into the
White House. The "field of honor" for Washington duelists
was in suburban Bladensburg, which was also, incidentally,
the scene of the most humiliating battle American forces
have ever fought. The battle, if it can be called that, occurred in 1814 when fifteen hundred British invaders met
more than five thousand American defenders at Bladensburg,
five miles east of Washington. The Americans promptly ran
away, almost without firing a shot, and the burning of the
Capitol and the White House ensued. The battle was subsequently sardonically labeled "the Bladensburg races," and it
is not a battle children read much about in the standard
texts.

Violence also frequently occurred, on a more informal
basis than on the Bladensburg "field of honor," on Capitol
Hill (which was known originally as "Jenkin's Hill"). Republican Congressman Matthew Lyon of Vermont, an aggressive Irishman described by a Federalist poet as "a
strange, offensive brute, too wild to tame, too base to shoot,"
was one of the principals in the first fight to occur on the
floor of Congress. The other was a Connecticut Federalist,
Congressman Roger Griswold. As Roger Butterfield de-

scribes the historic battle in *The American Past*, Griswold "made an insulting remark about Lyon's Revolutionary record, and Lyon bristled up to him and spat in his face. Two weeks later Griswold worked up enough courage to attack Lyon with his cane, and Lyon hit back with a pair of tongs from one of the Congressional fireplaces."

Lyon was later arrested, under the Alien and Sedition Acts, for writing that President Adams had an "unbounded thirst for ridiculous pomp, foolish adulation, and selfish avarice." He was put in jail, but the Vermonters re-elected him from jail by a landslide, and Jefferson helped to pay his fine.

There were other scenes of violence in Congress, especially before the Civil War, when the slavery issue aroused violent passions. Senator Henry S. Foote of Mississippi threatened the antislavery leader Senator Thomas Hart Benton with a pistol. Benton bared his breast, shouting, "Let the assassin shoot. He knows I am unarmed," and Foote scuttled away. In 1856 Senator Charles Sumner of Massachusetts, another antislavery leader, was beaten almost to death by a gutta-percha cane wielded by Representative Preston Brooks of South Carolina. In 1902 Senator "Pitchfork Ben" Tillman, also of South Carolina (these Southerners are hot-blooded), beat up a fellow Senator in the well of the Senate, and President Theodore Roosevelt, to show his disapproval, canceled Tillman's invitation to a state dinner at the White House.

In modern times, the mad fusillade of Puerto Rican revolutionaries from the House gallery in 1954 fortunately killed no one, though it was a close thing. Otherwise, in recent memory, there has been little public mayhem on Capitol Hill, although from time to time, especially in the bitter McCarthy era, there seemed to be the makings of a fist fight.

But the violent feelings that political issues can arouse in the breasts of men are still there, boiling away beneath the surface, and although political conflict these days rarely takes physical form, the drama that conflict produces is still the central theme of Washington life.

5

THE SAD STATE OF STATE

Fruits and treachers, the place is full of 'em.

··

There is one way for a poor man to live like a very, very rich man. That is to join the State Department's Foreign Service as a young man, and work his way laboriously up through the ranks until he becomes an ambassador.

An American ambassador in one of the great foreign capitals—London, Paris, Rome, Moscow, Tokyo, Bonn—lives in a luxury unmatched by any but a handful of enormously rich Americans. He lives in a huge, handsomely furnished house. A chauffeur-driven limousine is available at any hour. He has what even the very rich lack in this country—a staff of a dozen servants or more. The staff includes a first-class chef, and the ambassador (if he and his wife have any sense and discrimination at all) sets an excellent table. (Officially, he is supposed to serve American wines as his contribution to closing the dollar gap, but of course he doesn't—he serves good French or German wines.) In short, the American ambassador to a major post abroad lives very high on the hog indeed.

Of course, the American ambassador to a major post may be rich already. He may have reached his embassy, not through the toilsome Foreign Service route, but through the much simpler expedient of contributing handsomely to the campaign of the incumbent President. In the old days, rich contributors occupied most of the major posts. But as the foreign relations of the United States have become increasingly complex and increasingly important to the United States, the tendency has grown to appoint professionals— Foreign Service Officers—to the big-power capitals. The embassies of four of the six cities named above are occupied by professionals, as this is written. Of the other two, David Bruce in London, although he is not a Foreign Service Officer, is in fact one of the half-dozen most experienced and professional American diplomats; while the mission of Texas millionaire George McGhee in Bonn has been chiefly marked by a steady deterioration in U.S.–West German relations.

Over all, about 75 percent of the 110 U.S. ambassadors are career Foreign Service Officers. A career ambassador even to one of the real misery spots—Chad, say, or the Central African Republic—is likely to live in a state of reasonable comfort, and even a rather junior FSO abroad lives reasonably high by U.S. standards, with a roomy house or apartment, and a cook, a maid, perhaps a nurse. It would be hard to imagine a pleasanter place for a man who liked sea and sun and gentle tropical winds to spend his declining years than the embassy residence in Nassau, say, or the American Consul General's big house perched on the hills above Hong Kong. But, alas, there are drawbacks.

An ambassador's house is by no means his castle; or it is an ill-defended and easily breached castle at best. The American ambassador in Paris or London can expect more than a hundred members of Congress, plus dozens of representatives of the higher reaches of the executive bureaucracy, to descend on him every year, mostly in the more salubrious months. To these official visitors are added more hundreds of Very Important Persons—or those who regard themselves as Very Important Persons—from outside the government.

Even the minor embassies are constantly deluged with important or self-important American visitors, who expect as a matter of course to be entertained at the residence, and who are certain to be annoyed at being fobbed off with an invitation to a reception or cocktail party.

There are other drawbacks as well to the rich ambassadorial life. It is not true—or not necessarily true—that an American ambassador is a mere messenger boy, without influence on policy. A strong-minded and knowledgeable ambassador can strongly influence policy. Charles Bohlen, for example, has had a real influence on American policy toward the France of Charles de Gaulle; he persuaded the Johnson administration that in respect to de Gaulle it was best to adopt the Biblical rule: "It is useless to kick against the pricks." Llewellyn Thompson has had a deep influence on American policy toward the Soviet Union, and other ambassadors have also helped to shape U.S. foreign policy in important ways.

But it *is* true that Washington will treat an ambassador like a messenger boy if Washington can get away with it. The Washington bureaucracy has an ungovernable compulsion to breathe down any ambassador's neck at all hours of the day and night. It was on a long tour of Africa some time ago that I first became fully aware of how the Washington bureaucracy hog-tied an American ambassador in the field. There was, for example, the incident of the Guinean students.

The Communist-leaning Guinean government had designated four hundred Guinean students as eligible for foreign scholarships. Immediately, an East-West scramble for these future Guinean leaders developed, and the American Embassy managed to get thirty-two boys assigned to scholarships in the United States. The boys assigned to the Soviet Union and Eastern Europe were whisked off immediately by plane, and those assigned to Western European countries (mostly Britain) followed soon after. But when I arrived in Guinea, the boys assigned to the United States were still in Conakry, the capital. They had been there, twiddling their thumbs, for several weeks, while all Conakry snickered about that fabled "American efficiency."

It turned out that there was something called the DSP66 Form, which had to be filled out in triplicate, sent back to Washington, "processed" through the bureaucratic sludge, and then returned to Conakry. But the real trouble was the "security check." The security problem was complicated by the fact that Guineans are unoriginal about names, and most of the boys had the same surnames and no first names at all. It was several weeks before the welcome news came back to Conakry that Washington's copious files contained no "derogatory information" about these teen-age boys fresh out of the Guinean bush. At long last the boys were allowed to emplane for the land of the free. In the meantime, of course, the Ambassador of the United States had been made to look just plain foolish.

Soviet ambassadors abroad, contrary to the widespread myth that they must check everything down to dinner invitations with Moscow, operate with remarkable freedom in some respects. In Africa and other underdeveloped areas, they not only offer scholarships freely; they also commit the Soviet Union to aid on major projects, dams, stadiums, and the like, seemingly on their own initiative. By contrast, one

American chief of mission in Africa seemed to be spending most of his time arguing alternately with his strong-minded wife and the State Department administrative services about the interior decoration in the living room of his new residence. His wife, quite rightly, found the color scheme detestable, but Washington refused to change it, and there was nothing the poor chief of mission could do about it. "I've got to cable Washington for permission to go to the bathroom," another chief of mission in Africa complained bitterly, and his complaint is echoed by American chiefs of mission the world over.

The mindless impulse of the Washington bureaucracy to try to run everything at long distance has operated most powerfully in Vietnam. In Saigon the pressure from Washington to find some magic formula to get the war over with is so heavy that it is known as "the blowtorch." Vietnam also provides a striking example of the urge of all Washington departments and agencies to shoulder the State Department aside and to get into the foreign policy act. The little country, as this is written, is crawling with representatives of at least three dozen Washington departments, bureaus, and agencies.

To cite one specific example, the provincial town of Mytho in the Mekong Delta in 1964 harbored precisely one representative of the American civilian bureaucracy—a very young and very junior State Department man, whose office was his jeep. A couple of years later, there were more than twenty American civilians from half a dozen departments and agencies in the place—more than three times the number of French civilian officials in Mytho when the colonial era was in full flower. They had all the appurtenances of the American official abroad—offices, vehicles, villas, and organization charts to establish the pecking order.

From Mytho right around the globe to Conakry—or Paris

—the conduct of American foreign policy abroad has one absolutely consistent fault: there are too many Americans involved in it. On this score the testimony is abundant and unanimous. Henry Villard, a retired Foreign Service Officer, cites various eyebrow-raising statistics in his *Affairs at State*. For example, the U.S. diplomatic mission in Bujumbura, capital of the new African state of Burundi, came to more than sixty Americans—more foreigners than there were in the whole country when the Belgians ran the territory. Again, "the collective American representation in Rome is between 800 and 900," while the British and the French somehow each make do with less than eighty.

On this subject, former Ambassador (to several countries) Ellis Briggs has been more eloquent than anyone else. "Practically every United States diplomatic mission in the world," he has written, "is so stuffed with unnecessary personnel that the handful of State Department officials trying to perform substantive diplomatic functions can scarcely find a chair to sit on, or a desk on which to stack the papers."

To prove his point, he tells the story of the Science Attaché in Brazil and the Coast Guard mission in Greece. When he was Ambassador to Brazil, he received notification that a science attaché, a Ph.D. in physics, was about to be assigned to his mission. He cabled the State Department: "The American Embassy in Rio de Janeiro needs a science attaché the way a cigar store Indian needs a brassiere." The Deputy Under Secretary for Administration replied frostily, "Your telegram did not amuse the White House." In time, the Science Attaché duly arrived, although there was really nothing for him to do.

Briggs went from Rio to Athens, his last post as ambassador. In Athens he found that the Coast Guard maintained an office in the U.S. Embassy. This was, after thirty years in the diplomatic service, a new experience for Briggs. He diligently inquired what function the Coast Guard contingent was expected to perform. He found no sensible answer, and sent a message to the State Department requesting their removal. This, too, was a futile gesture. How futile is suggested by the fact that whereas in Briggs' day the Coast Guard detachment was run by a mere lieutenant commander, it has now been upgraded and is headed by a full commander; and in Brazil there is, as this is written, no longer one science attaché—there are two science attachés.

In late 1967 a successor of Ellis Briggs as Ambassador to Brazil, John Willis Tuthill, received a telegram from Washington which, the optimists in the State Department hope, will have historic consequences. The telegram requested a survey on "bats and noxious birds" in Brazil. Ambassador Tuthill blew up.

He sent a telegram to Under Secretary of State Nicholas Katzenbach citing the bats-and-birds telegram as an example of the kind of bureaucratic nonsense that had swelled his mission to almost a thousand Americans and more than a thousand Brazilian employees. He proposed that State approach each of the twenty or more departments and agencies represented on his mission, and request that their staffs in Rio, both American and Brazilian, be reduced by at least a third and preferably a half. Katzenbach agreed enthusiastically, and as this is written "Operation Topsy" (so named because the vast U.S. mission in Brazil "just grew like Topsy") is going forward.

If the Rio experiment works, similar cutbacks are to be made in all the major U.S. foreign missions, and thus the incredibly luxuriant American bureaucracy abroad will be pruned back. So runs the script. If the past is any guide, the drama will follow the script only very briefly. The Rio Embassy will be pruned a bit, and there will be some pruning elsewhere. But in time—and not too much time—the rich jungle growth of the bureaucracy will again resume, more than compensating for any pruning. Most of this jungle is not the State Department's; in the missions abroad, the State Department men are a beleaguered minority.

"One of the things that truly startled me when I first came here," Under Secretary Katzenbach has said, "was to learn that no less than 80 percent of the people officially representing the United States overseas were working for agencies other than the Department of State."

Before the war the United States was actually represented in foreign lands by the State Department, but after the war, "abroad" became bureaucratically fashionable, and every department, bureau, and agency wanted to get into the act. Moreover, the various MAAG (Military Advisory Assistance Groups) and other military missions abroad helped to solve one of the oldest of military problems: what to do with the military when they have no war to fight.

A "slot" could always be found for Colonel So-and-so or Commander Such-and-such in an MAAG or as an attaché in an embassy. The trouble was, of course—and still is—that a great many countries all over the world were soon fairly pullulating with Americans in uniform, conspicuous in their large new American cars. This has been very helpful to the Communist propagandists, whose favorite theme is "American neo-colonialism."

The military are the most conspicuous members of American missions abroad. But they need never be lonely. As Briggs writes: "In addition to the propaganda, handout, and skulduggery agencies, all abundantly overstaffed, practically every executive department in Washington has permanent or temporary representation abroad." The representatives abroad, in order to prove their usefulness, keep up a massive correspondence, mostly by cable, with the home office, while the home office keeps them happy and busy with queries like the one about the bats and noxious birds. It is surprising that any serious diplomatic work ever gets done at all.

The State Department could hardly have stemmed entirely the urge of its bureaucratic rivals to get into the foreign policy act. The department has always been a weak sister politically—it has no natural political constituency in the United States, and it thus swings less weight on Capitol Hill than, say, the Civil Aeronautics Bureau or the Bureau of Indian Affairs. Moreover, with the exception of Christian Herter, the postwar Secretaries of State have had very little interest in the mechanics of the conduct of foreign policy.

The late John Foster Dulles was especially prone to regard the entire State Department much as the Roman generals regarded the *impedimenta* of wives, prostitutes, and traders who accompanied their armies on the march—as unavoidable but annoying excess baggage. Once, while attending a Pan-American meeting of foreign ministers in Brazil, Dulles made an important decision which deeply involved American policy in Europe. An aide suggested that the decision be conveyed to the appropriate regional desks of the State Department in Washington.

"Why?" Dulles inquired in mild surprise. "I'm here."

Dulles regarded the whole business of administering the State Department, or defending its interests in Washington's unending imperial wars of the bureaucracy, as no business at all of his, and in varying degrees other Secretaries of State have adopted a similar attitude. One result is that, in the postwar years, other bureaucratic empires, from the Pentagon and the CIA to the Agriculture or Treasury Departments, have forced on the beleaguered State Department a series of nonaggression treaties staking out their role in the conduct of foreign policy.

An American embassy abroad is thus festooned with bureaucrats from outside the State Department, ranging from the "spooks" of the CIA to specialists in shrimp production from the Fish and Wildlife Service. Under the circumstances, the ambassador, the official representative of the President of the United States, has no easy task remaining the master in his own house, since most of these supernumeraries look to their own agencies or departments for orders and promotions.

Soon after he became President, John F. Kennedy wrote a letter to each American ambassador firmly instructing him to be chief of his own mission henceforth, in fact as well as name. Under this dispensation all communication with Washington was to be routed through the ambassador's office, and to be approved by him. Thus the practice of completely by-passing the chief of mission, to which the CIA and the military had been particularly prone, was supposedly ended. This Kennedy order did help to make an ambassador, theoretically at least, *primus inter pares*. But the effectiveness with which an ambassador rides herd on his "country team" depends very heavily still on his personality. To be master in his own house, he must be willing to be cordially detested by a lot of the people he sees every day.

These are some of the reasons why the life of an American ambassador, despite his high living style, is not as enviable as it might seem. Another is that his tour of duty in his post is not likely to be long. The British, the French, the Russians, and most other major powers like to keep one man in the same post for five or six years, or even longer. Except for the half-dozen most important posts, the State Department habitually plays a rapid game of musical chairs, in which an ambassador from the career service rarely lasts longer than a couple of years *en poste*.

The purpose of this game of musical chairs is to make the maximum number of ambassadorships available to qualified Foreign Service Officers. This ought to be easy, for American ambassadors have experienced a population explosion of their own. In 1940 there were 19 American ambassadors; in 1950, 58; now, 110. But it isn't easy, thanks largely to what is known in the department as "the Wriston bulge."

In 1954, in compliance with the recommendations of a distinguished committee appointed by President Eisenhower and headed by Dr. Henry Wriston, the State Department endured the most disastrous in an unending series of "reforms" and "reorganizations." About 2,400 State Department employees of one sort or another—civil servants, administrators, specialists, and so on, most of whom had never served abroad and had little or no experience in diplomacy —were made Foreign Service Officers as by the touch of a magic wand. The size of the Foreign Service was thus tripled, from around 1,200 people pre-Wriston to around 3,600 today.

This "democratization" of the Foreign Service had a shattering effect on the morale of the service, already harried by the attacks of Joseph R. McCarthy. In the McCarthy era, a Foreign Service Officer had to endure being widely regarded as a homosexual, or a traitor, or quite possibly a homosexual traitor. Once, during the height of the McCarthy era, I took a taxi to the State Department, and as the taxi drew up before the entrance, I heard the driver muttering something.

"What did you say?" I asked.

"Fruits and treachers," he said. "Nothin' in there but treachers and fruits. I see 'em goin' in and out all day, in their tammyshanters and their fur-covered shoes. Fruits and treachers, the place is full of 'em."

Presumably he had seen Frenchmen in berets or Englishmen wearing reversed-calf shoes. When I repeated his remark to Foreign Service friends, they were at best faintly amused. They were not even faintly amused by another story that I found amusing, and that may be true. McCarthy and such imitators as Senator Kenneth Wherry of Nebraska, known at the time as "the merry mortician," had started attacking the State Department for harboring homosexuals, after a State Department underling, testifying before a Senate committee, had unwisely revealed that a dozen or so homosexual employees of the department had been fired.

According to the story current at the time, someone in the Republican National Committee read the late Dr. Kinsey's report on the sexual habits of the American male and reached the horrifying conclusion that "the homosexual vote" was almost as big as "the Negro vote" and much higher than "the Jewish vote." The word was passed to McCarthy and company to "lay off the pansies," and they duly complied. The story may be apocryphal, but it is true that McCarthy dropped the homosexual line of attack, suddenly and completely.

To the beleaguered members of the Foreign Service, there was nothing even faintly amusing about the McCarthy era. With some lapses which he later regretted, Secretary of State Dean Acheson ("the red Dean," McCarthy called him) stood up bravely to the attack. John Foster Dulles, by contrast, unwisely supposed that McCarthy could be appeased, and as a result some very able Foreign Service Officers were cast to the wolves. The most conspicuous was John Davies, a brilliant Far Eastern specialist, who was dismissed and denied his pension rights in 1954. His chief sin lay in having expressed views on China policy sharply at variance with those of Republican doctrine, in those days of the "unleashing" of Chiang Kai-shek.

The sacrifice of Davies, and other similar surrenders to McCarthyism, certainly did not improve morale. At the time, in a courageous letter of protest to Charles Saltzman, the Eisenhower-appointed Under Secretary of State for Ad-

ministration, veteran FSO Robert Joyce summed up sentiment in the Foreign Service:

The feeling is widespread in the Foreign Service that Davies
was not a loyalty or security risk or any kind of risk other than a
public relations risk. . . . I need not add that there is a deep
feeling of revulsion at the fact that Davies was summarily
dismissed without a pension at the age of forty-seven and with a
wife and four young children.

In those days, the Foreign Service regarded itself as a
corps d'élite, and the external attack by McCarthy and his
fellow Neanderthals had a unifying internal effect, as Joyce's
indignant letter suggests. The FSOs who survived Mc-
Carthy's attacks and Dulles' too-frequent surrenders to Mc-
Carthy had a sense of having been through the fire together.
Wristonization destroyed the *esprit de corps*—the *esprit* of a
corps can hardly survive if the size of the *corps* is arbitrarily
tripled overnight. Many of the Wristonees turned out to be
able people, and even the old-guard FSOs agree that an
occasional transfusion of new blood into the Foreign Service
is badly needed. But this was more a drowning than a
transfusion, and almost everyone now agrees that the net
result was badly to demoralize the morale of the service.

With the size of the Foreign Service tripled overnight,
there were not enough good jobs to go round. This is truer
today than ever. Many able Foreign Service Officers and
Wristonees who were young men at the time of Wristonization are now reaching the age when they ought to become
chiefs of mission—or else mark down their life story as a
failure.

William Attwood, an able journalist, who served as
Ambassador to Guinea and Kenya, has described some of the
consequences of the "Wriston bulge":

From what I have seen of the State Department, the greatest concentration of executive talent can be found in the 35–45 age bracket. But most of these men and women are upper middle-level FSO-2's. With about 36 ambassadorships available each year, of which a quarter are filled by political appointees, the chances of a substantial number getting top jobs in their most productive and vigorous years are practically nonexistent. . . .

Some officers who manage to reach the top after long years of patient subordination tend to become martinets—like British Public School boys hazing their juniors because they were once hazed themselves. And their wives can be even more dictatorial: I have known of some who ordered the wives of staff members around like servants; one who put a hairdresser off limits to other wives because she didn't like him; one who insisted the staff speak to her in French; one who would whimsically appropriate a cook or piece of furniture from subordinates. A book could be written about the dragon-ladies who have dominated some of our embassies in the past.

As Attwood's words suggest, in order to become an ambassador, a Foreign Service Officer must climb a long, slippery, and above all tedious ladder. An FSO may be well up in middle age before he has done much more than stamp visas, shuffle papers, concur in reports, and remember to be politely respectful to his superiors—and above all to those "dragon-ladies," the wives of the superiors. A chief of mission (or sometimes a Mrs. chief of mission) who dislikes a junior officer can blight his career, however irrational the dislike may be. Partly because of the competitive pressure of the "Wriston bulge," selection boards seize on anything adverse in an FSO's personnel file as a reason, or an excuse, to hold him back. Thus a single adverse report may well be enough to ensure that an FSO will never make Class One, the mark of a successful career.

A good many able young FSOs, after a year or so of paper-shuffling, get out before it is too late. Recently, the attrition rate among young officers became so alarming that a survey was taken, in which those who had resigned were asked their reasons. A typical response was as follows:

"The fact that I more than doubled my total remuneration was not what caused me to leave the Foreign Service. What did cause me to leave was that after four years of Foreign Service training, I was the second of two visa officers in Rome. After six months' training in industry, I took over as manager of an oil company producing 35,000 barrels per day."

Quite naturally, the tendency of the young officers who stay with the service is to play it safe, to avoid controversial positions, to adopt a policy of blandness, until blandness becomes a way of life. Not all Foreign Service Officers are bland, of course. William Sullivan, currently one of the youngest ambassadors in the service, is by nature anything but bland. His habit of speaking his mind with force and candor grated on more than one superior, and for years he languished in the lower grades. Then, in the Kennedy administration, he was assigned to the office of W. Averell Harriman, the Assistant Secretary for the Far East. Harriman, no admirer of blandness, immediately recognized his abilities, and Sullivan rapidly passed his more cautious contemporaries on his way to the top of the career ladder, going to Laos as Ambassador at the comparatively tender age of forty-two.

"If Bill hadn't happened to be assigned to Harriman," one of his colleagues has remarked, "you can be damned sure that he'd have retired by now—or else he'd be number two or number three at some minor mission."

Sullivan had good luck, but many FSOs have bad luck. One very able officer, with a very pretty wife, had the bad luck early in his career to be assigned to an ambassador, a political appointee, who was a lecherous alcoholic. When the FSO's wife resisted the ambassador's advances, the ambassador gave the FSO an "Unsatisfactory" rating, equivalent in the State Department to the kiss of death. It haunted his career forever after.

Aside from such perils, the poor young man who aspires to the rich ambassadorial life must survive service in the huge State Department Building in Washington, where he is likely to spend more than a third of his career. On a purely economic basis, service in Washington is a sad comedown from service abroad, for those Foreign Service Officers so improvident as to have failed to inherit money or to marry it.

Abroad, in all but the real hell-hole spots, a junior Foreign Service Officer is likely to live in reasonable comfort. In Washington a junior FSO must make do on a salary of $8,843 (Class Eight) to $10,602 (Class Five), sums which do not, after taxes, provide for many of life's little luxuries, especially for a married man.

Even the career ambassador, the Foreign Service's equivalent of a Duke of the Blood Royal, lives in Washington in a modest comfort which contrasts sharply with the luxury to which he is accustomed abroad. As this is written, there are eight career ambassadors (Charles E. Bohlen, W. Walton Butterworth, U. Alexis Johnson, Llewellyn Thompson, Foy D. Kohler, Douglas MacArthur, George V. Allen, James Riddleberger). They are paid $28,750 a year, which is enough for comfort, but only very modest comfort for those with children of school or college age. The same is true, only more so, of the next highest grades, career minister (54 of them, at $28,000 a year) and Class One (324 at $27,055 a year).

This contrast in comfort between service abroad and Washington service is one of the reasons why almost all

Foreign Service Officers assigned to Washington can hardly wait to get abroad again. But there are plenty of other reasons.

To many returning FSOs, the vast, eight-story State Department Building, which covers an area of four blocks between Virginia Avenue and C Street, soon comes to seem a nightmarish place. The older men recall with nostalgia the period before 1947, when the State Department occupied "Old State," now the Executive Office Building next to the White House. That endearingly hideous structure, with its marble floors, its nonfunctional Corinthian pillars, and its office fireplaces, was drawn to human scale, and almost everybody in it knew almost everybody else.

"New State," a dingy building originally built for the War Department, with a vast new addition tacked onto it, is hideous without being endearing. James Reston has observed that it "has about as much character as a chewing gum factory in Los Angeles." What character it has partakes strongly of Orwell's *1984*. The place is not drawn to human scale; it is a kind of computerized maze.

The elevators are "programmed" by computers, and they are impervious to any human will. They intermittently emit a strange, sullen buzzing noise. A visitor who wishes to reach the eighth floor, where receptions are held in suites which house some valuable French and early American furnishings, may be utterly frustrated if he takes an elevator which is not programmed for that floor—when he presses the "8" on the control panel, the elevator will buzz threateningly and balk.

A vast, impersonal cafeteria, obviously designed for Orwell's "proles," serves 3,380,000 customers and two million cups of coffee a year. The first floor boasts an Automated Data Processing Division, in which rows of computers keep a cool, impersonal eye on the activities of State's fifteen thousand American and ten thousand foreign employees, as well as the 32,000 Peace Corps and AID employees under the Secretary of State's rather nominal control.

According to a State Department handout, the computers determine "even the courses selected for each student at the Foreign Service Institute." Gone are the freewheeling days when an FSO, returning to Washington to further training at the Foreign Service Institute, was expected to choose his own courses.

In Old State, courtly Negroes in white gloves glided to and fro along the corridors, delivering messages from one office to another. They have been replaced in New State by an elaborate system of pneumatic tubes, through which documents are whizzed relentlessly and ceaselessly to sixty-five receiving stations. Whereas the slower-moving couriers might take upwards of half an hour to deliver a message from one office to another, nowadays it may take forty-eight hours or more to achieve the same purpose.

The daily wordage written, delivered, and presumably read by someone or other in the State Department is staggering. A random spot check for January 28, 1966, showed a total of 215,361 words, comprising 1,283 messages, sent and received by cable. Cabled wordage often goes higher than 500,000 words. This cable traffic is heavier than that of the Associated Press and United Press International combined.

Once in a long while, on orders from above, during a period of really dire crisis, the cable traffic is reduced to a mere trickle. This happens when, to clear the decks for the crisis, a "Limit-Tel" order goes out. Then no telegram can be sent from areas other than those involved in the crisis, except for reasons of genuine emergency. A Limit-Tel order was instituted, for example, during the Arab-Israeli war of June, 1967. The condition of the entire State Department, except for the small minority directly involved in the crisis, immediately became comatose.

"People had nothing to do," recalls a State Department working-level official. "There were no telegrams to initial or comment on. Everybody was going crazy, just sitting around reading the papers." The hiatus had no visibly disastrous effect on the conduct of foreign policy in areas other than the Middle East. But it raised the tedium level to a new high.

The tedium level is high enough at all times. Simple boredom is a main reason why almost all FSOs on Washington assignments can hardly wait to get abroad again. The State Department is the second smallest executive department (after Labor). But it boasts the most tedious and stultifying of all Washington's departmental bureaucracies, except perhaps for the Pentagon. For able men who have been assigned to one of State's numerous nonjobs, the sheer tedium of daily life within the bureaucracy is enough to drive them to drink, or to the brink of lunacy.

If you looked at an organization chart of the State Department, to be sure, you would conclude that it was sensibly and rather simply organized. By the same token, if you met and talked to the men who occupy the most prominent positions on the chart, you would conclude—correctly—that they were able and effective human beings.

The number one and number two men are of course (as this is written) Secretary Dean Rusk and Under Secretary Nicholas Katzenbach. Number three is Under Secretary of State for Political Affairs Eugene Rostow; number four, Deputy Under Secretary for Administration Idar Rimestad; and number five, Deputy Under Secretary for Political Affairs, Charles E. Bohlen.

Eugene Rostow, brother of Walt of the White House,

shares his younger brother's bounce and enthusiasm, as well as his intelligence. While Rusk and Katzenbach concentrate, almost obsessively, on Vietnam, he freewheels, concentrating on what was until recently the central area of American policy, and has now almost become the forgotten continent —Europe. Idar Rimestad, as will be noted later, inherited a powerful empire from his predecessor, William Crockett, a talented empire-builder.

Charles E. Bohlen is the number one Foreign Service Officer in the State Department hierarchy. As a former Ambassador to the Soviet Union and France—he served brilliantly in both posts—he is the government's leading Sovietologist and Élyséeologist, and an important policy adviser. He is also the Foreign Service's ambassador to the top brass, and, in an informal sense, the ambassador of the top brass to the press. Bohlen has often been at odds with journalists (like John Kennedy, he is something of a journalist *manqué* himself), but he has a natural talent for dealing with the crusty journalistic profession, partly because, like most reporters and unlike most professional diplomats, he loves a good, free-for-all argument.

The Policy Planning Council, headed by an intelligent, unassertive FSO, Henry D. Owen, is still officially a part of the top hierarchy. When it was headed by George Kennan, and later by Paul Nitze (it was then called the Policy Planning Staff), it was the central policy-making organ of the American Government. Kennan kept wanting to retire to an ivory tower (or rather to his farm in Pennsylvania) to contemplate his navel and think large thoughts about foreign policy, but because he was so brilliantly able, he kept being dragged back into the day-to-day business of dealing with crises. He played a key role in all the major decisions of the late nineteen-forties, and after Nitze took over from him on New Year's Day, 1950, Nitze also played a key role, notably in planning and arranging the secret negotiations which preceded the Korean settlement.

Since those days, the Policy Planning Council has been gently subsiding into obscurity. John Foster Dulles consulted policy planners Robert Bowie and Gerard Smith quite often, but he regarded policy planning as exclusively his function. Under Dean Rusk, the Council has become more moribund than ever before.

At the next hierarchical level, there are five "functional" bureaus (Economic Affairs, for example, and Education and Cultural Affairs) and five geographic bureaus (African, Inter-American, European, East Asian and Pacific, and Near Eastern and South Asian Affairs), all headed by Assistant Secretaries. Of these, William P. Bundy, brother of McGeorge, is probably the ablest and certainly—because of the eternal Vietnam nightmare—the most important. Aside from the Assistant Secretaries, there are various specialists, like Thomas Hughes, capable chief of the intelligence branch (now much reduced since CIA has gobbled up certain of its functions), or Angier Biddle Duke, who replaced handsome James Symington, for a second tour of duty as Chief of Protocol. It is Duke's duty to be endlessly polite and entertaining to foreign visitors of all shapes and sizes, a burdensome task he performs admirably.

With one or two exceptions, the hierarchy consists of skilled men who work very hard at their often unrewarding jobs. On paper, moreover, the division of labor seems to make sense. Yet working in Washington drives many career officers back from assignments abroad to the brink of lunacy all the same. If you ask them why, they will wanly reply that "it's the system."

The system spawns committees by the dozen, even by the hundreds. The State Department chairs no fewer than sixty-two interdepartmental committees, and sits on many others.

Among the committees chaired by State are, to choose a few at random, the Interagency Committee on International Aviation Policy (ICIAP), the National Facilitation Committee (whatever that is), the Advisory Committee on Documents on German Foreign Policy, the Government Advisory Committee on International Book Problems, the National Review Board for the Center for Cultural and Technical Interchange Between East and West, the Telecommunications Coordinating Committee (TCC) and the United States National Committee for the International Telegraph and Telephone Consultative Committee (CCITT).

Merely to read such a list is to feel an irresistible impulse to yawn. Actually to sit on one of the committees—and for hours at a time, days on end—must be an agony of tedium. And the interdepartmental committees are only a beginning. The intradepartmental committees—those within the department—are so numerous that no one can count them. When Averell Harriman first moved into the State Department at the beginning of the Kennedy administration, he headed a committee-killing task force. He went about his committee-killing task as manfully as any dragon-slaying knight, killing about three dozen useless committees in a few months. But the committee system is hydra-headed, and when one committee was killed two more would spring up to take its place.

There is certainly something in Henry Kissinger's observation: "The committee approach to decision-making is often less an organizational device than a spiritual necessity." Any fairly major foreign policy decision is loaded with booby traps, and no Foreign Service Officer with an eye to his future wants to end up as the booby. The system, by making decisions a collective responsibility, greatly reduces that risk.

It also produces the phenomenon which former Secretary of State Dean Acheson, that peerless phrasemaker, has christened "the waffle paper"—the policy paper which means all things to all men, and nothing very much to anyone. As George Kennan has observed, the result of writing policy papers in committee is "compromised language, obscurity, a hodgepodge inferior to any of the individual views out of which it was brewed."

To produce even the hodgepodge requires a Herculean effort and thousands of man-hours of wasted time. Former Secretary of State Christian Herter remarked of his experience of policy-making by committee: "Sometimes you get yourself so bogged down in the editing of a sentence or a word that you say, 'My God, why am I spending so much time on this?'"

The committee system also helps to account for the extraordinary quantity of red tape in the process of making foreign policy. President Kennedy (like President Roosevelt before him) was alternately irritated and mystified by the difficulty of getting any decision or action out of the State Department. Early in his administration, when the pro-Communist Cheddi Jagan threatened to turn British Guiana into a Communist state, Kennedy asked McGeorge Bundy to get the State Department to send over a paper on "our policy in British Guiana." Bundy picked up a telephone, called the appropriate desk, and asked for a policy paper that afternoon.

Consternation resulted. Perhaps in a week or two a paper might be available. But that afternoon? Impossible. Consternation at the State Department was matched by intense irritation at the White House.

When I heard about this incident, I asked a Foreign Service friend at the middle level for an explanation of why the State Department could not produce a policy paper for the President on a small country like British Guiana in a few hours. After all, with the threat of a Communist takeover so obvious, a lot of bright people must have been giving a lot of thought to what to do about it. My friend was genuinely appalled.

"But my God, man," he said, "you can't expect a subordinate officer to produce a policy paper out of his hat. It would be as much as his career was worth. First, a paper would have to be drafted, and then it would have to move up through the various levels of the office of Inter-American Affairs. Then there would be clearances and concurrences— European Affairs, International Organization Affairs, Intelligence and Research, Political Affairs. Then when it got up near the Secretary's level, there would be interagency clearances—the Pentagon, the Central Intelligence Agency, maybe Treasury or Commerce. And finally the paper would have to be cleared by the National Security Council. A policy in an afternoon? Good God!"

The system of "clearances and concurrences" shares with the committee system the responsibility for the enormous amount of waste motion in the process of foreign policy making. In theory, of course, the system makes sense. Its purpose is to let the right hand know what the left hand is doing. A policy on British Guiana that seems fine to the Bureau of Inter-American Affairs may seem perfectly horrible to the Bureau of European Affairs. And the Pentagon, the CIA, perhaps even Treasury and Commerce, have a legitimate interest in foreign policy decisions. The trouble is that the whole system has gotten out of hand.

One reason is that there are too many people in the State Department. Everyone who has ever had any experience at all with the department agrees on that point. Hans Morgenthau, George Kennan, and Ellis Briggs have all suggested that the department could operate more efficiently with half as many people, while Dean Acheson, William

Attwood and others have proposed a more modest cutback of about a quarter of the staff.

The trouble is not only that there are too many people in the State Department; there are too many *able* people. A bureaucracy hums along happily enough if it consists very largely of drones, content to shuffle their papers and collect their pay checks. But the presence of large numbers of intelligent and able people produces near-chaos. An able man wants to earn his salary, and when something important is afoot, he wants to get into the act. Getting into the act means attending the meetings of the committees and "task forces" (another, more activist-sounding name for committees) dealing with the major crises of the moment.

These committees thus keep getting bigger and bigger. To cite one example, in the early Kennedy period, a "task force" assigned to dealing with the Berlin crisis started with a half-dozen men, and grew as the crisis deepened to more than sixty. Because all the able and intelligent people attending them want to have their say, instead of sitting dumbly on the sidelines, the meetings become more and more interminable.

The State Department is fairly pullulating with able and intelligent people—its IQ level is certainly higher than that of any other department or agency, with the possible exception of the CIA. Foreign Service Officers have to be intelligent; otherwise they would not be Foreign Service Officers. Every year, on the average, some five thousand bright young college graduates volunteer to take the written and oral Foreign Service tests. Only about 165 emerge as Foreign Service Officers. This winnowing process ensures a high minimum intelligence.

The high level of intelligence helps to account for the fact that morale in the Service has probably never been lower—not even in the McCarthy days. An intelligent man well into middle age, or approaching it, hates to spend most of his time in waste motion. "The system" ensures that an FSO—especially if he is on Washington duty—does just that. There are FSOs who share the despair of George Kennan, who wrote in the nineteen-fifties that "only some form of catastrophe—natural disaster, financial collapse, or the atomic bomb—could dismantle [the system] or reduce it to healthier proportions."

The notion that the nuclear weapon might have to be used to reform a bureaucracy may be a counsel of excessive despair. But "the system" in the nineteen-sixties is now even more firmly embedded than when Kennan wrote his cry of despair.

A mysterious process has been at work in the State Department: the triumph of those who administer over those who *do*. The same process has been at work in many other areas of American life, but it has reached its finest flower in the State Department, where once the Foreign Service generalists—the professional diplomats and makers of foreign policy—reigned supreme. Now the administrators have enjoyed a total and probably irreversible triumph.

An ambassador is, in theory, appointed by the President, on the recommendation of the Secretary of State, and with the advice and consent of the Senate. The theory accords with the actuality where the vitally important embassies—Moscow, London, Paris—are concerned, or when the President wants to reward some worker in the political vineyard. But as a practical matter, until rather recently, most of the embassies and almost all the lesser posts in the Foreign Service were, in fact, distributed by the Director General of the Foreign Service and other members of the Foreign Service establishment. In George Kennan's heyday the Foreign Service ran the Foreign Service. That is no longer so. The administrators have now seized effective control.

The administrators decide who is to be ambassador to Ecuador; who is to be the Deputy Chief of Mission in Rangoon; who is to be recalled to brush up his Urdu at the Foreign Service Institute; who is to be the ANZ (Australia–New Zealand) desk officer; and who is to be given the choice between resigning and accepting an insultingly low-ranking post in some markedly unimportant and unattractive country.

The administrators were moving in hard even in the nineteen-fifties. But their final triumph occurred in the period between 1963 and 1967, when William Crockett, a brilliant bureaucratic empire-builder, became chief administrator, with the title of Deputy Under Secretary of State for Administration.

During this period the administrators not only established their right to have a decisive say in what Foreign Service Officer had what job. They have also established their right to breathe down the neck of the Foreign Service at all times and in all places.

Abroad, for example, an FSO, whether a chief of mission or a lowly Class Six, is likely to be subject to FAPS. FAPS is the Foreign Affairs Programming System. The purpose of FAPS is to measure the effectiveness of each foreign mission by feeding into computers voluminous details about how each member of the mission spends his time—whether chatting with the foreign minister, filling out forms, writing reports, spying on the host power, or, presumably, even just thinking. The notion that the effectiveness of diplomacy can be measured by computers is designed to enrage every self-respecting Foreign Service Officer.

Another invention of the administrators seems designed to the same end. When an FSO who has been subjected to FAPS abroad comes home to Washington, he is apt to be assigned to a "T-Group." A T-Group consists of a dozen or so FSOs, with a sprinkling of other State Department people, who are sequestered in a country mansion or hotel, for a week at a time.

The group is presided over by a "behavioral scientist," who stimulates the group to "unfreeze." Once unfrozen, the members of the T-Group, if all goes according to plan, confess their sins and expose the sins of others, in the manner of "socialist self-criticism," as practiced in the Communist countries. Some extroverted FSOs have rather enjoyed this exercise in soul-baring, but most bitterly resent it, as an outrageous invasion of privacy. One young and bold FSO organized all the FSOs in his T-group, pledging them to refuse flatly either to confess their own sins or to attack others. His particular T-Group was so abysmal a failure that the lady psychiatrist assigned to unfreeze it was reduced to tears.

The impression is widespread in the Foreign Service that the administrators, now that they have achieved effective control, are enjoying their revenge. For the members of the administrative branch used to be regarded by the lofty, policy-making Foreign Service generalists as a lesser breed —"pants pressers," they were called, by the old-guard FSOs. Now that the pants pressers are running the show, the FSOs have learned to be polite to them—very polite indeed.

It is no coincidence that the administrators scaled the heights of power during the reign of Secretary of State Dean Rusk. Rusk's approach to the business of running the State Department has much in common with that of John Foster Dulles, who at first wanted to remove himself physically from the department by taking an office in the White House. Rusk's idea was that he should occupy himself with policy matters, while his Under Secretary ran the department.

His first Under Secretary, Chester Bowles, actually performed a useful job in shaking up the department, helping to restore the authority of ambassadors over their "country team," and appointing able younger men to top positions. But then Bowles committed the sin of being right about the Bay of Pigs disaster while almost everybody else (including President Kennedy) was wrong; and the more unforgivable sin of making widely known the fact that he had been right. Moreover, day-to-day administration was by no means Bowles' forte. After Bowles was edged out, his successor, George Ball, tried his hand at running the department, and also performed usefully for a while. But Ball is an able and articulate man with strong convictions, and as time went by he found the job of running the department increasingly unfascinating. Thus a vacuum was created, into which Crockett and the administrators deftly moved.

When Ball was replaced by former Attorney General Nicholas deB. Katzenbach, Katzenbach was predictably appalled by his first exposure to "the system." He was baffled by the office symbols which are essential to communication by anyone caught up within its toils: "For a while I confused S slant S (S/S) with S slant S dash S (S/S–S) until I discovered that one was on one side of the hall and the other one on the other. But I confess I remain intrigued by S slant S dash EX (S/S–EX)." He was amazed that it required twenty-nine signatures to clear one routine cable dealing with the non-earth-shaking subject of milk exports.

It remains to be seen whether Katzenbach will succeed in his announced intention of reducing the system to "healthier proportions," the task which George Kennan said would require no human agent, but "some form of catastrophe." Katzenbach strongly supports Ambassador Tuthill's Brazilian "Operation Topsy," and he is determined to start Topsy operations in other missions. Perhaps he will succeed, where other reformers of the State Department system, back to the early nineteenth century, have failed. But it seems unlikely. It seems far more likely that, like his predecessors, Katzenbach will sooner or later abandon the Sisyphean task of trying to defudge the fudge factory, and turn to the greener pastures of policy-making.

Policy-making is, after all, the chief function of the Secretary of State and his alter ego, the Under Secretary. Foreign policy is so insanely complex a matter nowadays that a man deeply involved in the making of it has very little time left over to worry about who should be DCM (Deputy Chief of Mission) in Rangoon. Even so, it seems unlikely that the vacuum would have been so complete, or the triumph of the administrators so final, if Dean Rusk had been a different sort of man.

There is a curious passivity about Rusk's approach to the whole business of making foreign policy—in the department this cool passivity has earned him the nickname "the Buddha." Indeed, he looks a bit Buddha-like, with his round, balding head and his heavy-set body. He himself has said that he looks like "your friendly neighborhood bartender"— which he also does. As the remark suggests, Rusk has a sense of humor. He is, in fact, a man of genuine personal charm; he has a small, kewpie-like grin, which lights up the somber, round face. He is also a phrasemaker of parts. At the crucial moment in the great Cuban missile crisis, at a White House meeting, the news came in that one of the Soviet missile-bearing ships bound for Cuba had turned back.

"We're eyeball to eyeball," Rusk remarked to McGeorge Bundy, "and I think the other fellow just blinked."

There is no question at all about the quality of Dean Rusk's mental equipment. His special genius lies in identifying and summing up all the various elements in a problem succinctly, lucidly, and with total objectivity.

"He can sit listening to one of those interminable, wandering, confusing arguments that committee meetings often become," says one of his admirers, "and at the end he'll sum up all the important factors in five sentences, forgetting no relevant fact, giving due weight to all the options. It's a brilliant act."

His critics agree that it is a brilliant act, but they contend that the act lacks a climax; having brilliantly summarized the conflicting alternatives, Rusk never chooses between them. "He plays his hand so close to his chest," says one critic, "that I sometimes wonder whether he knows himself what cards he holds."

Rusk's subordinates, even at the Assistant Secretary level, complain that they never know what he thinks, what policies he favors. To get a positive decision, they say, it is necessary to adopt the old expedient of telling him, in effect, "Unless you disagree, I intend to do so-and-so."

Rusk himself defends his lack of communication with his subordinates as a matter of conscious policy. A Secretary of State who is known to feel strongly on one side or another of a major policy decision, he contends, inevitably influences the direction of the decision before all factors are weighed. Thus the Secretary should make his views known only to the President, and then only after all the options have been thoroughly examined.

After the Cuban missile crisis, for example, none of the other members of Ex Comm—the "Executive Commitee" of the National Security Council which had been created by the President to handle the crisis—could recall in retrospect just where Rusk stood, as between the "hawks" and the "doves." Rusk himself has explained that he carefully kept his own counsel; that he communicated his views to President Kennedy two days before the President's television address to the nation on Monday, October 22, 1962; and that the policy he recommended to the President was substantially the one which was adopted.

This may be so, but there is not much doubt that Kennedy

himself was more than once annoyed by his Secretary of State's disinclination to commit himself. In the early Kennedy period, an apocryphal story circulated about a meeting on the Berlin crisis between the President and Rusk, who were alone in the President's office. The dialogue was supposed to have gone as follows:

RUSK: "Mr. President, I believe that I have at last found the solution to the Berlin crisis."

PRESIDENT: "Fine. What is it?"

RUSK: "I should be delighted to tell you. But this is a most sensitive matter, and I believe it would be best if half of those present would first leave the room."

According to Arthur Schlesinger and others, President Kennedy became so annoyed by Rusk's habit of playing his cards so close to his chest that not even the President could see them, that he planned to replace Rusk in his second term, probably with Robert McNamara. Kennedy was certainly never on close personal terms with Rusk—it was not until a year or more after Rusk became Kennedy's Secretary of State that the President began to call him by his first name. As this is written, there are recurrent rumors that Rusk may be following McNamara out of the Cabinet. But the personal relationship between Rusk and President Johnson has undoubtedly been closer than between Rusk and Kennedy, perhaps because they are both Southerners who knew poverty as young men (Rusk was brought up on a hardscrabble Georgia farm).

No doubt there is another reason as well. The heaviest cross President Johnson has had to bear has been, of course, the war in Vietnam. Rusk has done whatever he could to lighten the load. For this is one subject on which he has been absolutely unambiguous. He is passionately convinced that the President's decision to intervene in Vietnam with American combat troops—the key policy decision of the Johnson years, and probably the key Presidential decision of all the postwar years—was absolutely correct. He is more convinced of its correctness, one suspects, than was McNamara —whose advice on this issue, as Secretary of Defense, was decisive—or than the President himself. Again and again, Rusk returns to his analogy between Nazi Germany and Mao Tse-tung's China.

"I'm not the village idiot," he told this reporter in 1966. "I know Hitler was an Austrian and Mao is a Chinese. I know all the other differences between this situation and the situation in the thirties. But what is common between the two situations is the phenomenon of aggression." This analogy, which infuriates the dove-liberals, has been much derided, notably by Arthur Schlesinger. But Rusk is passionately convinced that history will prove how accurate it is.

Except in this one respect, Dean Rusk has played a passive role. It is interesting to compare his long reign in the State Department with Robert McNamara's long, now ended reign in the Department of Defense.

In his years in the Pentagon, McNamara basically altered both the strategic doctrines of the United States and the methods by which those doctrines are shaped and determined. Aside from his unwavering line on Vietnam, Dean Rusk has left behind him no memorial whose merits will be argued by future historians—no Marshall Plan, no NATO, not even a SEATO or an Eisenhower Doctrine. No important new departure in foreign policy is clearly identified with his name. As for "the system," the State Department's policy-making mechanism, it is what it was before Rusk became Secretary of State—except that it has become even more cumbersome.

Everybody who has been exposed to "the system" agrees that *something* has to be done about it, that somehow the State Department has got to find a way to respond less slowly and bureaucratically to the enormous challenges which confront this country abroad. Most of those who have been exposed to the system agree at least on the broad outlines of what needs to be done. Ex-Ambassador Attwood, in an article in the *Atlantic Monthly,* came up with conclusions with which few would quarrel:

Revitalizing State would be difficult, but it would not be impossible under a reform-minded Secretary with full White House backing and a sympathetic Congress. The recommendations I have made . . . can be summarized as follows:

1. Get rid of deadwood and trim overstaffed posts and bureaus.

2. Promote FSOs on merit rather than seniority.

3. Make salary scales comparable with those offered by private industry.

4. Mimimize the production and distribution of paper.

5. Personalize (that is, decomputerize) personnel assignments.

6. Dismantle the AID bureaucracy, and put foreign economic assistance under the State Department.

7. Coordinate the activities of all federal agencies concerned with foreign affairs.

All these things certainly need to be done, though they would certainly take some doing. Another thing that needs very badly to be done, in this writer's opinion, is to return to the Foreign Service control over the Foreign Service. One of the Foreign Service's career ambassadors—a Foy Kohler, a Charles Bohlen—should be made directly responsible, under the Secretary of State, for running the Foreign Service. The administrators should be returned to the equivalent of pants-pressing—they should be sternly told that their job is to support the Foreign Service, not to run it.

For the pride and the prestige of the Foreign Service, which have been so badly eroded over the years, must be restored. The poor old Foreign Service has been regularly castigated as an "elite." It used to *be* an "elite," before Wristonization "democratized" it, and it was an elite that produced a great many men of very superior ability and great independence of thought—Robert Murphy, Charles Bohlen, George Kennan, Llwellyn Thompson, Foy Kohler. An "elite," after all, is a useful thing to have around—the word is defined in the dictionary as "the choice or best part, as of a body or class of persons." That rather accurately describes the kind of Foreign Service we need.

Time ought to help to make the Foreign Service an elite again. For time, in its ruthless way, will eliminate the middle-aged men now caught in "the Wriston bulge." They will be replaced by the younger generation of Foreign Service Officers, who are very bright and very able, and who have not suffered the traumas of McCarthyism and Wristonization. But the first prerequisite is to restore to the Foreign Service control of the Foreign Service, and then to leave it alone to sort itself out.

There are those, to be sure, who believe that it is already too late, that "the system" has an inner strength of its own; that it grows inexorably, like a blob from outer space in one of the television horror series; and that it is quite invulnerable to human attack. These pessimists believe that there is really nothing to be done—that the number of signatures required on a cable dealing with milk exports will creep up relentlessly from twenty-nine to some even more monstrous figure, while the days required to get a policy paper for the President on some such country as British Guiana will stretch into weeks, months, years.

And yet policy decisions do get made, after all. Sometimes —as in President Kennedy's decision to risk nuclear war in the Cuban missile crisis, or President Johnson's decision to send more than twenty thousand troops to the Dominican Republic—they are made in a matter of a very few days, even a very few hours. The more one examines how such key decisions are made, the clearer it becomes that when an important decision really *has* to be made, the whole decision-making process simply flows around "the system," as water flows around a boulder in a stream.

6

DEFENSE:

THE McNAMARA REVOLUTION

> VINSON (incredulously): *You will be able to tell us*
> *what we need?*
> McNAMARA (quietly confident): *Yes, sir.*

Power is what Washington is all about. Power is what attracts able men into government and politics, and keeps them working ten hours or more a day, and enduring ulcer-inducing pressures, year after year, for far less money than they could make elsewhere. Washington has many yard-sticks with which to measure a man's power. Two of these yardsticks are men and money. The more men a man "owns" —the more people he bosses in his bureaucratic empire— and the more money he spends, the more powerful he is thought to be.

By both these measures the Secretary of Defense is, next to the President, by a very wide margin the most powerful man in Washington. He spends more than anyone else in the government—indeed, he has more spending money under his direct control than any other human being in the world. His three nearest Cabinet competitors spend less than half the $70 billion-plus currently spent by the Defense Secretary.

127

The Secretary of Defense also "owns" more people by far than any other official. He is the boss of roughly 3.5 million military and one million civilians, who get their pay checks from the Department of Defense. Indirectly, the Secretary of Defense is by far the greatest employer in the land. The Defense Department annually grants contracts worth between $24 and $30 billion to private industry, and more people work in the defense industries than in the steel and automotive industries combined. Thus by the yardsticks of men and money, every competing bureaucratic empire is puny indeed by comparison.

Men and money are not the only measures of power in Washington, of course. If that were true, the Secretary of HUD would wield more clout than the Secretary of State, which of course he does not. The final, essential measure of a man's power is the degree of his influence on the great central decisions of government policy. This means, in the end, influence on the President, who is ultimately responsible for the great, central decisions. Of the eight men who preceded Clark Clifford as Secretary of Defense, there were one or two whose power, measured by this yardstick, was limited, and who therefore ranked well down in power's pecking order.

In the first Eisenhower administration, for example, Secretary of the Treasury George Magoffin Humphrey had far more real power than the Secretary of Defense, the late Charles E. Wilson. Eisenhower chose both Wilson, president of General Motors, and Humphrey, president of the Hanna Company, on the dubious theory that a man who had made a big success in big business would make a big success in big government. The mysterious workings of the human personality soon made George Humphrey, a steamroller of a man, top dog over the amiable Wilson.

Wilson was constantly torn between his uneasy feeling that the Soviets were outstripping the United States, especially in space, and George Humphrey's deeply held and thunderously expressed conviction that the government was "spending the country into socialism." Humphrey was giving tongue to the big businessman's Holy Writ of that era. Big businessman Wilson revered the Holy Writ, and so, for that matter, did the President. So Humphrey's Holy Writ constantly triumphed over Wilson's uneasy feeling, until at last the uneasy feeling was justified when the Sputniks roared into space in 1957.

James Forrestal, the first of the eight men who have served as Secretary of Defense, killed himself in despair. Two or three others have left the office with their reputations tarnished, or at least decidedly unpolished, the most notable example being the late Louis Johnson, Harry Truman's second Secretary of Defense, who really believed that he could ride the "economy-in-defense" issue into the White House. The Korean War proved him disastrously wrong.

It is not hard to be wrong, and even disastrously wrong, as Secretary of Defense. The job is complex to a maniacal degree. The ideal Secretary of Defense should combine the wisdom of Solomon, the political guile of Machiavelli, the military genius of Napoleon, and the mental equipment of the latest IBM machine. Consider the kind of questions a Secretary of Defense is expected to answer:

Are the military advantages of mining Haiphong Harbor sufficient to offset the political risks?

Is it better to buy four conventionally powered naval frigates or three nuclear-powered frigates with the same amount of money?

Should the Marines, in the interests of economy, be forced to abandon their traditional cordovan shoes in favor of the black shoes worn by the other services?

Can one tactical aircraft serve both the Air Force and the Navy equally well?

Should the United States spend upwards of $30 billion on

an antiballistic-missiles system, which might save as many as sixty million American lives in case of all-out nuclear war—roughly $500 per life?

Should $15 billion or so be spent to build a manned strategic bomber, to replace the B-52?

Should still another military installation be placed in the area of Charleston, South Carolina, in order to appease Mendel Rivers, the powerful chairman of the House Armed Services Committee?

This is a very small sampling of the kind of questions that one Secretary of Defense—Robert S. McNamara, who served in the office longer than any other man—was called upon to answer. McNamara answered them all—briskly, without undue delay, and on the basis of what he calls "reason, not emotion." In the opinion of this writer, he answered at least two of them (the ones about the Marines' shoes and the Navy–Air Force plane) quite wrongly. But most reasonably objective observers would agree that, given the insane complexity of the questions he had to answer, his question-answering batting average was remarkably high.

Moreover, in several deeply important ways, the Pentagon which Clark Clifford has inherited from McNamara, and which *his* successors will inherit, even unto the third and fourth generation, will be a very different place from the Pentagon which McNamara inherited from President Eisenhower's last Secretary of Defense, Thomas S. Gates.

Physically, to be sure, the Pentagon remains unchanged; it is the same monstrous and gloomy structure built a generation ago to serve as the command center of this country's vast war effort. When in 1944 it became clear that World War II would surely end in victory, some thought was given, on orders from President Roosevelt, to the uses to which the Pentagon might be put after the war. No formal decision on this point was made before the President died, but it was generally agreed that the place would serve as a general hospital.

When the war ended, however, and the number of men in the armed forces was reduced to a quarter and at times a fifth of the wartime level of more than twelve million, the number of people in the Pentagon steadily increased. The proliferating Pentagon bureaucracy overflowed into other buildings, like the $17 million building for the recently created Defense Intelligence Agency, while the Pentagon itself reached and passed the bursting point.

A simple example of this proliferation of the military bureaucracy is provided by Room 4D1053, which is on an air well facing a yellow brick wall on the inside of one of the Pentagon's outer rings. In 1944, Room 4D1053 was occupied by Lieutenant Colonel R. S. McNamara, an Air Force backroom boy, or boffin, specializing in the recondite art of statistical control. Besides that dashing officer, Room 4D1053 sheltered one other officer and a WAC. Room 4D1053 has now been cut up into two rooms, with a shifting population of officers, enlisted men and civilian secretaries, crowded in desk to desk. At last count there were seven persons in the area once occupied by Lieutenant Colonel McNamara and two others—an "increment," to use a favorite McNamara word, of well over 100 percent.

The fact is that the military bureaucracy obeys Parkinson's Law with far more enthusiasm than any other bureaucracy. McNamara once remarked that the population of the Pentagon, now about 27,000, could and should be reduced by about half. The job could be done, he said, but if he took on the job, he would have to spend half his time doing it, and he had other, more important things to do. Thus Clark Clifford's Pentagon remains what it has been since the Second War—a depressing, oddly Orwellian place (one can almost hear Big

Brother's disembodied voice echoing through the seventeen and a half miles of corridor), bursting with majors and colonels and staff sergeants and civilian female secretaries and generals bustling busily about. Most of these bustlers are engaged in the task of taking in each other's bureaucratic washing.

In such ways, the McNamara Monarchy (as Hanson Baldwin of the *New York Times* dubbed the McNamara regime) left the Pentagon unchanged. But in certain more important ways, the Pentagon, and the military establishment of which it is the command center, was altered beyond recognition during the seven years of the McNamara regime.

In the first place, the defense establishment of the United States is run in a way quite different from the way it was run by the first seven Secretaries of Defense. Moreover, McNamara himself is convinced that the clock can never be put back, that the new way of running things which he imposed on the Pentagon cannot now be changed in any basic way.

In a talk with this reporter in 1966, McNamara harked back to his Detroit experience (he left Room 4D1053 to go to Ford, and had become president of the company just before John Kennedy summoned him back to the Pentagon in 1960) to explain his conviction that his system would outlast him. He compared his managerial revolution in the Defense Department to the managerial revolution which transformed General Motors from a failing company under its brilliant, erratic founder, Walter Durant, into the most successful automobile company in the world.

"Durant was running the company on an emotional basis," he said, "and the company was almost wrecked. The Du Ponts came in and rationalized the company and established the basic system. Now no president of GM—and there have been several who were no geniuses—could wreck the company."

His meaning was clear. Not even a reincarnated Engine Charlie Wilson (who was "no genius," either as Defense Secretary or president of GM) could change the "basic system" which McNamara imposed on the Pentagon. This "basic system" can be made (and has been made) to sound insanely complicated. In fact, it is essentially simple enough, and easy to understand.

The first change which McNamara imposed is this: The Department of Defense is now run by the Secretary of Defense. Barring the appointment of a weak or a stupid Secretary (and Clark Clifford is certainly neither weak nor stupid), the Pentagon will continue to be run by McNamara's successors. McNamara's "basic system" places the ultimate responsibility (short only of the President's responsibility in the great strategic decisions) squarely upon the Secretary, whoever he may be.

"I believe that a leader should lead," McNamara remarked shortly after he was appointed Secretary of Defense by John F. Kennedy. He promptly suited the action to the word, considerably to Washington's astonishment. It may seem astonishing that Washington should be astonished by a Secretary who actually ran his department. But in the Pentagon there was no precedent for the kind of leadership McNamara had in mind.

A wonderfully McNamara-ish exchange took place between McNamara, old Carl Vinson, chairman of the House Armed Services Committee, and Republican Representative Leon Gavin of Pennsylvania, in February, 1961, within a matter of weeks of McNamara's appointment. Here it is:

VINSON: Mr. Secretary, you use the President's famous statement in his inaugural address: "Only when our arms are sufficient beyond doubt can we be certain beyond doubt that they will never be employed." How much is enough, when it boils down? Now will you be in a position to advise the President that we have a sufficiency beyond a doubt?

McNamara: Yes, sir. That is the objective of our studies. As I stated earlier, we expect to complete them at the time scheduled—that is, the end of the month.

Vinson: You will be in a position to tell the committee, then, from your study, what we need in the field of missiles, aircraft, and vessels?

McNamara: Yes, sir.

Vinson (*incredulously*): You will be able to tell us what we need?

McNamara (*quietly confident*): Yes, sir.

Gavin (*breaking in, also incredulously*): And hardware?

McNamara: Yes, sir.

McNamara's thrice-repeated "yes, sir" was startling to Gavin and old Carl Vinson for a simple reason. No previous Secretary of Defense had ever been able to answer Vinson's question—"How much is enough, when it boils down?"— with any real conviction or assurance. For the question has a corollary—"Enough for what kind of war?"—and no man, then or now, could predict what kind of war the United States might become involved in. Yet here was McNamara promising to come up with a firm answer to Vinson's question within a few weeks of taking office.

Vinson's question, moreover, involved the basic issue of "roles and missions"—which service would do what in case of war. The battle over roles and missions had been going on ever since the Department of Defense was created and the services ostensibly "unified" in 1947. The first Secretary of Defense killed himself in part because he had despaired of getting the services to agree on a joint strategic plan, with the roles and missions of each service defined in advance, in case of war with the Soviet Union. When McNamara took over in 1960, the issue had never really been resolved by Forrestal's successors; it had simply been swept under the rug.

When McNamara found out that this was so, he was surprised. In the Ford Company, he remarked, he would have put a committee or task force to work on the matter, with instructions to come up with a solution in a couple of weeks. This remark of McNamara's, which was widely repeated, caused much amusement among knowledgeable Pentagonians. Amusement changed to amazement when the issue (plus a couple of hundred lesser but vitally important ones) was in fact resolved, and within a matter of a few months after McNamara took office.

McNamara's issue-resolving technique was very simple. He would pose a question, which might range from "How do you stop leaks to the press?" (something of a McNamara obsession) to "How many fatal casualties would the United States suffer in an all-out nuclear war?" (on the order of 135 million, by the most recent estimate) or "Which service should be responsible for the military uses of space?" (McNamara's answer: the Air Force). He would then put a task force to work, with instructions to come up with the answer on a specified date. If there were two or more answers, as often happened, McNamara would then settle the issue with three key words: "I have decided . . ."

This system is so simple that it may seem rather strange that none of McNamara's seven predecessors, who included some very able men, had ever put it into practice. In fact, two new factors made it relatively easy for McNamara to settle the Pentagon's issues with his three key words, and almost impossible for his predecessors to do so. One was the Defense Reorganization Act, passed in 1958. The original National Security Act of 1947, which established a Department of Defense, gave the Secretary of Defense responsibility without authority. He was not really boss of his department. He was a mere "coordinator," a referee without the power to enforce his rulings. The military men, the august Chiefs of Staff, had implicit authority to by-pass the Secretary and appeal directly to the President. This unworkable system, of which ironically James Forrestal had been a chief advocate, helped to drive Forrestal, in frustration and despair, to his grave.

The 1958 act made the Secretary of Defense the master in his own house, and McNamara's immediate predecessor, Thomas Gates, had begun tactfully to assert this mastery even before McNamara took over from him. The other new factor was more gradual and imprecise, but no less important. It was the fading from the scene of the giants—the great military leaders thrown up by World War II. The first three Chiefs of Staff after the war were General Dwight D. Eisenhower, Admiral Chester Nimitz, and General Carl ("Toohey") Spaatz, immortals all. Other chiefs of the postwar era were men with such famous names as Generals Omar Bradley, "Lightnin' Joe" Collins, Matthew Ridgway, Hoyt Vandenberg, Nathan Twining, and Tommy White, and Admirals Forrest Sherman, Robert Carney, Arthur Radford, and Arleigh Burke.

Consider the unhappy situation of a mere civilian, newly appointed Secretary of Defense, overruling the military decisions of much-decorated men with names like those listed above. It is no wonder that Charles E. Wilson and most of McNamara's other predecessors shied away from what Wilson called "all that military stuff." The trouble is that every major decision which confronts the Secretary of Defense boils down in the end to "military stuff." If he avoids decisions on the "military stuff," the Secretary is not master in his own house. He is a mere administrator—a kind of janitor.

By the time McNamara took over, only two World War II giants were still active on the national scene—General Maxwell Taylor, former Army Chief of Staff, and General Curtis LeMay, who became Air Force Chief of Staff in June, 1961.

On McNamara's recommendation, Taylor became Mc-Namara's second Chairman of the Chiefs, after General Lyman Lemnitzer, his reputation blemished by his failure to advise against the Bay of Pigs adventure, was exiled to NATO. Taylor and McNamara worked closely together. In fact, McNamara's strategic doctrines (of which more later) were deeply influenced by Taylor's book, *The Uncertain Trumpet*, a *cri de coeur* warning against the Eisenhower era doctrines of "massive retaliation" and a "bigger bang for a buck." Taylor and McNamara are the same sort of men, and although they had occasional differences, they became allies in Washington's jungle warfare, and personal friends.

As for LeMay, the rough-spoken, cigar-smoking, flak-defying combat commander of World War II was not at all the same sort of man as Robert McNamara, the wartime specialist in statistical control. LeMay and McNamara rarely saw eye to eye, and were frequently eyeball to eyeball, and McNamara was not desperately unhappy when LeMay, the last of the giants, left the Pentagon and active service in 1964.

The World War II giants were not all that gigantic when seen at close range. This writer remembers one of them poking a cigar in his face and remarking idiotically: "The only difference between this coming war and the last, Alsop, is that some of you civilians are going to get killed." Another met all the cogent technical arguments against spending billions to develop military capabilities for space vehicles by repeating *ad nauseam* that "the first thing any plebe learns in West Point about military strategy is to seek the high ground."

And yet, gigantic or not, the World War II commanders *seemed* gigantic, and their names carried vast weight on Capitol Hill and with the public. By contrast, two of the present chiefs were mere lieutenant colonels—like Mc-Namara himself—during World War II, and it will be a very knowledgeable reader who can name more than one or two of the five members of the current Joint Chiefs of Staff.

But the 1958 Defense Act and the fading of the giants explain only in part the all-but-total mastery which McNamara so quickly achieved in his own house. Another part of the explanation was that "basic system" which McNamara imposed on the Pentagon, as the Du Ponts had imposed their basic system on General Motors. The McNamara system removes the real power of decision from the generals and admirals, and places it in the OSD—Office of the Secretary of Defense. Under Clark Clifford it seems likely to remain there.

Part one of McNamara's "basic system" had its genesis shortly after he took office. The Navy staged for him one of those briefings, complete with movies, charts, recordings, offstage voices, and ritualized jokes, which have become a Pentagon art form. The briefing was on the target system of the Polaris nuclear submarines. Halfway through, McNamara asked an obvious question: How did the Polaris targets tie in with the target system of the Strategic Air Force?

The assembled admirals were aghast. Air Force targets? But that was strictly the business of the Air Force. If the Secretary wished to know about the Air Force target system, he should request a briefing from the Air Force. McNamara stomped out of the room, and shortly thereafter nine principal *interservice* missions were designated. The most important of these interservice missions were: "Strategic Offensive" (meaning nuclear attack, combining the Navy and the Air Force); "Strategic Defensive" (nuclear defense—Army and Air Force); and "General Purpose" (conventional warfare—including all three services).

The rationale underlying this part of the McNamara system is that the traditional division into air, sea, and ground, or Air Force, Navy, and Army, is outdated—that what matters is the mission itself, not which service performs it. This makes sense. It also clearly tends to take the final power of decision out of the hands of the chiefs of the individual services and place it in the hands of the Secretary of Defense.

The significance of the other parts of the McNamara system can be understood only in terms of how the system used to work in the pre-McNamara era. In those far-off days, months before the time for submitting the Defense budget to Congress arrived, the Joint Chiefs would hold a long series of meetings, to prepare their budget submissions for the Secretary and the President. An interminable argument would ensue, with each Chief and his retinue of Indians defending the inflated claims of their own service and attempting unsuccessfully to deflate the equally inflated claims of the other services. At the end of this process, a vastly inflated over-all figure would be submitted in the name of the Joint Chiefs to the Secretary of Defense and the President. There would be gasps of horror, the Secretary of the Treasury and the Budget Bureau would be consulted, an arbitrary ceiling would be decreed on the over-all budget, and the budget would then be divided between the three services on the principle of the distribution of the weapons in *The Wind in the Willows*. But the rat, the mole, and the badger did not get equal shares. Here is how General Maxwell Taylor described the end result of this nonsensical process in *The Uncertain Trumpet*:

I always found Mr. Wilson and Mr. McElroy anxious to give each service its day in court and receive a thorough briefing upon the effects of the budget guidelines on that service. But although these sessions generate a tremendous amount of discussion, I have never seen any evidence to suggest that they influence much the ultimate outcome. Regardless of the eloquence expended by the service representatives, as we have seen, the fixed percentage allocations of the budget have remained the same for years—

Army 23 per cent, Navy and Marines 28 per cent, Air Force 46 per cent.

Each of the three services then spent its money more or less as the Chiefs and the Indians saw fit, on a year-to-year basis. This 23-28-46 system of arbitrarily splitting up the arbitrary yearly total allocated for defense of the United States was just plain silly. What is more, it tended to commit the American Government to vast future expenditures which nobody bothered to estimate seriously in advance. Developing a weapons system may take anywhere from five years to ten years. In the first year or so the system may be relatively cheap, but as the stage of "buying hardware" is reached, costs skyrocket. Such estimates as were made were usually based on cost projections of companies bidding for lucrative defense contracts, and in the nature of things these projections tended to be wildly optimistic. Just how optimistic they were is suggested by a study made in 1966, which showed that aircraft weapons systems cost as much as six times the estimates, and missiles systems fourteen times the estimates.

McNamara changed this silly system in two ways. First, he abandoned the custom of splitting up an arbitrary defense pie into arbitrary slices on an arbitrary annual basis. Instead, the Joint Chiefs now produce a hallowed document called a JSOP (pronounced "Jaysop") for Joint Strategic Objectives Plan. The Jaysop tries to peer five years into the future, to forecast the U.S. defense requirements for that period. The results of this crystal ball gazing are then "costed out" by the Systems Analysis Office, headed as this is written by Alain Enthoven, a rather reserved intellectual in his mid-thirties. Because of his hold on the purse strings, Enthoven is currently the most influential of the "defense intellectuals" or "whiz kids" (the latter appellation is preferred by the crustier general officers) whom McNamara recruited into the Pentagon.

The result of this system is a reasonably coherent long-term defense plan. The plan is of course subject to change, for no one can foretell what the defense requirements of this country will be five years from now—by that time the country may be at peace, or, alas, engaged in a very much larger and more lethal war. But at least the system, instead of being just plain silly, is "rational," to use one of Mc-Namara's favorite words. Again, this system, while it gives the Joint Chiefs a voice in planning the "Jaysop," leaves the final power of decision in the Systems Analysis Office, directly controlled by the Secretary of Defense.

Another part of the McNamara-created "basic system" is also designed to rationalize defense planning. This is the much-debated use of "cost effectiveness" as a yardstick for buying weapons systems. The system has been attacked by those who do not understand it as a way of putting considerations of cost before considerations of national security. It is nothing of the sort. Consider the question cited earlier. Is it better to buy four conventionally powered naval frigates or three nuclear-powered frigates with the same amount of money? This is a typical exercise in planning by "cost effectiveness." The system forces the military planner to ask himself this question: "Instead of buying *this* weapons system, can I not buy for the same amount of money *another* weapons system which would do the job better?"

Charles Hitch, who preceded Enthoven as McNamara's chief money man and leading defense intellectual, maintains that cost effectiveness has always decisively influenced the choice of weapons systems. In his booklet, *Decision Making for Defense,* Hitch points out that the armored knight of the Middle Ages had been developed into a "highly effective weapons system." Each knight "required upwards of two hundred pounds of hammered plate for himself and his horse, plus a large retinue to keep him in the field." Despite his high cost, the knight was such an effective weapons system that "in the eleventh century a force of about seventy knights conquered the ancient and civilized kingdom of Sicily."

But the armored knight fell victim to "cost effectiveness," in the Battle of Crécy. In that battle the longbow, a very much less costly weapons system than the armored knight, proved much more effective, and "over 1,500 French lords and knights fell as compared to a few dozen archers." Then the bow in its turn fell victim to the "cost effectiveness" of musket and gunpowder. This was not because the musket was a better weapon than the bow; it had "less range and accuracy than the bow and a much lower rate of fire." But more troops could be armed much more cheaply with the musket, and thus far greater fire power could be achieved. Throughout history, in short, "cost effectiveness" has determined the outcome of wars and the balance of power between wars.

In its modern application, "cost effectiveness" can be a good deal more complicated than these illustrations from a simpler past suggest. To decide between the four conventional frigates and the three nuclear frigates, for example, involves all sorts of recondite factors of speed, range, fire power, and the like. But for a really complex example of "cost effectiveness" at work, consider an analysis which McNamara ordered in 1965 of the comparative advantages in five potential theaters of war of airlift, sealift, and prepositioning. (Prepositioning means having the stuff there already when war breaks out. The Army, for example, has all needed supplies for two divisions prepositioned in Europe, and the "bodies," or trained troops, can be married to the supplies within two weeks of the order being given.) All sorts of conditions had to be imagined in all five war theaters —revolts in allied or enemy territory, bases knocked out by nuclear attack or for political reasons, and so on.

A "mathematical representation of the world," consisting of an immense stack of IBM cards, was devised. The cards were fed into the computers, and the computers were asked, in effect, what was the best and cheapest way to "get thar fustest with the mostest."

One result of this exercise in cost effectiveness was to force the Navy to face up to the fact that the Air Force's C-5 cargo plane threatened to make sealift, one of the Navy's chief reasons for being, obsolete. The C-5 is an immense jet which can carry 600 troops or 250,000 pounds of cargo anywhere in the world at almost 500 miles an hour, at very reasonable cost compared with the traditional sea convoy.

Far too often for the Navy's comfort, the computers clicked out the answer that the C-5 provided the best way to "get thar fustest with the mostest." So the Navy, as an answer, devised the RO-RO (roll-on, roll-off) system. RO-RO works essentially like a two-way car ferry, and it enables the Navy to linger offshore more or less indefinitely where trouble threatens, and to deliver supplies in airtight containers on short notice directly to a landing area. To the Navy's relief, the computers have given RO-RO a hearty nod of approval.

Again, "cost effectiveness," like every other element in McNamara's "basic system," tends to remove the power of decision from the Chiefs and their Indians, and to concentrate it in the hands of the Secretary of Defense, and his technicians, back-room boys, and boffins. It is they, after all, not the admirals and generals, who decide what weapons systems to test, and who feed the questions to the computers and read and interpret the answers.

Hitch agrees with McNamara that the McNamara system

will survive intact McNamara's departure from the Pentagon. "I will readily admit," he writes,

that to push through the development of the programming system in so short a time and make it work required a Secretary as strong and decisive as Robert S. McNamara. But I believe that the programming system can be adapted without too much difficulty to almost any style of leadership we are likely to have in the future. Every Secretary will have his own style. . . . But I cannot imagine a Secretary of Defense who would willingly forego the assurance, provided by the new planning-programming-budgeting system, that his military plans are in proper balance and actually provide the capabilities that his military planners are counting on.

Another Pentagonian, who has closely observed the growth of the McNamara system, dissents: "McNamara has created this monstrous machine, and he's the only one with the driver's license." The real danger is not that the machine will break down for lack of a licensed driver, but that the driver's seat will be occupied by the back-room boys, the specialists, the experts—call them what you will.

McNamara is himself an expert or specialist par excellence. His mastery of detail is downright breath-taking. His seven years of testifying on Capitol Hill provide convincing evidence that this man has a mind unlike the minds of other men. As you read the testimony, you wait in suspense for the inevitable bobble, for McNamara to get lost in a syntactical thicket, or to forget a fact. It never happens. What is the "current production rate of the UH-IB/D Iroquois helicopter?" The Secretary knows the answer—for last year and the year before as well as this year. How does "discrimination radar" work? The Secretary explains, clearly and concisely. What is the difference in cost between the mobile-based and the stationary solid-fuel missile? The Secretary has it to the last penny. What is the "Soviet damage potential in terms of millions of U.S. fatalities in an all-out nuclear strike?" The Secretary knows the horrible, if still theoretical, answer in detail.

His remarkable mental equipment served as sword and buckler to McNamara in his scraps with Congress, which became increasingly bitter as the years passed. To bury criticism under a flood of facts is an old technique, but no one mastered it better than McNamara. But the McNamara mental equipment also served as reinsurance against a takeover by the specialists. No specialist was likely to bemuse or outtalk him by a display of professional expertise, because he could use his total recall to outspecialize any specialist.

There is no assurance that his successors will enjoy a similar protection. And this is dangerous. For the specialist, however brilliant and dedicated, tends always to get wrapped up in his specialty, and to be thus blind to the wider horizons of the national interests.

Indeed, in a sense this is what happened in the years when the Joint Chiefs of Staff and their Indians really ran the Defense Department, and when the doctrine of "massive retaliation" and the "bigger bang for a buck" prevailed. The military are specialists by definition. In the days when the United States had a monopoly or near-monopoly of nuclear power, the big-bomber men of the SAC-dominated Air Force had become the dominant specialists, partly because the money-saving aspects of the "bigger bang for a buck" theory were particularly seductive to the civilian political leadership. The result was the rigid 23-28-46 Army–Navy–Air Force ratio of Defense expenditures. This ratio reduced the nation's ability to fight non-nuclear wars to near zero. This was as true of the Air Force itself as of the Army—TAC (tactical command) was pared away until it had almost ceased to exist, in order to feed the ravenous demands of the big-bomber men in SAC.

The American atomic monopoly was broken in September, 1949. And yet ten years later, by reason of a sort of military-cultural lag, the United States was almost wholly dependent for its defense on a weapons system which could be employed only at the risk of national suicide. This despite the fact that the man who was President of the United States during most of the decade of the nineteen-fifties had made his career as an Army general; and despite the further fact that the Korean War had very vividly demonstrated the limitations of nuclear power, even while the United States enjoyed a near-monopoly of that power.

Here we come to the second of the great and lasting changes which McNamara imposed on the American defense structure. He changed the "basic system" under which the Pentagon is run, just as the Du Ponts changed the system under which General Motors was run. But he also changed the underlying *theory* of how to defend the United States and maintain the world balance of power. He produced in the process two interlocking strategic doctrines, each bearing the indelible McNamara imprint.

To understand this second change, it is useful to glance back at a bit of half-forgotten history, and to compare a decision which confronted President John F. Kennedy in 1961 with another decision, which confronted President Lyndon B. Johnson in 1965.

The decision which confronted President Kennedy in 1961 was this: whether or not to intervene directly with American ground troops in Laos. Vietnam seemed at the time comparatively secure, but Laos appeared about to fall to the Communist Pathet Lao. In March of 1961 Kennedy made a decision-in-principle to intervene in Laos, if necessary, in order to prevent a Communist takeover. In late March, at a press conference largely devoted to Laos, he hinted very broadly at this decision. On a big map, for the benefit of the television cameras, he traced the areas already Communist-controlled. He insisted on the strategic importance of the little country—the safety of Laos, he said, "runs with the safety of us all." Under the SEATO treaty, he said, the United States was obliged to oppose Communist aggression in Southeast Asia, and "I know every American will want his country to honor its obligations."

The Marines and the Seventh Fleet were alerted for the intended intervention. Pakistan, then the firmest American ally in the Far East, promised eight thousand troops, and the Kennedy administration assured the Pakistani that airlift would be available when the time came. The Thais, the Filipinos, the Australians, the New Zealanders, and even the British, who had promised a token battalion from Hong Kong, had agreed to come in. But the intervention never took place. Why?

The Bay of Pigs disaster, which occurred in April, 1961, largely answers that question. Before the Bay of Pigs, the President and those around him had trusted more or less implicitly the information and the judgment of the professional civil servants and military men. They had accepted the assurances of the professionals that a few hundred Cuban refugees would bring down the Castro regime without direct American intervention; and they had therefore never asked the hard questions about the operation which, in retrospect, cried out to be asked.

The professionals of the permanent government were unanimous for Plan Five, the plan for intervention in Laos. But the professionals had been unanimous for the Bay of Pigs operation too, and Kennedy and those around him had learned their lesson. They asked the hard questions, and demanded hard answers. This question-and-answer process, as reported by this reporter at the time, went about like this:

Q: If we go into Laos, how many men could the United States and its SEATO allies put into the country?
A: About 30,000.
Q: If the other side intervened openly, how many men could they put in?
A: About 120,000 from Vietnam. From China, God knows.
Q: Suppose our side was threatened with being overrun, what could we do?
A: Use nuclear weapons.
Q: Where and against what?
A: That's up to the President.

As a result of this question-and-answer exercise, the United States did not intervene, and accepted instead the Geneva agreement neutralizing Laos.

Almost everybody—certainly including the President himself—expected at the time that the agreement would mean a rather rapid Communist takeover in Laos. Moreover, the failure to intervene in Laos, coming on the heels of the Cuban disaster, made President Kennedy look like a bluffer twice in succession, thus inviting Nikita Khrushchev to call another American bluff (which wasn't a bluff at all) in Berlin. These dangers were fully recognized by President Kennedy. But once the question-and-answer exercise had been completed, Kennedy had no real choice.

He did not intervene in Laos because he could not intervene in Laos. With an Army of eleven understrength divisions and the other skeletal conventional forces which he had inherited from the previous administration, he simply lacked the non-nuclear power to intervene and make the intervention stick.

Now consider the rather similar decision which confronted Lyndon B. Johnson in the spring and early summer of 1965. By March of that year it was clear that the only alternative to Communist victory in Vietnam was active American intervention with ground troops. With agonizing reluctance—for almost three months, he refused to admit, even to himself, that there had been any "basic change" in the American mission in Vietnam—President Johnson decided to commit American ground troops. The first two battalions were sent to the area of Danang in March, and from that first commitment there was no possible turning back. One result was later described to this reporter by Secretary McNamara:

"We moved 100,000 troops 10,000 miles in about 120 days, with all their supporting matériel, and those troops immediately began operating damned effectively and with tremendous morale. I consider that quite an accomplishment."

It *was* quite an accomplishment. Moreover, the thing was done, and the troop commitment was doubled and tripled, without the declaration of national emergency which then legally had to precede a call-up of the reserves—McNamara's assurance that a reserve call-up would not be needed was a major reason why President Johnson, with whatever reluctance, agreed to commit U.S. combat troops. And this was possible because McNamara, in the years since Kennedy had decided not to intervene in Laos, had beefed up the true conventional strength of the U.S. forces by something like 100 percent.

In short, Kennedy decided not to intervene in Laos because he couldn't and Johnson decided to intervene in Vietnam because he could. It is almost as simple as that. As one of McNamara's subordinates remarked: "If McNamara hadn't increased our conventional capability all along the line, we probably wouldn't have gone into Vietnam, because we couldn't. You could argue that we went into Vietnam because we *could* go into Vietnam, just as you could argue that we dropped the bomb on Hiroshima because we had the bomb to drop."

McNamara himself disagrees; he believes that we would have intervened in Vietnam with ground troops under any circumstances, simply because the national interest demanded intervention. In any case, McNamara undoubtedly had more to do than anyone else with the contrast between the situation which confronted Kennedy in 1961 and that which faced Johnson in 1965. That contrast relates directly to the twin McNamara strategic doctrines: "the doctrine of the controlled response" and "the doctrine of the conventional option."

The Eisenhower administration also had a couple of strategic doctrines: the John Foster Dulles doctrine of "massive retaliation" and the Humphrey-Wilson doctrine of "a bigger bang for a buck." Under the Humphrey-Wilson doctrine, the conventional power of the United States was cut back heavily, in the name of economy. The theory was that this country would respond to any threat bigger than a very small brushfire war with "massive retaliation . . . at times and places of our own choosing"; in other words, by starting a nuclear war.

Even before they took office, both Kennedy and McNamara had strong doubts about both doctrines. The Bay of Pigs disaster and the Laos crisis powerfully reinforced those doubts. "Is that *really* all I've got?" the President asked when he realized how little uncommitted conventional power he had available, for use in Laos or elsewhere. And he was even more incredulous when it turned out that the best next step the military professionals could propose, if that little were not enough, was to start a nuclear war.

"The only thing that surprised us when we got into office,"

Kennedy later remarked with that unforgettable grin, "was that things were just as bad as we had been saying they were."

The twin McNamara doctrines of the "controlled response" and the "conventional option" were designed to make "things" less bad. In the Kennedy years, in order to achieve the "conventional option"—i.e., the power to fight wars without recourse to the nuclear weapons—McNamara upped the level of spending on the non-nuclear forces by a margin of about $9 billion. As proved by the aftermath of President Johnson's decision to intervene, McNamara has indeed achieved the "conventional option" in such limited-war situations as that in Vietnam.

But the conventional option is by no means an unlimited option, as the Korean crisis of January, 1968, served to emphasize. When the North Koreans seized the *Pueblo* and its eighty-three-man crew, a second round in Korea became a clear and present danger. Partly because of the McNamara policy of minimum mobilization for Vietnam, there was very little wherewithal, in available men and matériel, for another limited war. Some of the military warned privately, and some Senators publicly, that in case of a second round in Korea the United States would have no choice but to use tactical nuclear weapons. If they were right, the option in Korea was no longer conventional.

Nor is there a true "conventional option" in Europe. McNamara tried hard to achieve it. He argued repeatedly, and with irrefutable logic, that if the NATO allies so chose, Europe could be defended by conventional means. If the nuclear weapon had never been invented, he pointed out, it was ridiculous to suppose that Western Europe, supported by the United States, could not be defended against a Russian attack. The chief effect of this wholly logical argument was to arouse European suspicions that in case of threatened war with Russia the United States would abandon Europe to its fate rather than risk nuclear devastation.

Instead of making the effort necessary to achieve a genuine "conventional option" in Europe, the British and the Germans cut back their force goals, while General de Gaulle withdrew his feeble forces from the NATO command. Thus, instead of achieving a true "conventional option" in Europe, McNamara had to settle for a substitute theory—the theory of "the pause," or the "threshold." According to this theory, there is enough conventional power in Europe, not to fight a non-nuclear war, but to ensure a "pause" before both sides pass the "threshold" between conventional and nuclear war. Before passing that hideous threshold—so runs the theory— the pause will last long enough so that both sides can be absolutely sure that there really is no alternative to the mutual suicide of nuclear war.

The doctrine of the "controlled response" concerns what happens if the threshold of nuclear war is passed. Soon after McNamara became Secretary of Defense, one of the highly trained specialists whom he brought with him into the Defense Department paid a visit to the headquarters of the Strategic Air Command in Omaha, Nebraska. A SAC general gave him one of the elaborate briefings which were a SAC specialty. The briefing was on SAC's "war plan," which amounted in those days to an operation designed to reduce all of the Soviet Union, within hours after the order was given, to a heap of radioactive rubble.

"General," said McNamara's specialist, "you don't have a war plan. All you have is a sort of horrible orgasm."

The "horrible orgasm" war plan, known to its critics as the "spasm response," was a natural outgrowth of the theory of "massive retaliation." McNamara set out to change the theory. This is how one of McNamara's back-room boys explained the change, not long after McNamara had taken office:

"Before McNamara, the President really had only two buttons to push—'Go' and 'No Go.' If he pushed the 'Go' button, the military took over with the spasm response. McNamara wants to give the President a whole series of buttons on his nuclear console, from strictly limited tactical nuclear war at one end, through several shadings to Armageddon at the other end. He wants to give the President a non-nuclear console as well. And he wants to make sure that the civilian leaders, not the military, do the button-pushing from beginning to end."

McNamara himself, in 1963, in a famous speech at Ann Arbor, Michigan, spelled out his own thinking on this subject:

Our nuclear strength . . . makes possible a strategy designed to preserve the fabric of our societies if war should occur. The U.S. has come to the conclusion that to the extent feasible . . . principal military objectives, in the event of a nuclear war . . . should be the destruction of the enemy's military forces, not of his civilian population.

In other words, the "controlled response" was to be substituted for the "horrible orgasm." McNamara reasoned that since both sides had an interest in avoiding mutual suicide, both sides, in case of mutual war, would try to hold back from an all-out, civilization-destroying attack, concentrating on military targets rather than on the great population centers. Another of McNamara's specialists explained McNamara's thinking to this reporter in these rather simple terms:

"This country and the Soviet Union are like two men with cocked pistols. Both know that if one trigger is pulled the other trigger will be pulled. Both want to be able to aim at the heart. But both have a mutual interest in avoiding death. So both will also want to be able to aim at the shoulder, say, or the hand holding the pistol, as in one of those duels where both duelists want to stop short of killing. The trouble, of course, is that to hit the shoulder and not the heart you've got to have a damn good aim. And if you aim at the shoulder, and the other fellow aims at your heart, you've got to have another bullet left to aim at *his* heart."

In his first years as Secretary, McNamara made a very great effort to make possible a "controlled response" in case of nuclear war. He insisted on a basic revamping of the whole "command and control" structure, to ensure against accidental war, and also to ensure that civilian control of the military would survive the outbreak of nuclear war. He made a vast investment in the Polaris submarine-borne missile system, and the underground Minuteman missile system, to achieve a "sure second-strike capability." This is McNamara shorthand for the ability to strike a devastating nuclear return blow even if the Soviet Union launched an all-out nuclear attack by surprise. "Second-strike capability" means, in other words, that the United States will always have "another bullet left to aim at his heart."

McNamara unquestionably achieved his "sure second-strike capability." And when he left office he still believed, in theory, that a nuclear war might be limited. But as the years passed, his doubts on this score deepened, and he came to suspect that nuclear war is like an inoperable cancer—once started, it cannot be stopped.

"It's important to assess the *possibility* of avoiding a full exchange in case nuclear war starts," he told this reporter in 1966. "But I must admit that possibility seems to me marginal. . . . Now people realize what hardly anybody realized five years ago—that it's impossible to win an all-out nuclear exchange. Once you realize this, you arrive at certain rational conclusions."

The Pentagon estimates of U.S. fatalities suggest why "it's impossible to win an all-out nuclear exchange." Given the present state of defense against nuclear attack, an all-out nuclear exchange would kill about two-thirds of the population. Given a major "damage-limiting effort"—an investment, on the order of $30 billion, in an antiballistic-missile system and fallout shelters—the fatalities might be reduced to about a third of the population. But McNamara himself strongly suspects that in both cases these hideous forecasts of death err on the *low* side.

"Our estimates of fatalities in case of an all-out nuclear attack are almost certainly conservative," he told this reporter. "They're based on AEC computations involving blast and radiation. These factors are measurable, in terms of experience in Hiroshima and Nagasaki, and controlled tests, on tethered animals and so on. But they do not include thermal effects—there is simply no way to measure thermal effects in advance—fire storms, for example. And they do not include fatalities resulting from chaos, disease, and so forth after an attack—again, there is no way to measure these effects. So even given a considerable damage-limiting effort, it's extremely important to realize that a full nuclear exchange could destroy both sides."

Such matters are sensitive, and the interview was sent to McNamara to check for accuracy. The paragraph above came back unchanged, except that the "c" in the word "could" in the last sentence was crossed out and a "w" neatly substituted. That substitution suggests the nature of the "rational conclusions" to which McNamara came, after peering long and intently at the hideous nuclear equation. One conclusion was that, since a full nuclear exchange "would" destroy both sides, despite whatever defensive measures either side might take, it was more "cost-effective" to invest very large sums in deterrent, or offensive, nuclear capacity than in defensive capacity. That conclusion was reflected in his decision in 1967 to overrule the Joint Chiefs, who wanted the $30 billion-plus anti-Soviet antimissile system, and to opt instead for the "marginal" $5 billion anti-Chinese antimissile system. That is a decision which Clark Clifford, or *his* successor, will be under constant pressure from the military to review and which, in fact, very much needs to be reviewed carefully and constantly, for it involves many millions of American lives.

But McNamara also clearly came to a much more basic conclusion, with enormous political and strategic implications. This was that nuclear war must be avoided at all costs, short only of national humiliation and defeat; and that because this is so the United States must have great nonnuclear means of exerting national power.

Whatever else it may prove, the Vietnamese war has at least proved that the United States is capable of fighting a long, hard war, half a world away, without recourse to nuclear weapons. The achievement of this "conventional option" is an important achievement. Quite apart from the question of whether or not the United States should have intervened with combat troops in Vietnam, and apart even from the eventual outcome of the struggle in Southeast Asia, the "conventional option" may rank in retrospect as the greatest achievement of a remarkable Secretary of Defense.

Remarkable he certainly is, but McNamara is no superman. He made his share of mistakes, and he left grave problems for Clifford to deal with. It is easy to prove, on the record, that he was more than once dead wrong about the course of the Vietnam war. His two most famous gaffes were his 1962 prediction (which, in fact, was rather carefully qualified) that the bulk of American forces could be withdrawn by 1965; and his 1965 forecast that the Marines (then just landed in Vietnam) would "not have to tangle with the Vietcong." In this reporter's opinion, there were two chief reasons for such demonstrable errors of judgment.

One was McNamara's conviction, which was severely weakened before he left the Pentagon, that a war can be "quantified," or measured statistically, as automobile production or sales might be measured. In the period when the Vietnamese war was "McNamara's war"—when at President Kennedy's request he had assumed the chief responsibility for Vietnam—McNamara insisted on imposing a system for "quantifying" the progress of the war. Under the system, every relevant statistic was supposed to be gathered, collated, and returned to Washington, so that the progress of the war could be measured. As a result, an American visitor to the remotest hamlet or Green Beret outpost in Vietnam would immediately be subjected to a formal briefing, consisting of endless statistics and charts, listing Killed in Action, Wounded in Action, Prisoners Taken, Weapons Lost, Weapons Captured, Population Lost, Population Brought Under Control, and so on and so on.

This vast mass of statistics eventually wound up, neatly tabulated, on McNamara's huge desk in the Pentagon. There McNamara would pore over the statistics by the hour, trying to use them to "quantify" the war's progress, much as he might have used the sales statistics of the latest Ford model to measure the success of a sales campaign. It didn't work.

Before his death in 1967, the late Desmond FitzGerald, one of the key men in the Central Intelligence Agency, recalled a small episode from this early period of the war in Vietnam. FitzGerald, who had been in the infantry in Asia in World War II, and who had spent many of the ensuing years in Vietnam or elsewhere in Asia, was called to McNamara's office intermittently to brief the Secretary on the progress of the war. One afternoon he found McNamara poring as usual over his "quantifications." FitzGerald briefed him on the CIA's current intelligence input on Vietnam, and as the briefing ended, McNamara shook his head, and remarked unhappily, "You know, it's hard to make *sense* of this war."

"Mr. Secretary," FitzGerald volunteered, "facts and figures are useful, but you can't judge a war by them. You have to have an instinct, a feel. My instinct is that we're in for a much rougher time than your facts and figures indicate."

"You really think that?" asked McNamara.

"Yes, I do," said FitzGerald.

"But why?" asked McNamara.

"It's just an instinct, a feeling," said FitzGerald. McNamara gave him a long, incredulous stare, as though FitzGerald had taken leave of his senses, and FitzGerald was never again asked to brief the Secretary of Defense.

Reporters in Vietnam knew that a lot of the quantifications being sent back to Washington were works of imaginative fiction, which is one reason for the long history of mutual hostility between the American press and American officialdom in Saigon. The Vietnamese, being polite people, did not want to disappoint their American "advisers." Moreover, those advisers did not want to tell their superiors in Saigon or Washington that the situation in their area of responsibility was going to hell in a hack—a captain quite naturally wants to become a major, and a major wants to become a lieutenant colonel, and to report failure is not a good way to get promoted. Thus the "quantifications," for simple human reasons, were often highly imaginative. But by the time the statistics arrived on McNamara's desk, all neatly collated and quantified, they had the ring of objective and immutable truth.

This suggests the other reason for McNamara's infrequent

but serious errors of judgment. Unlike FitzGerald, who had a magnificent combat record, McNamara did not know—he had no way of knowing—what war is really like. A World War II Air Force expert on statistical control, which is what McNamara was, cannot be expected to know what it is like to fight an infantry war.

Almost all the men around McNamara, military as well as civilian, were primarily staff men in World War II, with little or no experience of ground combat. Men who have no personal experience of war on the ground naturally tend to harbor the amazingly persistent delusion that wars can be won cheaply and bloodlessly from the air, instead of expensively and bloodily on the ground. That delusion largely explains the Bay of Pigs disaster, for example.

"There's only one real regret I have," McNamara remarked to this reporter in 1966, "looking back over the last five years, and that's the Bay of Pigs. As I told President Kennedy afterward, 'You know damn well where I was—I recommended it.' Of course, we'd only been in office ninety days, and none of us had had time to get on top of our jobs, but that's no real excuse for bad judgment."

The basic error in judgment on the Bay of Pigs was the assumption that control of the air would make it possible for a mere battalion of refugees to hold out on the ground against Castro's army. The Bay of Pigs disaster was the American counterpart of the British disaster at Suez in 1956. In *Suez*, an authoritative study of that disaster by Hugh Thomas, the following description of Musketeer, the plan for the Suez invasion, occurs:

This plan . . . laid special burdens of responsibility on the air task commander, Air Marshal Barnett . . . of wartime Bomber Command. . . . The plan assumed that Egypt could be conquered by forty-eight hours of bombing to destroy the Egyptian

Air Force, accompanied by eight to ten days of aeropsychological warfare—pamphlets and broadcasts "to break the Egyptians' will to fight," accompanied by bombing of troop movements and defences. After this, the allied fleet would surely be able to land the armies at Port Said without fighting. . . . Eden had found this plan appealing on the grounds that it would cut our casualties to a minimum.

Kennedy, McNamara, and Kennedy's other chief advisers found the Bay of Pigs operation "attractive" for essentially the same reason—that a major objective, the overthrow of Castro, could be accomplished on the cheap, simply by achieving control of the air. As the Suez disaster illustrates, the myth that wars can be won by air power alone is not confined to this country. But it has been remarkably persistent in this country.

When President Harry Truman decided to intervene in Korea, he was assured by his experts, military and civilian, that American infantry would not be needed; the job could be done with U.S. air and sea power, plus Korean ground troops. And although McNamara insisted that he never believed that the bombing of North Vietnam would in itself bring the Communists to the conference table in a mood to negotiate, he certainly hoped that it would.

Instead, in the end, Lyndon Johnson had to commit more U.S. ground troops to Vietnam than Harry Truman had committed in Korea. And as the bombing of the North continued year after year, while the fighting in the South grew increasingly bloody, the brisk self-confidence which McNamara had always displayed in his assessments of the progress of the war began to wear a bit thin.

Originally, McNamara had been the chief theoretician of the Vietnamese war. Over and over again, he explained to Congressional committees and to the press the official theory of how the war would end. It was only necessary to persuade the Communist side that "they can't win in the South." Then "we presume that they will move to a settlement, by negotiation or in other ways."

This theory, like its author, was eminently logical. It may even, in the end, turn out to be a correct theory. But when McNamara left the Pentagon, it was abundantly clear that the Communist side had no rational hope of military victory in the South. Yet there were no signs that the Communists were about to "move to a settlement," which Washington, much less Saigon, could accept. McNamara's theory did not allow for the possibility that Ho Chi Minh might not be as logical—or not in the same way—as McNamara. And McNamara himself had begun to develop doubts about the Vietnamese war, and especially about the effectiveness and usefulness of the bombing of the North.

That was one major reason why he left the Pentagon, the other being his own wholly understandable fatigue. When McNamara's imminent departure for the World Bank was announced late in 1967, there was much speculation and much obfuscation about the manner of his going. But there seems to be no reasonable doubt about the following points:

a. McNamara did want to go to the World Bank eventually, and so told the President.

b. He made it clear to Johnson that he would be willing to stay until after the 1968 election.

c. Instead of urging him to stay, the President nominated him for the World Bank post without telling him in advance that he was doing so.

d. McNamara's growing doubts about the war, especially about the effectiveness of the bombing, certainly played a key part in the President's decision to let him go.

In testimony before Congressional committees in 1967,

McNamara had stated flatly that the very heavy and very costly bombing of North Vietnam had "not significantly affected North Vietnam's war-making capability nor seriously deterred the flow of men and materials to Communist-led forces in South Vietnam." By late 1967, when he made the decision to replace McNamara, the President had made up his mind to continue the bombing short of some definite commitment to "mutual de-escalation" by the Communist side. He could not afford, especially in an election year, public testimony like that quoted above, from a doubting Thomas like McNamara.

There were three leading candidates to replace McNamara. One was Cyrus Vance, McNamara's very able former Deputy. But Vance had a bad back, and for that and other personal reasons he was quickly eliminated.

Another leading candidate was the Deputy Secretary of Defense, Paul Nitze. Nitze has the public reputation of being a steely-eyed hawk, and a professional "cold warrior." In fact, he has probably been more consistently right about the war in Vietnam—about which more people have been more consistently wrong than about almost any other war—than any other inhabitant of The Center.

Back in the early Kennedy period, he was the chief opponent of what President Kennedy called "Walt's Plan Six." Walt's Plan Six was put forward by Walt Rostow and General Maxwell Taylor after a joint expedition to Vietnam in 1961. It called for a "limited commitment" of U.S. ground troops to Vietnam, in order to "stiffen" the South Vietnamese Army.

Nitze argued vociferously that such a commitment could not be limited—that in a war it was not possible to be "a little bit pregnant." To commit any ground troops at all meant in the end to commit as many as might be required to ensure the security of those already committed. This process, Nitze argued, was open-ended, and could therefore lead to American involvement in a major ground war in Asia. Kennedy, mindful of General MacArthur's warning to avoid such a war at all costs, vetoed Walt's Plan Six. This early battle left scars which were not wholly healed six years later.

More scars were left by Nitze's articulately expressed doubts about both President Johnson's crucial decisions on Vietnam in 1965. These were the decisions to make a limited commitment of U.S. combat troops, and to bomb North Vietnam's industrial and communications net, while avoiding the bombing of Hanoi and the other population centers. On the first point, Nitze warned again, as he had six years earlier, that a commitment of any ground troops tended in the nature of things to be open-ended. On the second point, he drew on his experience as a member of the postwar Strategic Bombing Surveys. The surveys showed that in both Japan and Germany production and morale tended actually to improve while bombing was limited. Production declined and morale began to disintegrate only after the really brutal—and morally repugnant—bombing of population centers began.

These arguments did not make Nitze popular in powerful quarters—in Political Washington it is often more dangerous to be prematurely right than to be wrong. Moreover, Nitze's sometimes acerbic manner had displeased certain Congressional grandees, and as an Eastern Establishmentarian—Harvard, Wall Street, Old Money—he was never really on the Johnsonian wavelength. Finally, Johnson was disinclined to replace one doubting Thomas with another. For such reasons it appears inevitable in retrospect that Nitze should have been passed over.

In retrospect it also appears inevitable that Clark Clifford should have been chosen by President Johnson. Clifford is a man of undoubted ability and intelligence. His is the kind of intelligence that produces perfectly parsed sentences and balanced paragraphs even in social conversation—in the mind's ear one can hear even the semicolons and parentheses click into place. His baritone voice is oddly compelling—a room is likely to fall silent when Clifford speaks. His manner is one of bland and affable confidence—when he talks, he clasps his hands together, in a faintly sacerdotal gesture, in front of the double-breasted suits which are his trademark (he wore them even in the era when the men's fashion authorities had ruled them impossibly square). Aside from ability, intelligence, and an air of authority, Clifford has other assets as well.

As an intimate of three Democratic Presidents, starting as Harry Truman's youthful adviser, he is The Center's leading expert on the care and feeding of Presidents. He is an insider's insider, a member, along with Abe Fortas, Joe Fowler, and a few others, of the little group of lawyers who know and can reach everybody worth knowing in Washington, from the President on down. Unlike Nitze, he has no enemies on Capitol Hill, and many staunch friends and admirers. And unlike most inside men, he is a very competent outside man too—his public speeches and Congressional testimony are impressive.

He harbors, finally, none of the doubts about the Vietnamese war in particular, and the strategic situation of the United States in general, that worried Nitze and McNamara. He is a strong believer in air power—he is a close personal friend of Stuart Symington, chief Senatorial air power advocate, whose 1960 Presidential bid he managed. He is very unlikely to rock the boat with testimony like McNamara's, quoted above. Finally, he is very much on President Johnson's wavelength, in a way that McNamara, despite genuine mutual admiration, never really was.

Clifford is by no means a weak man, and he certainly will not be a weak Secretary of Defense. As this is written, it is really too early to make any sort of firm judgment on his performance. But two guesses seem sensible. One is that, as Secretary of Defense, Clifford will be President Johnson's man in a way that Robert McNamara was not. McNamara, after all, remained a close personal friend of Robert Kennedy, and before he told the President that he wanted out of the Pentagon, he had long, anxious discussions with Kennedy. As the 1968 elections approached, Lyndon Johnson tended more and more to see Kennedy as *the* enemy, and McNamara's frequent visits to Hickory Hill were not lost on the President. Clifford, by contrast, has no more than a nodding acquaintance with the Kennedy faction. As the chief strategist of Harry Truman's upset victory in 1948, in 1968 the new Secretary of Defense is likely to put first things first—the first thing of all being the re-election of Lyndon B. Johnson.

Another sensible guess is that Clifford seems unlikely to maintain the near-total mastery over the Pentagon, including the august Chiefs of Staff, that McNamara achieved. On one of his missions to Vietnam for President Johnson, Clifford came down with a severe and debilitating case of hepatitis, and he himself has said that as a result he does not have the "endurance" he once had. At sixty-one, he is unlikely to work McNamara's seventy-eight-hour week, and he lacks McNamara's passion for detail. The seventy-eight-hour week and the passion for detail were two of the secrets of McNamara's domination of the military. More important, Clifford has a less naturally skeptical and inquiring mind than McNamara. He is far less likely to question or oppose either the doctrines of the generals and admirals, or the views of the Congressional grandees of the Armed Services Committees. He believes in the doctrines, and he shares the views.

All in all, it seems probable that under Clark Clifford the Pentagon will be smoothly run, with a minimum of friction with either the military or Congress. At least during an election year, it seems improbable that the two most intractable problems, other than the war, which McNamara left behind him will be dealt with effectively. For these problems are intractable in part because they are so politically sensitive. They are the politically divisive and monstrously unfair system of American military recruitment and the galloping bureaucratization of the services.

McNamara himself was clearly unhappy with the draft, and with other aspects of the recruiting system. He was right to be unhappy, for the draft actively encourages the reasonably bright sons of reasonably prosperous parents to "hide in the catacombs of education," to quote President Kingman Brewster of Yale. But the problem does not end with the draft. All three services are in competition with each other, and even *within* each service, for promising recruits. As a result, over the years, an incredibly complex system of competitive recruitment has grown up. Its net effect is to offer boys with the necessary educational requirements, or boys who have the luck and the pull to get into limited-service National Guard or reserve units, either safe service, or short service, or both together. As a result, aside from the adventure-lovers or idealists who volunteer for combat jobs, only the poor and the uneducated get shot at. The result of this slyly discriminatory system is that, to quote President Brewster again, "national morality has been exposed to collective self-corruption."

As for the bureaucratization of the services, the bulging Pentagon is its outward and visible symbol. But it is an inadequate symbol. McNamara, as noted earlier, believed that the armed services could comfortably dispense with half of the 27,000 inhabitants of the Pentagon. Instead, the population of the Pentagon itself has grown inexorably every year, while four new "little Pentagons" have been built or are being planned to house the overflow.

The total headquarters and administrative staff of the Defense Department comes to more than 73,000 employees in the Washington area alone, according to a compilation by Don Oberdorfer of the Miami *Herald*. This represents enough "bodies" to man five combat divisions. The staff structure in all three U.S. services—the Army and Air Force especially—is such that the unfortunate officers and men who are expected actually to shoot at the enemy, and to get shot at, constitute a tiny minority.

Part of the problem is that the ratio of officers to men, in the Army especially, is higher than in any serious army in the world. Thus there are too many officers with nothing, or not enough, to do; the Army is so overofficered that an infantry officer is quite likely to have actual comand over troops in about one year in twenty during his career. To cite one astonishing statistic, there are more than *ten* field-grade officers—major and up—for every single command job requiring an officer of field grade.

Inevitably, underemployed officers, aided by the newest office equipment, make jobs for each other, principally by churning out great reams of paper. As a result, the American services have the most complex command structure, as well as the highest noncombat-to-combat ratio, the world has seen in all the long history of warfare.

McNamara was entirely aware of the tendency of the services to become vast self-feeding bureaucracies only remotely involved in the process of fighting and winning wars. He tried to deal with it, and he did succeed in getting in Vietnam a sharply increased return in combat capability on the huge manpower investment there. Even so, in Vietnam the $30 million mini-Pentagon in the Saigon suburbs serves as a symbol of the system, as the Pentagon itself does in Washington. Only the American military would build so vast a building, to house thirty-odd generals and their staffs, in order to fight what remains essentially a guerrilla war.

So McNamara's success was only partial, at best. The fact is that there is in all bureaucracies a fierce resistance to change, since the position, prestige, and even the livelihood of the bureaucrats is at stake in the existing system. Since the U.S. military bureaucracy is far vaster than any other, the resistance is far fiercer. And yet, though the problem of the galloping bureaucratization of the services remains unsolved, McNamara did bequeath to Clifford a genuine "conventional option." The fact that he bucked the system year after year to achieve his "conventional option" is perhaps the best tribute to his determination, persistence, and force of character.

Adlai Stevenson, as quoted by Arthur Schlesinger in *A Thousand Days*, warned President Kennedy of the "tremendous institutional inertial force" in Washington's permanent government, which "in the Defense Department has systematically absorbed a series of Secretaries of Defense." What Stevenson wrote was perceptive, for the great institutional bureaucracies of The Center do usually manage to "absorb" their Presidentially appointed chiefs by keeping them too busy to think.

McNamara was not absorbed by the Defense Department; the department was very nearly absorbed by McNamara. And McNamara, despite his habit of getting up at dawn to work twelve to fourteen hours, was never too busy to think. For seven years he thought, long and hard, about the basic and hideous problems of national defense in the nuclear age. It is because he had the courage to do so that, in this writer's opinion, he will certainly be recorded as one of this century's greatest public servants, despite his occasional errors of judgment and whatever the outcome of "McNamara's war."

Some years ago, someone remarked that the Pentagon is "like a log with thirty thousand ants on it, tumbling down a rapids, with each ant thinking he was steering the log." In the McNamara era the joke lost its point. No one had any doubt which ant was steering the Pentagon log. Moreover, the ant-in-charge thought a great deal, and with great intelligence, imagination, and intellectual courage, about the direction in which the log must be steered. It will be interesting to see how well and in what direction his successor ant, Clark Clifford, steers that huge log.

7

THE PRESS:

FASHIONS IN THE NEWS

For men may come and men may go,
But I go on for ever.

....

Allen Drury's Washington novel, *Capable of Honor,* is
enough to give any political journalist a swelled head. The
protagonist of the novel is a newspaper columnist called
Walter Dobius, also known as "Walter Wonderful." Dobius
exercises such prodigious political power that he can curtly
summon Presidential candidates to his palatial Virginia
estate on a moment's notice, and even the President himself
is not above a bit of groveling for a kind word from "Walter
Wonderful."

No journalist in Washington's history has ever exercised
anything remotely resembling the power of a Walter
Dobius. The fact is that the gentlemen of the press—even
such important gentlemen as the nationally syndicated political columnists—operate on the periphery of power. They
have influence, but as Alexander Hamilton pointed out,
"Influence is not power." Real power means the power to
make the great policy decisions, and although Washington's
press corps may praise or criticize or explain or even some-

170

times obliquely affect those decisions, the press does not make them.

Even so, as Patrick O'Donovan of the London *Observer* has written, "Most strangers are astonished by the power . . . of the Washington press. It fulfills an almost constitutional function." O'Donovan confused power with influence, but the confusion was natural enough. The British especially are inclined to be "astonished" by the position of the Washington press, since British journalists are accustomed to being regarded in the still-rigid British hierarchy as about on a par with dentists.

This reporter's columnist brother, Joseph Alsop, contends that political journalists don't even have much influence; that only the facts really influence events; and that what columnists and other commentators say about those facts doesn't really matter much. It is certainly true that the facts about what has happened—i.e., the news—have far more impact than what columnists or other commentators say about what has happened. But although the news is what matters most, reporters and editors decide what is news and what is not, and what commentators say about the news influences this decision.

The influence of the Washington press corps is the greater because it is a continuing influence. The press shares one characteristic with the upper bureaucracy of the permanent government Establishment: it survives elections. The Washington press can boast with Tennyson's brook:

> I chatter, chatter, as I flow
>   To join the brimming river,
> For men may come and men may go,
>   But I go on for ever.

Presidents may come and Presidents may go, but a James Reston or a Marquis Childs goes on forever. The simple fact of having been a part—and an influential part—of Political

Washington while four or five Presidents have come and gone (or, as in the case of David Lawrence, eleven Presidents have come and gone) imparts to a successful political reporter a certain status and authority—and on occasion, to tell the truth, a certain pomposity as well.

The key relationship of the Washington press is, of course, its relationship with the government. But the relationship of the press with the press is also important—much more important than most outsiders realize. Although there are strays and nonconformists, the Washington press tends to travel in a pack. Indeed, the Washington press corps has long seemed to me to bear a certain resemblance to a pack of beagles. There is even a physical resemblance: not all reporters have stumpy legs and prominent tails (though some do), but almost all develop in time the anxious, preoccupied, self-important air of beagles. The resemblance, however, is more spiritual than physical.

The beagle is a highly competitive dog, but he is always ready to follow uncritically any other beagle who claims to have smelled a rabbit. When one beagle gives tongue, all the others instantly join in, and off the whole pack scurries, each beagle yelping like mad in order to convince the onlookers that he was really the first to pick up the scent. Sometimes the scent is actually that of a rabbit, but quite often the beagles, as they chase each other around in circles, giving tongue lustily, are simply smelling each other.

In the same way, when one political journalist writes something which is—or which seems to be—new or important, the rest of the press corps immediately begins to follow the same story. Certain reporter-beagles are by nature followers of the pack, while others—not many—are more apt to be the first to find the trail and give tongue. James Reston of the *New York Times* is one who has snuffled first along many a trail, leading the whole pack behind him.

My brother, Joseph Alsop, has often led the pack, although he has just as often stubbornly panted along his own trail, while the whole pack yelped like mad in quite another direction. Walter Lippmann was followed for years by a small private pack of reporter-beagles, who trotted obediently behind him no matter where the trail might lead.

The first duty of any political reporter is to read what his colleagues and competitors are writing, and this encourages the tendency of the Washington press to travel in a pack. So does the fact that most journalists spend a good deal of their time talking with other journalists. This is often mutually beneficial, for what is mere chaff to one reporter may be grist to another's mill, and vice versa. An agency man may have a revealing story about the President, for example, which he can't use but a columnist can, while the columnist may have a useful lead to a hard-news story to offer in exchange.

This incestuous relationship of the press with the press finds its outward and visible expression in the various journalistic gathering places. There is the National Press Club, for example. The Press Club now consists largely of ex-reporters who have abandoned journalism for public relations or some other financially rewarding trade, but for reporters with offices in the press building the club bar provides a useful central market for the exchange of information. (Ladies are not admitted as members of the National Press Club, so the lady journalists support *two* press clubs of their own.)

There is the Gridiron Club, which stages an annual show at which the great men of politics are "roasted." The Gridiron Club is largely a status symbol, but it is an important one, for it is important to a bureau chief to be able to ask his publisher to the show, to rub elbows with the great men who are being roasted. The status symbol is taken so seriously that members participating in the show spend long hours writing and rehearsing it, sometimes with genuinely funny results.

Then there are various luncheon clubs, and small groups of like-minded and congenial journalists who get together informally to talk with some local mover and shaker. The most important of the luncheon clubs is the Overseas Writers, which meets two or three times a month to hear some important official or visiting fireman make a short speech and answer questions, on a strictly off-the-record basis. And there are various clubs which are not primarily for the press, but at which the press meets the press.

All the leading syndicated columnists belong to the leading Establishment club, the Metropolitan (except for the ladies, who are not admitted, and one or two males, like Drew Pearson, who has stepped on too many Establishment toes, and doesn't want in anyway). A great many newspapermen also belong to the new Federal City Club.

The Federal City Club was started by a journalist, Charles Bartlett, in 1964. Bartlett and George Lodge, son of Henry Cabot Lodge, invited George Weaver, a high government official and a Negro, to lunch with them at the Metropolitan. When the cave dwellers among the members (cave-dwelling Washington is very Southern-oriented) insisted that they be sharply reprimanded, Bartlett resigned and organized the Federal City Club. Bartlett has jokingly remarked that the main dining room of the club ought to display prominently a portrait of Weaver, as "Our Founder." Rather ironically, when Weaver was asked to join, he refused. About a third of the members of the Federal City Club are journalists of one sort or another.

The tendency of the Washington press to travel in a pack helps to create one of the most striking phenomena of

Washington journalism: the fashions in news. One subject—Alger Hiss, or the Middle East, or the CIA, or the Peace Corps, or the poverty program, or what have you—will suddenly become journalistically fashionable. Then, just as suddenly, it will go out of fashion. A good example of this peculiar process was provided by the "conspiracy" of which the late Joseph McCarthy was the self-proclaimed victim.

In the early nineteen-fifties, for months and months on end, while the Korean War was being fought and very important things were happening elsewhere, McCarthy was *the* fashionable Washington story—this although the reporters who covered the McCarthy story were aware that the news McCarthy generated was false news. Then, all of a sudden, after he was censured in 1954, McCarthy ceased to be journalistically fashionable. He just wasn't news any more, a fact which helped to kill him.

When his lies and distortions, which had so recently made streamer headlines, went unreported, McCarthy screamed that he was the victim of a "conspiracy of silence" by the press. There was no conspiracy. No mastermind passed the word not to write about McCarthy any more. Instead, after he was censured, the whole Washington press corps all at once stopped covering McCarthy, just as a whole pack of beagles will suddenly and collectively realize that the scent is false, stop yelping, break stride, and give up the chase.

The herd instinct of the Washington press, which creates fashions in the news, has its dangers. After the commitment of American combat troops in 1965, the war in Vietnam became the all-dominating foreign news story. As one result, other parts of the world were inadequately covered. In the forties and fifties, for example, the Middle East had been a highly fashionable foreign news story. In 1951 *Time* magazine even chose Iran's mad old Mohammed Mossadegh as its

Man of the Year, and before the Vietnam war junketing Washington journalists regularly included the Middle East on their itinerary.

But after 1965 political writers on reporting trips abroad would make straight for Saigon, skipping such way stations as the Middle East. This concentration on Vietnam was natural enough, since American troops were fighting there. But the result was that the great Middle Eastern crisis of the spring of 1967 came as a sudden shock and surprise to most newspaper readers, and to most reporters too. There are many other instances of this underreporting of unfashionable areas—notably in Latin America, which has always been, for mysterious reasons, totally out of fashion journalistically.

The same tendency to overreport one subject and underreport others affects domestic news coverage too, of course. The interrelated problems of big-city poverty in the North, the malignant growth of the Negro ghettos, and the rapid decay of the cities at the core, all began to come to a head in the nineteen-fifties. But these problems, which have now become very fashionable journalistically, were ignored at the time—the fashionable story then was the civil rights struggle in the South.

Events themselves, of course—war, a crisis, an election—are the basic factors in determining what the Washington press corps writes about. But more than ever before, the Washington press concerns itself with what the events mean.

In the days before the invention of the syndicated column, reporters were expected to deal only in statements of demonstrable fact—what Senator X said on the floor, the size of the budget estimates, the outcome of an election. The reporter was expected to be strictly an impersonal conveyor belt for such statements of undeniable fact. David Lawrence, the first of the syndicated columnists, recalls, when he was a young man working for the Associated Press, writing a story in which he reported that President Wilson "frowned" on receiving a piece of unwelcome news. Lawrence got a sharp reprimand from the home óffice for "editorializing" in the news column.

Those were the days of the *who-what-when-where* formula of news writing. The formula still prevails to some extent, of course, especially in the Associated Press and United Press International. But even in the news services a *why* has been added to the formula, and in many news stories it has tended to become the most important ingredient of the formula.

This is partly because of the increasing complexity of the news; for the reader to make any sense of what is happening, the *why* must be answered as well as the *who-what-when-where*. But there is another reason as well. The more ambitious a political reporter is, the more likely he is to emphasize the *why*, because the *why* is more likely to lead to a syndicated column.

The syndicated political columnists—those who are taken seriously and have eighty papers or more—are the dukes and marquises of the Washington press hierarchy. Television and radio journalists are in a special niche of their own—a well-upholstered niche, since a successful television journalist makes far more money than even the most successful of the political columnists. Some of the television journalists, like David Brinkley (who is reported to make $500,000 a year), Eric Sevareid, William Lawrence, Edward Morgan, Elie Abel and others, are highly regarded in the trade. But because journalists still instinctively respect the written word, their standing is not quite as ducal as that of the major columnists. Almost all the television journalists were once newspapermen, and several, like Sevareid and Morgan, do some column-writing on the side.

In another separate niche, less well upholstered, are the magazine columnists. Bureau chiefs of big papers or national news magazines are also ranking members of the upper press hierarchy. So are reporters with nationally distributed by-lines, especially those who cover (in about that order) the White House, the State Department and foreign affairs, the Hill, and the Defense Department.

Then there are the specialists. The humor columnists have the most difficult of all the specialties, and at least two of them—Art Buchwald and Russell Baker—brilliantly succeed in the impossible task of being continuously funny about the increasingly unfunny national and international scene. Both Buchwald and Baker are more, of course, than funny men; they are political satirists of the first order. Politicians, with good reason, very much dislike being made fun of, which is one reason why Buchwald and Baker have as much real influence and impact in Washington as any of the "serious" columnists.

Other specialists range from reporters who cover the Supreme Court (who invariably acquire a judicial mien) to the reporters who make it their business to know what is going on inside the federal agencies and the minor departments. Washington society is another specialty. Society reporters like Betty Beale and Maxine Cheshire are respected and even feared, and they are considered must reading by most dining-out Washington ladies and a surprising number of Washington males.

Finally, there are the foreign correspondents who cover the Washington scene. A good many foreign reporters in Washington do their reporting the easy, lazy way, merely rewriting, according to their own political prejudices (which are rather often rancidly anti-American) the stories that interest them in the *New York Times* or the Washington papers. Once prestigious European papers have latterly been particularly addicted to the easy, lazy way of covering Washington. But a few foreign correspondents, notably Henry Brandon of the London *Sunday Times* (who has become, after eighteen years in Washington, a recognized member of the Washington Establishment) and Adalbert de Segonzac of *France-Soir*, are very much part of the Washington scene, and do a first-rate reporting job.

The whole Washington press corps comes to about fifteen hundred people, of whom about half cover the major domestic and international news—the rest are specialists. The needs of the press corps are catered to by well over three thousand government public relations specialists of one sort or another. The total bill to the taxpayer of all the activities of all the government's busy flacks was estimated by the Associated Press in 1967 at well over $400 million. This despite the fact that, except on rare occasions and for special reasons, self-respecting reporters rarely consult the PR men —a good reporter will always go, or try to go, straight to the main source of a story.

Reporting, of course, is the Washington press corp's *raison d'être*, and that remains true of those dukes and marquises, the nationally syndicated political columnists. Most columnists started as newspaper reporters. (Not all of them. Walter Lippmann never wrote a straight news story in his life.) Many reporters begin to make an important reputation by scoring important news beats. James Reston, for example, who started as a sportswriter, made a long series of beats (thanks to some communicative Chinese Nationalist delegates) during the Dumbarton Oaks Conference at the end of the war. But news beats are not enough. To aspire to a syndicated column, a reporter must also prove that he can interpret the meaning of the news both readably and convincingly.

It is not possible to interpret the meaning of the news

simply by reading the newspapers and pondering on the significance of the news contained in them. Walter Lippmann has been generally considered an ivory-tower columnist, far removed from the humdrum business of reporting. In fact, although he never wrote a straight news story, he did some of his era's most brilliant reporting, as in his fascinating reports of his day-long conversation with Nikita Khrushchev in 1961. In his last "Today and Tomorrow" column, he thus explained his decision to stop writing a Washington column on a fixed deadline.

For about two years I have been coming to the conclusion that this immediacy and this continuity was too much of a strain. It was not a physical strain to write. But it was a strain to be so continually alert, so attentive, so up to the minute. More and more I have come to wish to get rid of the necessity of knowing, day in and day out, what the blood pressure is at the White House and who said what and who saw whom and who is listened to and who is not listened to. The work of a Washington columnist requires that kind of constant and immediate knowledge, and it is only too obvious that the job should be done by men in the prime of their lives.

These words accurately describe what a political writer must do, over and above the reading of newspapers carefully, if he is to stay on top of his job. It is indeed "a strain," and it is easy to understand why Walter Lippmann, in his mid-seventies, chose not to endure it any longer.

In the Washington press hierarchy, until he chose to fade away to New York and Europe, Walter Lippmann was generally acknowledged to be *primus inter pares*. He was never *primus* in money terms—Drew Pearson, David Lawrence, and several other political journalists consistently made far more money than Lippmann. He was *primus* in prestige. His prestige survived the fact that a good many officials and former officials, and some journalists, have long maintained that Lippmann's judgments on international affairs have been consistently and demonstrably wrong—that he has been, to borrow the phrase of an old antagonist, Dean Acheson, "a commentator whose judgments over the years have been singularly error-prone."

Indeed, only a Walter Lippmann could have maintained his standing as an oracle in view of some of his more astonishing positions, like his serious proposal, shortly before the entry of the United States into the Second World War, that the size of the U.S. Army be sharply reduced. Lippmann's prestige was compounded less of the retrospective wisdom of the positions he took than of age, experience, integrity, personal style, and, above all, literary style. No current practitioner of the trade of journalism approaches him as a master of expository prose.

The "strain" of which Lippmann wrote is real. Writing a column is something like climbing a ladder without a top—when one column is finished and filed, there is always the next one to think about. And yet, unlike most work which involves strain, there seems to be something peculiarly preservative about column-writing—old columnists, to paraphrase General MacArthur, never die; they only fade away.

For some years after the Second World War, Mark Sullivan and Frank Kent, both well up in their eighties, were still turning out their columns. Lippmann (b. 1889), Lawrence (b. 1888), Arthur Krock, (b. 1886), Drew Pearson (b. 1897), and Gould Lincoln (b. 1880) are other examples of the preservative effects of column-writing. Perhaps there is something about climbing that topless ladder which keeps a man tapping away at his typewriter when other men have long since retired or gone to their eternal rest.

In any case, all the successful columnists endure "the strain of constant and immediate knowledge." They have to.

No man's mind is so rich a kingdom that it can produce several thousand words of interesting political commentary each week strictly on its own. As Ernest Lindley has pointed out, political writing is an exercise in "compulsory plagiarism," and a political columnist is in constant and sometimes desperate need of facts and ideas to plagiarize. In this sense, column-writing is a specialized form of reporting. All the successful columnists, even those who most emphasize analysis and opinion, remain essentially reporters. When a columnist stops reporting, his column quickly ceases to be worth reading.

A good deal of Washington reporting has much in common with paleontology. A paleontologist will dig up a couple of square inches of skull, a wrist bone, and a rib, and from these morsels he will confidently reconstruct the entire skeleton of some prehistoric animal. In the same way, a reporter may come upon a few seemingly unrelated facts, and be able, from his knowledge of the whole situation, to construct a hypothesis which he can then confirm with a few interviews or telephone calls.

The object of the exercise is to confirm the hypothesis, and many stratagems and knavish tricks are used to this end. One knavish trick, ancient but effective, was used by Murrey Marder and Chalmers Roberts of the Washington *Post* to score a beat over the *New York Times* toward the end of the Cuban crisis in 1962.

Marder and Max Frankel of the *Times,* rather to their surprise, had been asked to attend as guests a White House luncheon for Chancellor Adenauer of Germany. At this point the Soviets had agreed to remove their missiles from Cuba, but their Il–28 bombers were still there, and the American Government was pressing hard to have them removed also.

After the luncheon Marder and Frankel stopped to chat with McGeorge Bundy in the hall. Bundy fell to complaining about the eternal nosiness of the Washington press, which made it almost impossible to carry on delicate and secret negotiations. As a matter of fact, he remarked, he was sitting at that very moment on a red-hot secret, which ought to remain secret, and he gave it a half-life of about forty-eight hours. Marder asked Bundy jokingly whether he'd take even odds against the story being in the next morning's *Post*, and Bundy smilingly agreed to the bet.

At this point Marder and Frankel already had their square inch of skull—they knew there *was* a story, and although they did not know what the story was, they were pretty sure that it had to do with the Cuban crisis. On their way out of the White House, they ran into George Ball, then Under Secretary of State, who was wearing a small grin.

Marder asked Ball what he was looking so cheerful about, and Ball replied airily that things weren't going too badly. Ball's grin was the wrist bone. Marder and Frankel knew that Ball was deeply involved in the effort to have the Il–28 bombers removed. They both instantly constructed the same hypothesis—that some message had been received from the Soviet side promising to remove the bombers. Both returned to their respective offices, and began trying to confirm the hypothesis.

The vast *Times* staff got on the telephone to ask all sources whether it was true that Kennedy had received a message from Khrushchev promising to remove the bombers. Marder, back at the *Post*, recruited the help of Chalmers Roberts, the able *Post* foreign affairs specialist, and they decided to try a different tack. Their question was: "What was in the message from Khrushchev to Kennedy about the Il–28s?"

On about his fifth call, Roberts hit pay dirt: "For Crissakes, how did you know about that? I can't tell you what was in the message." That was the rib—now Marder and

Roberts knew their hypothesis was essentially correct. A little more checking, and Roberts was able to write a hard story, carried in the bulldog edition of the Washington *Post*, to the effect that Khrushchev had sent a message to Kennedy agreeing to remove the planes. Within minutes after the paper had hit the streets, Roberts got an angry call from Bundy, who was in a considerable state of perturbation.

The *Post* story, Bundy said, was all wrong. Did Bundy mean to deny that there had been a message from Khrushchev, or that Khrushchev had agreed to remove the bombers? No, but there were qualifications. What qualifications? Well, for one thing, Khrushchev was demanding a public promise that the U.S. would not invade Cuba. After a few further exchanges, Roberts was able to write a story for the later editions of the *Post* describing the Khrushchev offer in some detail, and beating the *Times* all hollow.

There is an ironical footnote. Bundy has since ruefully acknowledged that the Khrushchev message was not the secret he had in mind at all—his secret was by comparison minor and pedestrian.

As this episode suggests, there are times when the government and the press seem to be playing a rather childish game, with the officials shouting tauntingly, "Hah, hah, I've got a see-crut *you* don't know," while the reporters shout back, "Yah, yah, that's what *you* think." Many officials do undoubtedly get a childish pleasure out of knowing "see-cruts"; to them, the Top Secret stamp is a status symbol. By the same token, many reporters get an almost equally childish pleasure out of revealing the government's secrets—as the CIA, more even than State or Defense, has learned to its sorrow.

Sometimes, of course, the interests of officials and reporters run on parallel lines: the officials want to put out information which supports their policies, and the reporters want to write about the information. This is most likely to be so when an administration in power has firmly made up its mind what it wants to do and why, as in the creative period of policy-making during the first Truman administration, which produced the Truman Doctrine, the Marshall Plan, and the beginnings of NATO. Never since have relations between government and the press so closely approached a partnership. Tension tinged with bitterness is the normal relationship.

As Charles Bohlen has said, the government is naturally retentive, and the press naturally extractive. Various techniques of retention and extraction have been developed on both sides. So have certain mutually accepted ground rules. In some ways, the government-press relationship has become almost as ritualized as life at the court of Louis Quatorze.

For example, an official asked to lunch by a reporter knows that this is not a social occasion. The luncheon table is in Washington the most important meeting place between press and government. But dinner, unless otherwise specified, *is* a social occasion, and a reporter who does most of his reporting over the brandy and cigars soon has few friends left among either officials or fellow journalists.

Even at lunch, the rule which all journalists must obey at all costs—"Protect your sources"—applies, and it is understood that the official cannot be quoted without his permission, or identified as the source of any information whatever. Unless otherwise specified, the same rule applies to interviews in an official's office. Sometimes reporters from New York or elsewhere, who do not know the Washington ritual, create havoc. "My God, he *quoted* me by name," a Senator was heard to moan after an interview with a New York columnist.

Newcomers among politicians and officials are also sometimes unaware of the Washington ritual. Soon after his arrival in Washington, Senator Percy attended a "backgrounder" with several reporters. One reporter asked to what source any information which might be produced by the conversation should be attributed. "Why not to me?" said Percy. The reporters were astonished by this novel suggestion.

The "backgrounder" has become in recent years a Washington institution—and a deplorable one, in the view of a good many officials and reporters. Here, too, the rules are elaborate. The reporters are warned, for example, that the backgrounder is "deep background," or that the "Lindley Rule" applies—this means that any information or ideas must seem to spring, God-given, from the reporter's own brow. Or the information can be attributed to "a high government source," or "those acquainted with the President's views" (this often means the President himself) or, more specifically, to "State Department officials" or "Pentagon officials."

Those in the know, whether journalists, officials, or the Russian KGB or British MI–6 station chiefs in Washington, have little trouble identifying the source. For example, when McNamara was Secretary of Defense, a defense-related story in the Friday papers was based, in all likelihood, on one of the brisk weekly backgrounders Secretary McNamara customarily held at three o'clock on Thursdays. A foreign policy story on Saturday is based on one of Secretary Rusk's 5 p.m. Friday backgrounders (which are popular and well attended, in part because good Scotch is in liberal supply). The only trouble, as McGeorge Bundy has pointed out, is that although those in the know are aware of the source of the story, and can therefore assess its bias or reliability, the general public is not in the know.

The backgrounder ritual sometimes produces funny coincidences. For example, in October, 1966, the Washington *Star* printed a column by Crosby Noyes (a first-rate journalist who tends to be underestimated because his family has a partial interest in the paper). Noyes wrote: "Even such a relatively sophisticated leader as Russian Premier Alexei Kosygin is known to have told Britain's Prime Minister Harold Wilson that the American people would rise up in November and 'overthrow' Johnson's Administration."

Immediately below Noyes' column was another, by Charles Bartlett, in which Bartlett said almost exactly the same thing. The reason for this funny coincidence was, of course, a backgrounder attended by both Noyes and Bartlett. A good guess at the backgrounding official: then Press Secretary Bill Moyers.

Most officials will not say anything at a backgrounder that they would not be willing to have attributed to them publicly. (This is one reason why many journalists—Joseph Alsop and Rowland Evans, to name two—rarely if ever attend backgrounders.) If an official produces some really controversial news at a backgrounder, it is very likely to be hung around his neck like a particularly malodorous albatross.

This happened, for example, soon after Robert NcNamara took over as Secretary of Defense. He rather casually announced at a backgrounder that, after a good look at the facts, he had concluded the "missile gap" was a "myth." Since the new President had made a great deal of the "missile gap" in his campaign, this was hot news. Within a day or so, McNamara was publicly named as the source.

The same thing happened, to name three prominent victims, to Admiral Robert Carney when he was Chief of Naval Operations, to Richard Nixon as Vice President, and to the late John Foster Dulles as Secretary of State. The way it happens is always about the same. When there is a big story from an unidentified source—like Admiral Carney's prediction at a backgrounder in 1957 that war with the Chinese Communists was coming in a few weeks—reporters who were not at the backgrounder immediately begin checking on the source. This is seldom difficult. Reporters like to talk. As soon as the name of the source is published—even if it is published in some obscure paper or magazine—the lid is off. The rest of the press, usually with the prestigious *New York Times* leading the pack, immediately publishes the name of the loquacious official, and all hell breaks loose.

As the examples given above indicate, officials these days have become less loquacious at backgrounders. This is partly because in spirit they hear Lyndon B. Johnson breathing heavily behind them. But it is also because sophisticated officials have learned the danger of saying anything really interesting at a backgrounder. The usefulness of the backgrounder is thus sharply reduced, to both officials and reporters. A reporter who wants interesting information should see the official alone, and an official who wants to put out interesting information without being named as the source should see the reporter alone. But the institution of the backgrounder lingers on, as part of the press-government ritual dance.

One reason for its lingering is that it lends a certain prestige to reporters who enjoy one of Washington's favorite games, name-dropping. ("As Dean said to me the other evening . . ." "Dean who?" "Dean Rusk." "Oh, I thought you meant Pat Dean.")

Aside from the backgrounder, there are many other ways of getting information. Russell Baker once listed fourteen main techniques, ranging from lunch ("No lunchee, no newsee") to friction ("the art of rubbing two natural enemies together to make sparks"). But the essence of reporting is simple: you ask questions of people who know something important or interesting you don't know, and you listen to the answers. (A common and sometimes fatal disease of Washington journalism is to get the process reversed.) It is important to know what questions to ask, and how.

In this respect, standards as to what is and what is not cricket differ. In 1962 Charles Bartlett and I collaborated on a *Saturday Evening Post* article (which created a tremendous ruckus at the time) about the Cuban missile crisis. We both lunched together with a key source—a member of Ex Comm. I had carefully framed in advance a series of questions, leading up to one key question. No matter how the source answered the key question—by a smile, a refusal to comment, a shrug, or an ambiguity—it would tell a good deal about the true answer. When I sprang my key question, there was a moment of silence, and then Bartlett intervened.

"Gee, Stew," he said, in honest embarrassment, "that was a sneaky question." We all laughed, and the question might as well never have been asked.

Except perhaps for Bartlett, almost all reporters ask sneaky questions. The sneaky question is an essential extractive tool, the question asked by Marder and Roberts being an excellent example of how the tool is used. All reporters also develop their own particular question-asking techniques —James Reston is the acknowledged master of the "of-course-I-know-the-answer-anyway" ploy, while my brother Joseph Alsop is the foremost practitioner of the technique of the question framed as a statement. (If the source agrees, the statement is confirmed, and if he disagrees, that is equally informative.)

Bartlett himself has developed an odd but effective question-asking technique. After asking a nonsneaky question, while the source is pondering the answer, Bartlett makes a susurrant, or whuffling, noise, much like the noise a groom makes when he is brushing a restive horse. The noise seems to have a wonderfully calming and relaxing effect—I have seen normally suspicious officials and politicians answer Bartlett's questions with remarkable ease and candor.

The aftermath of the article Bartlett and I wrote together (besides popularizing two unpleasant and subsequently overused phrases, "eyeball to eyeball" and "hawks and doves") told a good deal about how the Washington press operates. The article seemed to me a rather routine "reconstruction piece," as this kind of after-the-event article is known in the trade—every major crisis produces such retrospective accounts by the bushel.

We wrote that the late Adlai Stevenson had suggested in the Ex Comm meetings a deal with the Soviets to deactivate the Guantánamo base and other foreign bases in return for "neutralizing" the missiles in Cuba. This was true (and not very surprising, since it was an obvious idea), as Arthur Schlesinger and others have since confirmed. We also quoted one of Stevenson's "nonadmirers" in the Kennedy administration (he had a good many) as saying that "Adlai wanted a Munich." The quote was accurate, and although the custom of quoting an official without identifying him by name may be a sinful custom, the sin is one of which every reporter in Washington is, by necessity, repeatedly guilty.

After the article appeared I went to the Caribbean on a reporting tour, and I was amazed to find that the article made such a row that for a few days it was the lead story even in the Spanish-language press. There seem to be two reasons, in retrospect, why the article made such a loud noise.

The first was that there was a news drought at the time; nothing much was happening, and during a news drought political journalists become desperate for something to write about. The other reason was more important: everybody knew that Bartlett was a close personal friend of President Kennedy. As Russell Baker wrote at the time, nobody would have paid much attention if Bartlett's name had not been on the article. As it was, it was assumed by the ever-suspicious and jealously competitive Washington press that Kennedy had inspired the piece, and that he was the anonymously quoted "nonadmirer."

He didn't and he wasn't. This was one of those times when the reporter-beagles of the Washington press pack were smelling, not a rabbit, but each other. But it is true that Kennedy read the piece for accuracy, and proposed a couple of minor changes. The most important suggested change (which was conveyed to Bartlett through the President's military aide, Major General Chester Clifton) was that we eliminate the name of Theodore Sorensen from our list of "doves." There had recently been a small row in Congress about Sorensen's wartime record as a pacifist, and Kennedy did not want to awaken any sleeping dogs.

Later, I was amused to read, in the section of Sorensen's book on Kennedy which deals with the ruckus about the Alsop-Bartlett article, that President Kennedy "was unwilling to repudiate his friends or cause more damage by specifying where they erred." We had indeed erred, in omitting Sorensen's name—at the President's request. In any case, it is entirely obvious in retrospect that the President himself did not at all anticipate, any more than Bartlett or myself, the ruckus the article would cause.

Having a President as a friend complicates life for any reporter. This is true only to a somewhat lesser extent of any important politician or high official. A reporter who likes and admires a politician or official is inescapably influenced in what he writes about him. This is one reason why it is an old, but rather frequently broken, rule of political journalism that close personal friendship with high officials must be sedulously avoided.

The rule was most frequently and most importantly broken when Kennedy was President, for the President had a good many personal friends in the press, and friendship, great personal charm, and the aura of the Presidency were an overwhelming combination. The combination was all the more overwhelming because Kennedy was a good source as well as a good friend—"The only ship that leaks at the top is the ship of state" was the current wisecrack. Information is to any journalist what water is to a perpetually thirsty man, and when a politician or official is a supplier of information as well as a friend, it is impossible to be objective.

"I always had the feeling," says Rowland Evans, one of Kennedy's reporter-friends, "when I was writing about President Kennedy that he was standing right there behind me, watching the words come and waiting to bore in. No question about it, friendship with a President can be a burden on a reporter's professionalism."

It is not surprising that the phrase "news management" first became current in the Kennedy administration. Kennedy, of course, was by no means the first President to try to manage the news. Thomas Jefferson, Andrew Jackson, and other early Presidents used their printing-contract patronage powers to subsidize friendly papers. The establishment of the Government Printing Office in 1860 deprived President Lincoln of this tool of news management, but he used as a very effective substitute the President's power to pass on exclusive information to friendly newspapermen—his ship of state also leaked at the top. Joseph Medill of the Chicago *Tribune* and for a time Horace Greeley of the New York *Tribune* were the chief beneficiaries of this Presidential largess.

As power has centered increasingly in the Presidency, the President's power to manage the news has—at least in theory—grown with it, especially since a new weapon of news management was added to the government's arsenal during and after the Second World War. This is the "Top Secret" stamp, a commodity almost unknown in the era of our isolation and innocence.

Especially since the last war ended, an intermittent but ferocious struggle has been going on between the press and the government about what is and is not properly secret. Certainly the press has not always been right. The government has authentic secrets, and the right to protect them. The press has no God-given right to nose around such subjects as technical defense information which might be useful to a potential enemy, or order-of-battle information in wartime, or secret diplomatic negotiations to end a war, or a number of other categories of secrets.

But it is remarkable how often the great "security flaps" have occurred because information is published which is certainly known to a potential adversary, or which comes from open sources, or even out of the reporter's overfertile imagination. When my brother and I were working together, we were the subjects of six or seven major security investigations. (Every Washington reporter worth his salt has been investigated, and reporters refer with false modesty to their investigations, like combat veterans talking about their medals or wound stripes.) Most of our investigations resulted from publishing information about Soviet weapons advances, which the Soviets obviously knew about, but which the administration in power did not want American citizens to know about.

But two of our investigations—one in the Truman administration, the other in the Eisenhower administration—illustrate a curious delusion among upper bureaucrats and high officials. This is the notion that a reporter cannot possibly reach the same rather obvious conclusions that government officials have reached unless the reporter has had illicit access to secret information. This delusion is even more widespread in Lyndon Johnson's Washington than in Truman's, Eisenhower's, or Kennedy's.

Our Truman era investigation occurred a few months after the Soviets exploded their first atomic bomb in September, 1949. This first atomic blast blew Secretary of Defense Louis Johnson's economy-in-defense policy halfway out of the water (the Korean aggression, in June, 1950, blew it entirely out of the water). Johnson and a couple of his cohorts on Capitol Hill were passing the word that the Soviet test was a fake, that it was not a true nuclear explosion at all.

When Senator Owen Brewster in a public speech echoed this nonsense, it occurred to us that there might be a column in the answer to the question, "How do we know that the Soviet test is not a fake?" My brother and I tried this question on several government sources, but we drew a blank—the subject was "sensitive," they said, and they clammed up. Then I had a bright idea. I called Georgetown University, asked for the head of the physics department (whom I had never laid eyes on), and asked him our question. He gave the answers which would be obvious to anyone with a working knowledge of nuclear physics: split nuclei in air samples, seismographic confirmation, and so on.

We published a column on the subject, which must have seemed very dull and technical to our readers. Unfortunately, the same question which had occurred to us had also occurred to President Truman. A paper had been prepared for him, and, as we learned later, it precisely paralleled the paper we had written—since physicists have a special language of their own, some phrases were actually identical.

Truman instantly concluded that we had purloined his Top Secret document, and he ordered the FBI into action. The FBI, finding no evidence of a government leak (there was, of course, no evidence to be found), adopted at last the desperate and unusual expedient of sending a couple of agents around to ask us how we got the story. The agents had obviously been carefully chosen—they were polite and intelligent young men, and one of them was even capable of discussing my brother's French furniture rather knowledgeably. But we did not tell them about the physics professor, and they left convinced, no doubt, that we had some still-open pipeline into the "secret places of the most high."

The episode in the Eisenhower era was even sillier. For some months, immediately after Eisenhower's re-election, and before the launching of the first Soviet Sputnik in 1957, a dispute raged within the Eisenhower administration about the U.S. missile effort. There was ample intelligence, based largely on a football-field-sized radar installation in Turkey, that the Soviets were testing very powerful missiles, capable of putting a satellite in orbit. The late Trevor Gardner, an Assistant Secretary of the Air Force, and one of the rather meager number of first-rate public servants of the Eisenhower era, was the chief protagonist of the view, strongly resisted in George Humphrey's Treasury Department, that a really major and expensive U.S. effort had to be made to match the Soviet effort.

I shared Gardner's view, and one day I dropped by the Pentagon to try out on him an idea I had for a column. (Most columnists pretest their column ideas in this way.) I had drafted a piece in which I quoted two wholly imaginary newspaper headlines: "SOVIETS CLAIM SUCCESSFUL LAUNCHING OF EARTH SATELLITES" and "U.S. RADAR CONFIRMS EXISTENCE OF EARTH SATELLITES." The idea was to suggest how disastrous to U.S. prestige it might be if the Soviets were the first to orbit the earth. Gardner liked the idea—more than I realized at the time.

My brother was abroad, and some days later, when the flow of columns from him ceased, I filed the column with the imaginary headlines. My brother arrived home the day after the column was published. A homecoming weekend had been planned for him at the country house of the late Frank Wisner, then a Deputy Director of the CIA. Richard Bissell, also of the CIA, was to be another guest. Wisner and Bissell were close personal friends, and we never discussed their business with them. But on orders from on high, the homecoming weekend was canceled—it subsequently became known as "the lost weekend." The reason, we learned much later, was that the President had been so enraged by the column with the imaginary headlines that he had ordered "an investigation to end all investigations."

Trevor Gardner, it transpired, had liked my imaginary headlines so much that he had incorporated them, virtually without change, in a National Security Council paper arguing the case for a greatly increased U.S. missile effort. The President read the column and the NSC paper on the same day.

"Goddammit," he was later quoted to us. "I don't like the Alsop brothers reporting what's in my NSC papers *after* I see them, but I'm damned if they can get away with quoting from my NSC papers *before* I see them." It never occurred to him that the Alsops weren't plagiarizing from the NSC— that the NSC was plagiarizing from the Alsops.

As these ridiculous episodes suggest, tension between the press and the President is no new thing under the sun. Even in the administration of John F. Kennedy, who genuinely liked reporters, the tension rose steadily and inexorably. Kennedy's cancellation of his subscription to the New York *Herald Tribune,* one of the few really silly things he ever did, was an expression of the profound irritation, the sense of being treated with gross unfairness, which all Presidents, from George Washington on, have felt toward the press, and with considerable reason.

As everybody knows by now, the tension between Lyndon B. Johnson and the press breaks all previous records. This is partly because Lyndon Johnson's conception of what is properly secret goes far beyond that of his predecessors.

All the postwar Presidents have used the "Secret" stamp to conceal the inconvenient—to conceal, for example, information that would tend to throw doubt on the wisdom of the defense or foreign policies of the administration in power. But, at least in theory, the national security provided the *rationale* for government secrecy. There is no serious pretense that the secrecy which President Johnson imposes—or tries to impose—on the government is necessarily related to the national security.

Any accurate forecast of anything the President intends to do—an appointment he intends to make, a trip he is planning to take—throws the President into a rage. He will go to almost any lengths simply to prove the forecast inaccurate. Many trips have been canceled, and a dozen or more major government appointments rescinded, for the sole purpose of proving the reporters who predicted them wrong.

A case in point was a story Philip Potter of the Baltimore *Sun* wrote for his paper in 1965 about the prospects for aid to India. Potter accurately forecast the amount of aid the President intended to ask Congress to provide. The amount was generous, the need desperate, the story involved no conceivable consideration of national security, and it put the President in a good light. Moreover, Philip Potter, a reporter of rocklike integrity, was one of Lyndon Johnson's few real remaining friends in the press corps. Despite all this, the President was so angry that he quite seriously considered canceling the whole Indian aid program, or at the least cutting it back very sharply. Only after the President's anger had had time to simmer down a bit were his aides able to persuade him that it would be shortsighted to force several million Indians to go hungry in order to make Potter look foolish.

In addition to his consuming passion for secrecy, another reason why the tension between this President and the press is higher than ever before is that Lyndon Johnson has never really understood the press.

Although John Kennedy was often irritated and sometimes infuriated by the Washington press, he understood it better than any other President since Theodore Roosevelt. He knew what makes a reporter tick, in a way that Lyndon Johnson does not, and never will. Rowland Evans recalls two episodes which illustrate the difference between the Kennedy and Johnson techniques of dealing with the press.

In the summer of 1961, Evans wrote a Sunday story, obviously based on a talk with the Foreign Relations chairman, Senator William Fulbright, to the effect that Fulbright was becoming increasingly disenchanted with the foreign aid concept in general, and President Kennedy's foreign aid bill in particular. On Saturday night, Evans went to a party at Robert Kennedy's Virginia place, Hickory Hill. On Sunday morning, before nine o'clock, the telephone rang in the Evans bedroom, and Evans sleepily answered it.

"How was the party?" said a familiar voice. Then the President, without mentioning the Evans story, began to talk about his foreign aid problem; asked Evans how he thought Fulbright would deal with the problem; asked how he, Evans himself, would handle the matter; listened carefully to Evans' freely proffered advice (just as Kennedy was a reporter *manqué*, most reporters are Presidents *manqué*); chatted amiably a few more moments, and then hung up.

It is no wonder that during the Kennedy administration

Evans at the typewriter felt the President "standing right there behind me, watching the words come"; and no wonder either that a lot of other journalists who knew and admired him felt the same way, and tended to write accordingly.

About six weeks after Kennedy's death, Evans got a call from Pierre Salinger, who had stayed on as President Johnson's press secretary. The press in those days was still handling the new President with very soft kid gloves. But Evans and Novak had written some mildly critical pieces about the President's flimflammery with the budget estimates. Salinger and Evans were old and close friends, and Evans greeted Salinger cordially.

"Rowly," said Salinger coldly, "why don't you get wise and play ball with us? Things have changed, you know—you don't have a pipeline into the White House any more."

Much later, after Salinger had left the White House, Evans confirmed what he had suspected at the time: Salinger was acting on the President's specific orders, probably with the President sitting at his elbow. The net result, inevitably, was that the criticism of the President was markedly less mild in subsequent Evans-Novak columns. Salinger, of course, knew that this would be the result—but not Lyndon Johnson.

I was first exposed to the curious obtuseness of Lyndon Johnson where the press is concerned on a trip to the LBJ Ranch in 1958, for an article on the then Majority Leader for the *Saturday Evening Post*. My wife and I had flown to San Antonio, where Senator and Mrs. Johnson met us at the airport, greeted us cordially, took us to a political dinner where the Senator made a speech, and then drove us to the ranch. Johnson was at the wheel, driving at a furious pace, and I was in front with him, while my wife was in the back seat with Mrs. Johnson.

Throughout the long drive, Lyndon Johnson relentlessly

stressed the same theme. The *Saturday Evening Post* was a conservative, Republican magazine. He knew, of course, that therefore I couldn't write a fair, objective article about him. He knew I would have to belittle him, and downgrade him, and stick a knife between his ribs. He knew, but he wouldn't hold it against me—a man has a job to do, and he has to do it. And so on . . . and on.

Finally I could stand it no longer.

"What you have been saying," I burst out, "is just as insulting as though you'd called my wife back there a whore."

There was a stunned silence. The car slowed to a crawl. After a few minutes, a long arm reached out, and began kneading my shoulder. Thereafter, the Majority Leader, a prickly subject for an article, then as now, went out of his way to help, and gave me a rare and rather fascinating on-the-record interview—all, I suspect, as a result of my outburst. But what is significant is that Lyndon Johnson was quite genuinely surprised that I should have resented what he said.

Perhaps it is not altogether surprising that he should have been surprised. Reporters on certain Texas papers are not noted for their journalistic independence—it is widely believed in the press corps that when Johnson was Majority Leader, reporters from Texas papers friendly to him actually submitted their copy to him before filing it.

Moreover, throughout his reign as Majority Leader, Lyndon Johnson generally enjoyed a good press, even in the national news weeklies and the big metropolitan dailies in the North. The symbiotic relationship of press and politicians is closer on the Hill than elsewhere in the government, and generally less antagonistic. The Senate especially is a small world of its own, and reporters as well as Senators learn the value of Sam Rayburn's old rule: "To get along, go along."

Reporters covering the Senate soon learned, moreover, to go to almost any lengths to avoid being subjected to what was then known as "Lyndon's Treatment A." I first experienced Treatment A in 1957. Here is my contemporary account of the experience, related when it was still painfully vivid in my mind:

This reporter experienced Treatment A during the post-Sputnik era, when Johnson's defense hearings were dominating the headlines. The reporter wrote an article, to the effect that Democrats as well as Republicans were vulnerable on the defense issue, which contained the following two fatal sentences: "As for Johnson, his voting record on defense has been good. But he is obviously open to the charge that he only summoned his Preparedness Subcommittee to make a serious inquiry into preparedness after the issue had been dramatized by the Sputniks."

On the day the article appeared, the reporter was summoned to the Majority Leader's small, ornate, oddly impressive office in the Capitol. Treatment A started quietly. The Majority Leader was, it seemed, in a relaxed, friendly, and reminiscent mood. Nostalgically he recalled how he had come to Washington in 1937, a mere freshman Congressman, and how Franklin D. Roosevelt had prevailed on the chairman of the Naval Affairs Committee to put "young Lyndon Johnson" on his powerful committee. That was, it seemed, the beginning of Johnson's interest in the national defense, which had continued ever since.

By gradual stages, the relaxed, friendly, and reminiscent mood gave way to something rather like a human hurricane. Johnson was up, striding about his office, talking without pause, occasionally leaning over, his nose almost touching the mesmerized reporter's, to shake the reporter's shoulder or grab his knee. Secretaries were rung for. Memoranda appeared and then more memoranda, as well as letters, newspaper articles and unidentifiable scraps of paper, which were proffered in quick succession and then snatched away. Appeals were made, to the Almighty, to the shades of the departed great, to the reporter's finer instincts and better nature, while the reporter, unable to get a word in edgewise, sat collapsed upon a leather sofa, eyes glazed, mouth half open. Treatment A ended a full two hours later, when the Majority Leader, a friendly arm around the shoulder of the dazed journalist, ushered him into the outer office. It was not until some days later that the reporter was able to recall that, excellent as Johnson's record on national defense undeniably is, the two sentences he had written had been demonstrably true.

In his Senate days, most of the reporters who covered Johnson were personal friends or at least friendly acquaintances. Most of them liked him, and even those who didn't were heavily dependent on the Majority Leader for news—or on the men around him, like Bobby Baker and George Reedy. Several days a week, after the Senate adjourned, eight or ten reporters would crowd into Johnson's small, impressive, Brumidi-decorated office on the gallery floor; or later, into the vast, unimpressive, Texas-decorated office suite off the Senate floor, known as "the Taj Mahal," which Johnson co-opted for himself in 1959. Drink would flow generously, courtesy of the Majority Leader (who drank Scotch and soda, and complained constantly that his soda wasn't fresh enough), amidst much talk, almost all of it Johnson's. Even in those days Lyndon Johnson would never tip his hand, and he was not much use as a news source. Even so, the gatherings were pleasant and often amusing, and a certain family feeling grew up between the Majority Leader and the Senate reporters.

A similar feeling has never grown up between the President and the White House reporters—quite the contrary. The lack of this feeling at first surprised, and then angered, President Johnson. For a while, after he inherited the Presidency, Johnson tried hard to establish the old ambiance on a much wider scale. (More even than most men, the President is a prisoner of his past, and tries ardently to re-create it.) He would invite the regular reporters into his office, or onto the

Truman balcony, for drinks or coffee, and he would invite publishers, columnists, and the like for lunch in the private dining room, often preceded by a swim in the White House pool and followed by talks which might last all afternoon.

But the relationship between the press and a President is inherently different from that between the press and a Senator, however important the Senator, and this effort by the President to re-establish the relationship with the press of his Senate days was inevitably a failure.

The failure irritated the President all the more because the press is actually installed inside what Lyndon Johnson sometimes refers to as "my place"—the White House. (Theodore Roosevelt, who came closer than any other President to managing the news successfully, was the first to set aside a room in the White House for the press.) Because the reporters were actually inside the White House, the President, according to one who knows the workings of his mind well, thought of them as *his* men, in much the same category as his staff. Thus when a White House reporter wrote something he disliked, he felt as though he had been nourishing a viper in his bosom.

This was true above all when a reporter wrote something like Philip Potter's aid-to-India story—an accurate account of something the President intended to do. President Johnson has never understood how this sort of story gets reported and written; he has never understood the paleontological method of reporting, by which a few details and a few telephone calls make it possible for a shrewd reporter to reconstruct a whole situation.

When a newspaperman wrote an accurate story of a certain complicated decision affecting future action in the foreign policy field, McGeorge Bundy, then still the chief White House foreign policy staff man, read it, and asked the reporter a favor. "Would you mind giving me a memorandum on how you came to write that story?" he asked. "I'd like to show it to the President. I know you got the story legitimately, but this President never believes a reporter can get a story like that unless a secret paper is filched or a Cabinet member suborned." (The newspaperman said he would think it over, but finally decided that he could not write a convincing memorandum and protect his sources at the same time.)

Quite often, of course, the President himself is the chief source of a major story. For example, in 1966 the President at a news conference said: "We must continue to raise the cost of aggression at its source."

Philip Geyelin, then with the *Wall Street Journal*, drew the obvious conclusion: that major U.S. air strikes against North Vietnamese targets were imminent. He did some careful checking around, confirmed his conclusion, and wrote a piece to that effect which was sent out over the Dow Jones ticker. The President, reading the article, instantly concluded that there had been a security-compromising leak, and ordered the FBI to investigate. There had, indeed, been a leak—and the leaker was Lyndon B. Johnson.

Latterly, the President has abandoned all attempts to re-create with the press the family atmosphere of the Senate days. He has three surviving personal friends among the journalists—William S. White, Max Freedman, and Marianne Means (who, on an early visit to the LBJ Ranch, made the immortal remark: "Oh, Mr. President, you're *fun!*"). These three are invited to Camp David, and attend social and/or state functions at the White House rather regularly.

He also sees a select group of newspaper and television reporters quite often on a business basis. These include: Hugh Sidey, able White House correspondent of Time-Life; Edward P. Morgan; Merriman Smith of UPI (the President was genuinely moved, and did what he could to help, when

Smith's son was killed in Vietnam); Charles Roberts of *Newsweek;* occasionally Max Frankel of the *New York Times;* quite often Ray Scherer, White House correspondent of NBC; Garnett Horner of the Washington *Star;* Dan Rather of CBS; Frank Reynolds of ABC; Frank Cormier of AP; and a few others. He also regularly grants audiences to important visiting firemen—for example, C. L. Sulzberger, foreign correspondent for the *New York Times,* almost always sees the President when he comes to Washington.

But these contacts are strictly business; except for his three surviving personal friends, the family atmosphere is all gone. The President has come to regard the press as a cross he has to bear. In this respect he is no different from his predecessors, except that he resents his cross-bearing more than any of them. He expressed his true feelings about the press when, in 1967, he strode into the White House press lobby with the King of Thailand, who was on a state visit to Washington.

"This is the press room," he told the King. "This is where they try you and convict you and execute you all at the same time."

As for the feelings of the press about the President, a few reporters deeply admire him, and a few dislike him to the point of hatred. The feelings of most are a mixture of admiration and dislike. The reporters who cover him talk about the President endlessly, and the quality of their ambivalence is suggested by a series of remarks which I jotted down in my notebook during one of the President's off-year election forays in 1966:

"I never know if he's looking at me—you can't tell by his eyes."

"Ever notice his blink rate? He hardly ever blinks."

"He's a man who always does the right thing, always in the wrong way."

"Think there's any chance he might step down in sixty-eight? He might just do it, you know, just to prove us all wrong."

"He could go out of office the most unpopular President in history—and one of the best."

"You know, there's something pathetic about the old bastard—he wants so much to be loved, and he never will be."

Looking at the President making a speech to a crowd in a street in Des Moines: "By God, maybe we're all wrong. These people just love that corn."

"I always wonder whether we're being unfair to him."

There are a great many people all over the United States who share Lyndon Johnson's distaste for the Washington press—and especially for the syndicated political columnists. Former President Eisenhower never got a bigger hand at any Republican Convention—not even when he accepted his own nomination in 1952 and 1956—than when he attacked "the sensation-seeking columnists and commentators" at the convention which nominated Barry Goldwater in 1964. It is an article of faith on the Republican right that virtually the entire Washington press corps is the willing handmaiden of the "liberal Establishment."

There may be a little bit—just a little bit—of truth in this theory. For it is true that a majority, and probably a rather large majority, of journalists tend to be Democrats and liberals at heart. This is partly because journalists, who make their living by the written words, are often quasi intellectuals, and—at least until rather recently—the Democratic Party has been the party of the intellectuals.

Moreover, the Democrats have always been more adept at dealing with the press. This is at least in part because the Republicans have generally tended to share with Lyndon Johnson and the Communist Party the notion that publishers dictate what their political reporters write. This has never been true except in very special cases, and it is less true now than ever before. Not even the Chicago *Tribune* would nowadays indulge in the kind of front-page partisanship that was thought perfectly respectable in the 1936 campaign, when the New York *Herald Tribune* displayed banner headlines every day, warning that there were only so many days left "to save the American way of life."

Because most publishers are Republicans, Republican candidates have tended to avoid the reporters who actually wrote the news, while basking in the warm glow of approval on the nation's editorial pages. For precisely the same reason, the Democrats with an instinct for survival have tended to cultivate the working press, and in the process to provide the working press with news.

A striking example of the difference was provided by the 1948 Presidential campaign. Thomas E. Dewey, supported by a vast majority of the papers, relaxed happily in the assurance of certain victory. Meanwhile, Harry S. Truman was out on the hustings giving 'em hell, making news, and incidentally making fools out of every political journalist or self-appointed political prognosticator (including this one), except for Alice Roosevelt Longworth, statistician Louis Bean, and then Secretary of the Senate Leslie Biffle.

Another example was provided by the 1960 campaign. There is no question but that a lopsided majority of the reporters who covered that campaign personally favored John Kennedy over Richard Nixon. But the reporters favored Kennedy far more for personal and professional reasons than for ideological reasons. Kennedy was readily accessible, and a fine source. Nixon kept the press at a long arm's length, and he made the same speech at every stop, so that the weary reporters would murmur together each sentence of "the speech" before Nixon uttered it, in a sort of anticipatory litany. As a result the reporters with Kennedy were happy, not only because they liked Kennedy but because they had a lot to write about. The reporters with Nixon were unhappy, not so much because most of them disliked Nixon as because they had nothing to write about. It is at least conceivable that this difference in attitude affected the minuscule number of votes needed to change the outcome of the election.

The distaste for the Washington press is not confined to the Republican conservatives. It is shared by the intellectuals of the New Left. The Communists of the Old Left, of course, have traditionally regarded reporters as "presstitutes" or "whorespondents," truckling in terror to the demands of their capitalist employers. The attitude of the New Left is essentially similar, but a bit subtler. Here, for example, is the *New York Review of Books* on the Washington press corps:

> In ways which journalists themselves perceive only dimly or not at all, they are bought, or compromised, or manipulated into confirming the official lies: not the little ones, which they delight in exposing, but the big ones, which they do not normally think of as lies at all, and which they cannot distinguish from the truth.

The "truth," of course, is that the government of the United States is ruthlessly imperialist, and that it is wholly controlled by the "military-industrial power structure."

Again, there may be a little bit of truth—just a little bit—in the notion that the Washington press is "bought, or compromised, or manipulated." Some reporters do have a rather overcozy relationship with their main sources. Because the press is dependent on its sources, and because the main source of news is the government, any administration is probably presented in a somewhat better light than it really deserves to be (a notion that would amaze President Johnson and virtually all of his predecessors). Moreover, the Washington press tends to a certain tunnel vision.

Most Washington reporters (including this one, as this book bears evidence) concern themselves primarily with the White House, the Hill, State, Defense, and to a lesser extent Treasury, the CIA, the Supreme Court, and the major embassies, with an occasional side glance at the lesser departments and the federal agencies. This leaves vast areas of political Washington unreported or underreported. This is especially true of the federal agencies, whose decisions can make or unmake great fortunes, and have vast impact on the economy. The federal agencies are covered, by and large, by the trade press only. The trade press, having a natural affinity for the industry which supports it, is not naturally inclined to lead crusades. Thus the federal agencies have an increasingly cozy relationship with the industries they are supposed to regulate, and this relationship is hardly reported at all, except when the surface is broken by some scandal.

And yet in fairness it must be added that the reason for the tunnel vision of most Washington reporters is that the tunnel they see is what their readers want to read about. A reporter who wrote a great deal about the Federal Power Commission, or the Federal Communications Commission, or the Civil Aeronautics Board would end up without very many readers, simply because not many readers are interested in such matters. And in the areas where the great central decisions of domestic and foreign policy are made, the simple fact that the Washington press is intensely competitive acts as a corrective. A story strongly distorted for or against some policy, agency, department, or public figure almost automatically stimulates a corrective story.

If a reporter gets and publishes a lot of information supporting the thesis that vast sums must be spent for an antimissile defense, for example, another reporter is sure to go to an opposing source, and get all the reasons why to spend the money would be a "tragic waste." This process can lead to confusion, but readers who are interested in the basic decisions confronting the government can at least blurrily discern the facts on which those decisions must rest. A citizen who really wants to, in other words, can get a pretty good idea of what is going on.

That is more than a traveler arriving in London in the afternoon can do. It is wildly frustrating, in the middle of some major international crisis, to find yourself limited to the budget of news supplied by, say, the London *Evening Standard*. Even if war impends, all the afternoon press in London is likely to provide is a rich diet of rape, murder, sexual orgy, or other wrongdoing. The very best British papers—the *Telegraph*, the *Observer*, the *Sunday* (not the daily) *Times*, and a few others—compare with the best American papers, and the very best writers in British journalism are better writers (but not better reporters) than the best American journalists. But the upper layer is thin. The popular press, which is what the vast majority of British citizens read, contains less real news than most small-city dailies in the United States, and even that news is distorted, romanticized, or shamelessly editorialized.

The very best French journalism is also very good, but most of it is, like the little girl with the curl, horrid. As for the rest of the world, as far as the news is concerned, as anyone who has spent a lot of time traveling can attest, it is like being blindfolded at the bottom of a deep hole.

About the best definition of the correct relationship between the press and the government was made in 1851, by the London *Times*, then the greatest paper in the world. Here, as quoted in the *Columbia University Forum*, is what the *Times* had to say:

The Press can enter into no close or binding alliances with the statesmen of the day, nor can it surrender its permanent interests to the convenience of the ephemeral power of any Government. The first duty of the Press is to obtain the earliest and most correct intelligence of the events of the time, and instantly, by disclosing them, to make them the common property of the nation. The statesman collects his information secretly and by secret means. . . . The Press lives by disclosures.

How well does the Washington press perform its "first duty"? A remark by President Kennedy suggests a rather ambivalent answer to that question.

According to an account by Clifton Daniel of the *New York Times*, President Kennedy made his remark to Turner Catledge, managing editor of the *Times*, in the course of a White House meeting of leading press executives convened by the President two weeks after the Bay of Pigs disaster. Kennedy castigated the press, and especially the *Times*, for prior disclosure of the government's secret preparations for the Bay of Pigs invasion. Then, in a surprising aside to Catledge, he said: "If you had printed more about the operation, you would have saved us from a colossal mistake."

The remark is worth pondering. There are times when government secrecy is absolutely essential, as during the first crucial days of the Cuban missile crisis. But there are also times when the government, operating "secretly and by secret means," can, as it were, hypnotize itself. Virtually the entire policy-making level of the U.S. Government—the new Kennedy men as well as the upper civil servants in the CIA, State, and Defense—approved the plan for the Bay of Pigs invasion. For reasons explained in the CIA chapter, the plan was not really so harebrained as it has been pictured. Even so, it is astonishing in retrospect that so many very able, very intelligent, very experienced men could have brought themselves to believe that Castro could be brought down on the cheap by sending a couple of battalions of refugees against him.

It is just as astonishing that so many able and experienced British politicians and civil servants could have brought themselves to believe that Nasser could be brought down on the cheap at the time of the Suez fiasco in 1956. When the first tentative air strikes against North Vietnam were approved, and the first couple of battalions of Marines were committed to South Vietnam early in 1965, the U.S. Government clearly believed—or at least strongly hoped—that Ho Chi Minh could also be brought down on the cheap.

This was why the whole government, from Lyndon Johnson on down, kept insisting that there had been "no change in the American mission in Vietnam." This self-hypnosis was insufficiently exposed by the press, and one result was that the American Government became committed to a major land war in Asia in the very worst way possible—crabwise, edging into the war without admitting it, even to itself.

It is the "first duty" of the press to prevent this kind of self-hypnosis, by obtaining "the most correct intelligence of the events of the time, and instantly, by disclosing them, to make them the common property of the nation." The record of the Washington press in performing this "first duty" is spotty, as the Washington coverage of the Vietnamese war and President Kennedy's aside to Turner Catledge both suggest. But it does seem safe to say that at least it is a better record than that of the press of London, Paris, or any other major capital.

8

CIA: *TRIUMPH*
OF THE PRUDENT PROFESSIONALS

> *Under the British system I would have to go.*
> *But under our system I'm afraid it's got to be you.*

More than 300,000 people work for the U.S. Government in Washington and its environs. The record of the recent past suggests that, of all the jobs held by these people, the most difficult and dangerous after the President's may be held by a conservative-minded, pleasant-mannered fellow of Greek descent named Thomas H. Karamessines.

Of the four men who held his job before him, one took his own life, one left Washington with a brilliant reputation sadly (and unfairly) tarnished, one died suddenly of a heart attack, and one went on to become the Director of the Central Intelligence Agency, and thus one of Washington's men of power. The story of the job now held by Thomas Karamessines is an interesting study of Washington's eternal interplay of power and personality.

In the Central Intelligence Agency, Karamessines is known, as were his predecessors, as "the DDP." The initials stand for Deputy Director, Plans, a carefully nondescript

213

title. The DDP is Washington's closest equivalent to James Bond's boss, "M." (The real-life "M," Sir Dick White, Chief of British MI-6, is actually known as "C.") Karamessines' share of CIA—the lion's share in both people and money—is called by detractors of the agency "the department of dirty tricks." He is the chief of espionage and clandestine operations.

All of the great rows and crises which have swirled about the Central Intelligence Agency since it was created in 1947—from the controversy over the CIA-promoted, anti-Communist coup in Guatemala in the early fifties, through the U-2 and Bay of Pigs crises, to the more recent rows about CIA subsidies to youth organizations, intellectual magazines, and labor unions—have been generated by the section of the CIA presided over by "the DDP." It is not surprising that the job involves a certain strain.

All four of the men who preceded Karamessines as DDP were men of quite exceptional ability (an opinion in which there may be some element of personal bias, since three of the four were close personal friends of the writer, and the fourth is at least a friendly acquaintance). The first DDP was Frank Gardiner Wisner, a handsome, stocky, intensely hard-working ex-lawyer, who was, in his hours of relaxation, a charming and entertaining companion.

Wisner was DDP throughout the coldest years of the cold war. Among a good many of the young who were never fully exposed to it, and among the mythologists of the left, it has become an article of faith that the cold war was a wicked American invention. In fact, especially in the Stalinist era, it was war indeed—war to the knife and for the highest strategic stakes—and in a more muted and polite form, with certain ground rules tacitly accepted by both sides, the cold war is still going on. It will go on as long as the goal of the Soviet Union and the other Communist states remains what

Nikita Khrushchev called "the great goal of Communism on earth."

There were times, especially in the late nineteen-forties and early nineteen-fifties, when our side came perilously close to losing the cold war. Our side would have lost a decisive battle if, for example, the Communist bloc had won the 1947 Italian elections; or if the Communist-dominated French and Italian labor unions had succeeded in sabotaging the Marshall Plan; or if Iran, the antechamber of the Middle East, had been captured by the Communist-controlled Tudeh Party. If these battles, or a number of other decisive battles of the cold war, had been lost, the whole world-power balance would certainly have shifted decisively in favor of the Soviet Union.

Frank Wisner, although his name is wholly unknown to most Americans, deserves a major share of the credit for the fact that the cold war was not lost. In the early days, although more visible personalities like General Hoyt Vandenberg, Admiral Roscoe Hillenkoetter, and General Bedell Smith were the titular chiefs of the CIA, Frank Wisner, for all practical purposes, ran the agency, and ran it well.

For a man in its front lines, like Wisner, the strain of fighting the cold war was in some ways as great as the strain of fighting a hot war. Frank Wisner was in the cold war's front lines for more than a decade. In 1956 the strain began to tell.

Wisner was in Vienna during the Hungarian uprising of that year. He saw the Hungarian rebellion almost succeed. Nikita Khrushchev, fearing the risk of war entailed in direct military intervention in Hungary, had tacitly agreed to a neutralist regime headed by Premier Imre Nagy, one of the leaders of the rebellion. Then the foolish French-British Suez adventure led Khrushchev to change his mind; he reasoned correctly that the Soviets could safely intervene, while the Western powers were preoccupied and bitterly divided by the Suez crisis. So the Soviet armored divisions moved on Budapest, the rebellion was drowned in blood, and Nagy was subsequently executed.

Frank Wisner had been deeply involved, emotionally as well as professionally, in the whole tragic episode. He returned to Washington seriously ill with hepatitis, but his illness was more than physical. In the years that followed, he fought with great determination and gallantry through several nervous breakdowns. He died by his own hand in 1965, as much a victim of war as any soldier killed in battle.

In 1957 Wisner was succeeded as DDP by his close friend, Richard Bissell, a tall, bespectacled, immensely articulate man, and a brilliant public servant. Before joining the CIA, Bissell had been, among other things, one of the architects of the Marshall Plan, and a deputy chief of the plan's offspring, the Economic Cooperation Administration. In the CIA, Bissell's most remarkable achievement was certainly the U-2 operation, perhaps the most effective operation in intelligence history.

The U-2 was born, in a sense, in Kapustin Yar, the first Russian missile-testing area, north of the Caspian Sea. In 1953 the CIA and British MI-6, which in those days worked very closely together, first received firm intelligence of Soviet long-range missile tests in the area of Kapustin Yar. By joint agreement, a British Canberra aircraft was sent on a dangerous mission. The Canberra flew at its maximum altitude from a base in West Germany over Kapustin Yar to a base in Iran, in order to take photographs of the missile site. The Soviets (who may have been forewarned by Kim Philby, the lifelong Soviet spy who had been placed in charge of anti-Soviet operations in MI-6) very nearly succeeded in shooting down the Canberra, which took several hits. It was clear that only a plane which could fly at a far greater height than any aircraft then in existence could be risked in future on such a mission.

The idea for a very light, very-high-altitude surveillance plane originated in a subcommittee on intelligence of a secret Committee on Surprise Attack appointed by President Eisenhower early in his first term. The committee was headed by Dr. James Killian of MIT, and the subcommittee by Dr. Edwin Land, president of the Polaroid Corporation. Land therefore stands *in loco parentis* to the U-2. But it was Bissell, then a special assistant to CIA Chief Allen Dulles, who got the plane built and thereafter, with Dulles' backing, pushed the idea of flying over Soviet territory up through the resistant layers of the bureaucracy, to President Eisenhower.

From a purely technical point of view, the U-2 was remarkable enough. Bissell got the go-ahead to build a prototype of the plane in December, 1954, and the plane actually flew in August, 1955—an incredibly speedy performance by Pentagon standards. Bissell had brilliant help, of course—notably from Land, who was principally responsible for the superlative photographic equipment which permitted the U-2 to take detailed pictures from seventy thousand feet; and from "Kelly" Johnson, the great airplane designer, a dead ringer for W. C. Fields, who built the plane from the ground up in his secret "Skunk Works" near Burbank, California. President Eisenhower gave the project for flying over Soviet territory a reluctant green light in June, 1956.

The green light was understandably reluctant; to overfly a hostile, nuclear-armed Soviet Union was a risky business. Eisenhower is said to have agreed to the first overflights of the Soviet Union after he was shown a photograph of the Augusta golf course, taken from seventy thousand feet. Every detail of the familiar, well-loved course was clear to the President, who delightedly picked out a golf ball on a green. After he picked out the golf ball, and after a heated internal debate within the administration, the President told Bissell he could have ten days to overfly Russia.

"Ten days of good weather?" asked Bissell.

"Ten days from today, period," said the President firmly.

By chance, the weather over Russia was generally clear in the succeeding ten days. The President was almost as delighted by photographs of the Kremlin, in which cars and people could be clearly identified, as by the picture of the Augusta golf course.

Ten days were wholly insufficient for the strategic mission for which the U-2 had been designed. That mission was to cancel out the great strategic advantage which the closed Soviet system (then more tightly closed than now) enjoyed over the open American system. Soviet intelligence could ascertain almost all the essential information on U.S. defense installations, or on aviation or missile developments, from the newspapers or from technical magazines like *Aviation Week*. U.S. intelligence had to depend for the same purposes on espionage, defectors, communications intercepts, and—mostly—guesswork. This left the U.S. in the position of the only blindfolded man in a game of blindman's buff. Because it was so clearly essential in the national interest to remove the blindfold, President Eisenhower authorized further flights of the U-2.

The flights continued throughout 1956 and 1957 without incident, and brought back thousands of rolls of invaluable and incredibly detailed photographs of the Soviet land mass. In 1957, with remarkable foresight, Bissell persuaded Dulles and the President that work must start as soon as possible on substitute techniques of surveillance.

A careful estimate of Soviet progress and potential in antiaircraft had indicated that within less than four years— quite possibly less than two years—the Russian air defenses should be able to reach the U-2's seventy-thousand-foot altitude, and claw the plane out of the sky. Bissell and Dulles therefore persuaded crusty old Clarence Cannon of the House Appropriations Committee, and a few other key Congressional figures, to approve secret appropriations for a satellite "spy in the sky." The Pentagon had been working on the "Samos" satellite, which was supposed to relay its pictures back by television. This method proved to have severe technical limitations. Bissell's technical advisers proposed that the nose cone of the satellite be recovered intact, and in 1957 work started on the CIA's surveillance satellite project.

Meanwhile, the U-2 flights had become milk runs. Initially, the plane had been equipped with an altitude-sensitive "destruct fuse" which would automatically blow up both the plane and the pilot if the plane descended below forty thousand feet over Soviet territory—the altitude the Russian air defenses were then able to reach. But as flight after flight was successfully completed, such precautions came to seem excessive. The destruct fuse was removed, ejection seats were installed, and the pilots were given the quite useless escape kits of the kind that Francis Gary Powers carried, when in May, 1960 his U-2 was knocked down by the Russian air defenses. That was the last U-2 flight over Russia. But thanks to Bissell's foresight in 1957, the nose cone of the first surveillance satellite was recovered, in August, 1960, complete with photographs almost as detailed as the U-2's. This, surely, was a near-miracle of timing.

The Powers episode, which Nikita Khrushchev used to break up the 1960 summit conference, was not a proud chapter in American history. But the embarrassment it caused was a small price to pay for what had been gained. Especially in the nuclear age, the military capability a potential enemy is *believed* to have is almost as important, in the total strategic balance, as what he *actually* has. As

Khrushchev was well aware, the myth of the "missile gap," which derived largely from wildly inflated Air Force estimates of Soviet missile production, was a great Soviet asset. The myth certainly encouraged Khrushchev to make his attempt to bluff the Western powers out of Berlin in 1959–61. The U-2, and later the surveillance satellites, exposed the myth, and greatly strengthened President Kennedy's hand when he decided to risk war rather than abandon Berlin.

"We'd show the Air Force generals the pictures," one CIA man recalls, "and say, 'Okay, so where are the missiles?' They'd mumble about camouflage, or say maybe they were in some corner of Siberia we hadn't covered, but of course it didn't hold water."

The exposure of the missile myth was in itself more than enough to justify the embarrassment of the Powers episode. But the U-2 also provided a kind of extra dividend in 1962, after Richard Bissell had ceased to be the DDP. For the elaborate trap which Khrushchev tried to lay in October of that year was uncovered when the CIA's U-2's picked up incontrovertible evidence that the Soviets were installing medium-range, nuclear-tipped missiles in Cuba. Without the U-2 Khrushchev's attempt to gain a great strategic advantage by making Cuba a forward nuclear-missile base might well have succeeded.

Bissell was also chiefly responsible for getting the money to start work on the A-11, a much speedier and longer-range surveillance aircraft. The A-11 was designed for surveillance in a sudden crisis, when the U-2 might be too vulnerable or too short-ranged. The surveillance satellites cannot be quickly switched from target to target in a crisis; it requires at least seven days to reprogram a satellite's flight, and launch it into orbit. The A-11 had very "long legs"—it could, for example, cover the entire U.S.S.R. from a base in Nevada, with one refueling. The A-11 could also be adapted for other purposes—for example, the delivery of lightweight nuclear weapons to essential targets without detection. Before his death, President Kennedy considered using A-11s to eliminate the nuclear plants then being completed by the Chinese Communists. The plants had, of course, been precisely located and repeatedly photographed.

For the U-2, the A-11, and the surveillance satellites (known as "Dick Bissell's private air force"), as well as other unsung feats before and during his tenure as DDP, Bissell deserves national gratitude. Under the traditional British system he would no doubt have been rewarded with a dukedom, a large fortune, and some such modest country seat as Blenheim Palace. Indeed, at the beginning of the Kennedy administration, Bissell was expected to succeed Allen Dulles as Director of the CIA (DCI, or Director of Central Intelligence, is the title used among the cognoscenti). In that case, Bissell would have been Washington's equivalent of a duke. Instead, he is now in private industry, and his brilliant talents as a government servant are wasted. The reason can be summed up in three words which still fall harshly on CIA ears: Bay of Pigs.

There has been, to quote Omar Khayyám, "much argument about it and about," and there will be no attempt here to recapitulate or disentangle the whole sad story of the Bay of Pigs. But one episode is worth recounting, because it tells a good deal about the peculiar way the Washington equation works.

The time was Sunday, April 16, 1961. The landing at the Bay of Pigs was set for Monday, the seventeenth. The planning for Operation Pluto—the Pentagon's code name for it—had all been squarely based on the assumption that Castro's air force would be completely destroyed before the first Cuban refugee set foot on Cuban soil. To that end, two air strikes were planned by the CIA, one on Saturday, April

15, the next at dawn on Monday. The Saturday strike—
billed as a bombing of Cuban airfields by defectors from the
Castro air force—had destroyed all but seven planes in
Castro's eighteen-plane air force. Overflights and espionage
confirmed that those seven planes were all foolishly concentrated, wingtip to wingtip, on an airfield outside Havana.

Bissell and the other CIA planners of the operation confidently expected the air strike planned for dawn, on Monday,
the seventeenth, to knock out these seven planes, leaving
Castro without a single aircraft. But two strange and malev-
olent coincidences upset their plans.

On Friday, April 14, a perfectly genuine Cuban defector,
Castro's personal pilot, landed his small passenger plane at
Jacksonville, Florida. The planes which took part in the CIA-
sponsored Saturday strike were supposed to land at Miami.
But the engine of one plane seized up, and it made an
emergency landing in Key West instead. Secretary of State
Dean Rusk somehow confused in his mind the Jacksonville
plane with the Key West plane. He therefore gave Adlai
Stevenson, U.S. representative at the United Nations, to
understand that the plane which landed at Key West was
piloted by a genuine Cuban defector. Stevenson, in a televised debate at the UN with Cuban representative Raúl Roa,
was therefore misled into pointing at the Cuban markings on
blow-ups of one of the CIA planes as proof that the defec-
tion was real. The markings, of course, had been painted
onto the plane by the CIA. When Stevenson learned that he
had been misled, he was understandably furious, and he
communicated his fury on Sunday to a worried Rusk.

Noon, Sunday, April 16, had been fixed as the "Go-No
Go" deadline for the operation. Bissell, McGeorge Bundy,
and others involved in the planning of the operation met
before noon and decided that there was no reason why the
operation should not go forward. Bundy so informed the

President, who was at Glen Ora, his country place in Virginia, and Kennedy gave the operation a rather reluctant "Go" signal.

At about six that evening, Tracy Barnes, Bissell's deputy, was summoned to Rusk's office in the State Department. Rusk asked Barnes to tell him just what Cuban planes had landed where, and which were real defectors and which part of the CIA operation. Barnes was doing so when Bundy came in, and Rusk asked Bundy for his understanding of the sequence of the various plane landings. Bundy precisely confirmed Barnes' version of events, and Rusk shook his head, and remarked, "I guess I got mixed up."

Rusk evidently realized that he had unintentionally misled Stevenson. Briefly, he discussed with Bundy whether he, Rusk, ought to join Stevenson at the UN, to give him support in the furious debate which was certain to break out on Monday. It was decided, instead, that Bundy should go to New York to backstop Stevenson. Rusk asked Barnes to go down to the floor below, where Stevenson's speech for the next day was being drafted, and to make sure that the speech contained no errors of fact.

Barnes did so, and went back up to Rusk's seventh-floor office at about eight o'clock. By this time, Bundy had left to fly to New York, and Rusk was alone. He remarked casually to Barnes that the second air strike had been called off. Bundy, it transpired, had telephoned the President, briefed him on the course of events, and explained that he was going to New York to backstop Stevenson in the UN, and to help him deal with the inevitable furor over the second air strike.

"What second air strike?" asked the President. He had been well briefed, but apparently he had forgotten this part of the plan. In any case, the evidence of American duplicity produced by the Cubans in the UN and Adlai Stevenson's anger at being misled had both deeply worried the President. So he told Bundy to order Rusk to cancel the second air strike.

When Rusk told Barnes there would be no second air strike, Barnes could hardly believe his ears. "You must be *kidding*," he said.

Rusk said that he was not kidding at all—the President had made the decision. Of course if there were some good operational reason for doing so, the air strike might be reinstated.

Barnes replied that there was the best operational reason possible for the second air strike: the ships carrying the refugees and their ammunition and supplies were "thin-skinned." They had no defense against air opposition, and the whole operation had been planned on the assumption that there would be no enemy air. With Rusk's assent, Barnes called his superior, Bissell, and asked him to come right over. He told Bissell of the President's order, but told him not to worry too much—the order made no sense and was sure to be reversed.

CIA Director Allen Dulles was in Puerto Rico, addressing a gathering of young business executives. His absence was part of the cover plan; it would make it more difficult—or so it was thought—for the Cubans to charge that the "notorious spy-master Allen Dulles" was responsible for the invasion. Bissell therefore called Lieutenant General Charles Cabell, Deputy Director of CIA, who was the acting head of the agency. Cabell called Rusk and asked for an appointment. It was nearly nine o'clock on Sunday evening when Cabell, Bissell, and Barnes met Rusk in his office.

Cabell, as the senior CIA representative, spoke first, reiterating the obvious arguments against the canceling of the second air strike. Then Bissell took up the argument, and with his accustomed force and eloquence he gave all the reasons why the second air strike was an integral part of the plan, and why, if the second air strike were not reinstated, the whole operation was likely to abort.

Rusk listened quietly, remarked that he was still unpersuaded, and picked up the white telephone on his desk. He was put through immediately to the President. He repeated, dispassionately but fairly, the arguments against the cancellation of the strike which the CIA men had advanced. He then told the President that he himself remained opposed to the second strike. The President said he agreed with Rusk and reaffirmed the cancellation of the strike. Rusk then asked the President to hold the line for a moment.

"Do you want to speak to the President?" he asked Cabell. Cabell looked at Bissell, and said something to the effect that there seemed to be no purpose in further argument. Rusk held the telephone out to Bissell, and for a moment Bissell had a strong impulse to take it and repeat his arguments. He held out his hand to take the telephone. Then he withdrew his hand and he shook his head.

The agreed "Go–No Go" point had been passed many hours before. The ships bearing the Cuban refugee battalion were by now approaching Cuban territorial waters, and it was probably too late to turn back. In any case, Castro's air force was more than half destroyed; perhaps, Bissell thought, the operation would succeed without a second air strike. Rusk spoke a few more words to the President, replaced the telephone on its stand, and the four men glumly parted.

In a later report on the episode, by a committee headed by General Maxwell Taylor, Bissell's failure to press his case for the second strike with the President was severely criticized. In retrospect, Bissell recognizes that he made a bad mistake. Indeed, it was the worst mistake of a brilliant career. But Rusk and President Kennedy made a mistake too, and their mistake is, in some ways, harder to explain.

Rusk, of course, was vividly and unhappily aware of having inadvertently misled Stevenson about the first air strike, and this no doubt increased his distaste for the second. As for President Kennedy, he had been unhappy about the whole operation from the very first—"It never did smell right to the President," one of the participants in the affair recalls. But as a new and very young President, Kennedy could not quite bring himself to trust his own sense of smell.

The whole plan had been put up to the Joint Chiefs of Staff, and if they had disapproved the scheme, it would undoubtedly have been a relief to the President. Instead, they ruled that the operation was "militarily feasible," and if thereafter the operation had been canceled, the President would have been open to charges of cowardice and vacillation—charges which could have been politically very damaging.

But the Presidential sense of smell continued to warn him against the plan, and the smell became very acute after the fiasco of the UN debate on the first air strike. As Kennedy's question to Bundy—"What second air strike?"—suggests, it may be that the President, instinctively disliking and distrusting the whole plan, instinctively shied away from mastering its details really thoroughly; and that therefore he never really understood the disastrous significance of his cancellation of the second strike.

At any rate, that moment when Bissell withdrew his hand was the sort of visible fork in history's road which appears frequently in books and movies about Washington, and very rarely in reality. If Bissell had picked up the white telephone, perhaps the President would have been persuaded to reverse his order canceling the second air strike. Or, just conceivably, he would have responded to his own sense of smell, and even at that very late date ordered the whole operation canceled.

If the second air strike had been reinstated, and all Castro's remaining planes destroyed on the ground, the course of events in the Bay of Pigs would surely, to some now undeterminable extent, have been quite different. Among the seven surviving Castro planes were three T-33 jet trainers left over from the Batista days, which Castro had astutely armed. The T-33s flew rings around the lumbering, propeller-driven B-26s which were supposed to give the refugees air support. After the B-26s were knocked out, and the thin-skinned ammunition ship sunk, the refugees were left nakedly defenseless on the beach.

If Bissell had picked up the white telephone and persuaded the President to reinstate the second air strike, would the final outcome have been different? Might the operation even have succeeded if all Castro's planes had been destroyed? Might a lodgment have been secured by the refugee forces, to serve as a base for a refugee government which the United States could then have recognized?

In this reporter's opinion, for the reasons suggested in the chapter on Defense, the Bay of Pigs plan was based on a persistent illusion—the illusion that wars can be won from the air. One way or another, it seems all but certain that the corporal's guard of anti-Castro refugees put ashore at the Bay of Pigs would have been destroyed in the end by Castro's hordes of infantry. But it is true that only three roads led through a virtually impenetrable marsh to the landing area. Given total control of the air, those approach roads might have been denied, at least for a time, to Castro's forces.

In any case, it is at least conceivable that the minimum objective of Operation Pluto—a base in Cuba secured for a refugee government—might have been temporarily achieved. It is also at least conceivable—though certainly very unlikely, given the time element—that the President might have decided to order a last-minute cancellation of the whole operation. In that case a good deal of national embarrassment and a great deal of personal pain would have been avoided.

The Bay of Pigs was not only a minor national disaster. It was also a major personal disaster to all those involved in it. Indeed, it was a disaster to the whole CIA, and even those who had never heard of Operation Pluto got hurt.

President Kennedy courageously took personal responsibility for the failure of the operation; and, in truth, he was in some considerable measure personally responsible for its failure. But for some time thereafter he felt, understandably, a smoldering resentment toward the CIA. For a week or so, he refused to have anything to do with the agency—he would not even read the intelligence reports.

"We were a sick dog then," recalls one veteran of the agency. "Anybody could kick us, and we couldn't bite back."

Various plans for putting the sick dog out of its misery, by breaking up the whole agency and parceling out its remains to the State and Defense Departments, were seriously examined. After Robert Kennedy and General Maxwell Taylor had had a careful look at these proposals, the structure of the agency was left largely intact. But the CIA was never the same again.

A process began after the Bay of Pigs which gradually transferred real power within the agency from one sort of man to another sort of man. No label precisely fits the two sorts. One sort might be given such derogatory labels as the Ivy Leaguers, the Socialites, the Establishmentarians. Let us call them the Bold Easteners. The other sort might be given such equally derogatory labels as the bureaucrats or the time-servers. Let us call them the Prudent Professionals.

Shortly after the Bay of Pigs, when the President had recovered his equanimity and his sense of humor, he called in Dulles, Cabell, and Bissell, and told them that he had decided that all three would have to be replaced, after a decent interval.

"Under the British system," he said with a grin, "I would have to go. But under our system I'm afraid it's got to be you."

Accordingly, on November 29, 1961, Allen Dulles was replaced as Director by John McCone. Cabell also resigned, and a couple of months later Bissell was replaced as DDP by Richard Helms. Thus the process of change began. In the Dulles-Wisner-Bissell period, which was also the period of the agency's greatest power, the CIA was dominated by the first sort of man, the Bold Easterners. The men of this sort came, for the most part, from the East; had gone to private schools in the East and to Ivy League colleges; had some money of their own; and brought to their jobs with the agency a certain spirit of derring-do, a willingness to take risks.

Of course not everyone in CIA fitted that pattern precisely. Frank Wisner, for example, was born in Mississippi. But generally the pattern held. There was a time when the CIA was positively riddled with old Grotonians, much as MI-6, the British secret intelligence service, was in its heyday riddled with old Oxbridgians.

Bissell and his deputy, at the time of the Bay of Pigs, Tracy Barnes, were both Grotonians. So was John Bross (who held, and as this is written still holds, a powerful administrative position in the agency). So was William Bundy, who was bravely defended by Allen Dulles against an attack by Joseph McCarthy in the early nineteen-fifties, and who went on to become Assistant Secretary of State for the Far East. So was Kermit Roosevelt, who, as our man in Teheran in 1953, almost singlehandedly foiled a takeover of Iran by the pro-Communist Tudeh Party. So was his cousin, Archibald Roosevelt, who has served as CIA station chief (head man) in London and in other important posts. So was W. Osborn Webb, who was in the Kennedy era responsible for collecting and editing the daily Top Secret intelligence reports to the President—a much more important job than it sounds. St. Mark's, St. Paul's, Milton, and other Eastern Establishment schools were also well represented in the agency, and so, inevitably, were Yale, Harvard, and Princeton.

The Bold Easterners flourished during the regime of Allen Dulles, not only because Dulles was himself very much an Eastern Establishmentarian (Princeton '14, former partner in Sullivan & Cromwell) but also because he admired boldness. Critics of Allen Dulles dismiss him as a romantic, a Walter Mitty playing the role of spy chief. This is nonsense—Dulles was the first thoroughly professional chief of clandestine operations this country has produced. But there is no doubt that, besides being a professional, Dulles greatly enjoyed his role.

"It was fun working for Allen," a CIA veteran has recalled. "He used to involve himself directly in operations, which could make life difficult, of course. He'd have us into his office, and we'd talk sometimes for hours. I can see him now, puffing at that pipe, and I can hear that loud guffaw. We were a band of brothers, but no one ever had any doubt about who was Big Brother."

The band of brothers began to break up soon after the Bay of Pigs. Dulles and Bissell were the first to go. They were followed a few months later by Robert Amory, Jr. (Milton

'32, Harvard '36). Amory, a lawyer and an imaginative and articulate intellectual, had held since 1953 the third most important job (in reality, though not in protocol) in the CIA hierarchy. He was "the DDI"—Deputy Director, Intelligence. The DDI owns no spies, launches no secret operations. It is his job to collect intelligence, both from the DDP and many other sources, including newspapers and history books; to evaluate the intelligence; and to be sure that it reaches its customers—notably the chief customer, the President.

The DDI is, in fact, the government's chief gazer into the crystal ball, since it is part of his job to try to discern the shape of things to come. Most, though not all, of the images which Amory discerned in his crystal ball turned out to be roughly accurate, notably when he was almost alone in predicting the Israeli attack on Egypt in 1956. But his most lasting contribution to the big business of intelligence is the National Photo Interpretation Center, which is housed in a large nondescript building in Southeast Washington. When Amory became DDI, the agency boasted just one full-time photographic interpreter. Working closely with Bissell, Amory created the Center, and by the time he left there were more than a thousand full-time photo interpreters there, busily examining the endless rolls of film brought back by the U-2s, the A-11s, and the surveillance satellites.

The photo interpretation system developed by the CIA is not simply a matter of looking at photographs. The interpreters work at consoles, and by pushing the appropriate buttons they can conjure up all sorts of data about the area being examined—previous aerial photographs, pictures from ground level, maps, statistics, and the like. This system has often paid off. For example, in the late nineteen-fifties at the time of the offshore-islands crisis, the Air Force reported to the President, on the basis of U-2 pictures of the Chinese mainland, that the Chinese had a previously unidentified long-range missile aimed directly at Taipei, capital of Formosa. Amory was able to report to the President the reassuring news that the missile in question was in fact a twelfth-century watch tower.

Unlike Dulles and Bissell, Amory was not directly a victim of the Bay of Pigs—it was one of the faults of Operation Pluto that the DDI was never given an opportunity to evaluate its chances of success. Amory resigned in part because he felt he had gone a bit stale in his job, but partly also because, having been at home in the atmosphere of the Dulles era, he was not at home in the atmosphere of the McCone era.

John McCone, a handsome, white-haired, forceful man, served as DCI from November, 1961, to April, 1965. A self-made multimillionaire from the West Coast, McCone is a conservative Republican, a devout Catholic, and a passionate anti-Communist. When he was appointed by President Kennedy (partly because Kennedy wanted to protect his right flank in Congress), CIA men feared he would be a crusader against "Godless Communism" first and foremost, and a secret intelligence chief only as a poor second. In fact, CIA veterans now agree almost unanimously in retrospect that McCone was a remarkably effective Director of Central Intelligence.

The CIA's role in the Cuban missile crisis, which occurred a year and a half after McCone had become DCI, was a great CIA triumph, second only to the U-2 operation, and without its embarrassing postlude. As McCone himself said later: "War over Cuba was avoided because every weapons system was correctly identified in time to give the President and his policy advisers time to think, to make a rational estimate of the situation, and to devise means of dealing with it, with a maximum chance of success and a minimum risk of global war."

McCone added to his personal reputation when, some weeks before the crisis erupted, on a Mediterranean honeymoon with his second wife, he kept experiencing a "gut feeling" that the Soviets were planning to place nuclear missiles in Cuba. McCone's gut feeling was contrary to the then prevailing official view, but McCone reported his feeling all the same, in a written message to his subordinates, and thereby established himself as at least a minor prophet. But no CIA veteran has ever said nostalgically, "It was fun working for John."

McCone was all business from the start. With him, there were no long pipe-puffing sessions and few guffaws. "I don't want to hear about your troubles," he would tell subordinates. "I want results."

In the McCone atmosphere, the Prudent Professionals quickly began to replace the Bold Easterners. Amory decided he had had enough one evening at about 8 P.M. That morning he had buzzed McCone on the telephone buzzer, which he often used to communicate with Allen Dulles, to give McCone an important piece of intelligence. As he was working late at his desk, a telephone repairman came into his office and removed the buzzer. The Director had given orders, the repairman explained, that all buzzers to his office be removed; henceforth he wanted only outgoing buzzers. Amory decided that this one-way communication was not for him, and shortly thereafter he resigned.

He was replaced by Ray Cline, a stocky, highly intelligent, Midwestern Ph.D. who was both more prudent and more professional than Amory. It was Cline who, in October, 1962, caught up with McGeorge Bundy at a dinner party and in cryptic words told him that U-2 photographs had confirmed the emplacement of Soviet missiles in Cuba, thus initiating the most dangerous crisis of the postwar years. But the key change was Helms for Bissell. The word "professional" is invariably used by CIA men asked to assess Richard Helms. "Dick's a *real* old pro," they say. "He really knows where the bodies are buried."

Helms is certainly prudent as well as professional. "There will be no Bay of Pigs under Dick Helms," a colleague said shortly after Helms had taken over from Bissell as DDP, "but there'll be no U-2 either." The forecast has proved correct.

Helms is a tall, black-haired, good-looking man, well preserved in his middle fifties, slim and athletic-looking (he plays a moderately competent game of tennis). He has been a professional intelligence man ever since he joined the wartime Office of Strategic Services (progenitor of CIA) in his late twenties, after a brief stint as a reporter. It has been said of him that, whereas Wisner and Bissell were operational men (viz., the Iranian and Guatemalan operations and the famous Berlin tunnel in Wisner's day, the U-2 and Bay of Pigs operations in Bissell's), Helms is an espionage man.

"Dick Helms would like to have a job like Dick White's," says one who knows both CIA and British MI-6 intimately. "MI-6 is almost entirely an espionage and intelligence show; they hardly ever mount major operations."

The CIA, of course, still maintains many major operations. Its biggest operation is probably in Laos, where the CIA runs two air fleets, Continental Air Service and Air America; finances a guerrilla army of ten thousand Meo tribesmen; and does a great many other things to keep the non-Communist government of Laos alive and kicking. But the Laos operation, like others in Africa and Latin America, was originated in the pre-Helms era. If the CIA has initiated any major operations since Helms took over, they have not come to light (which is, of course, as it should be), and there have been no major international crises generated by the CIA like the U-2 and Bay of Pigs crises.

Helms, to be sure, has had to deal with his share of rows centered on the CIA. One he caused himself, when he imprudently and quite uncharacteristically signed a letter to the St. Louis *Globe-Democrat*, congratulating the paper on an editorial defending the CIA and labeling a CIA critic, Senator William Fulbright, "a crafty Arkansan." The letter made quite a row, inevitably, and Helms had to apologize profusely and explain that he had signed the letter without reading it (which, it seems, was the simple truth).

The other rows centering on the CIA in the Helms era have all involved operations originated in the Dulles-Wisner-Bissell era, which belatedly came to light. For example, there was the row about the secret contracts signed with the University of Michigan and other universities in the late nineteen-fifties; or the hullabaloo about CIA subsidies to the National Student Association, the CIO and the AFL, for anti-Communist operations abroad. (AFL President George Meany vehemently denied that his organization had ever received so much as a tainted dime from the CIA, but no one knowledgeable in such matters believed him for a moment.) These operations were all originated in the pre-Helms era—the student association and union subsidies, for example, were started when Wisner was DDP. They made sense in those days, for it was surely entirely sensible to use such means to counter the Stalinist drive to take over all Western youth organizations and labor unions. But they were none of Helms' doing.

Helms and his Prudent Professionals are vulnerable to criticism all the same, especially as regards the subsidies to the students. For there was something peculiarly and surprisingly unprofessional about the way the operation was run. When it was first mounted, in the early nineteen-fifties, CIA men directly approached the three top elected leaders of the National Student Association (then in their early twenties, now middle-aged), explained the situation, asked for their help, and swore them to secrecy. For fifteen years the same procedure was followed. Under the circumstances, it is quite astonishing that the operation remained secret for so many years—boys in their early twenties like to talk.

The professional way to run the operation (as CIA professionals later ruefully acknowledged) would have been to establish a ".cutout" in the form of a single "charitable trust," to subsidize and control the student operation, giving the boys who were elected as chief officers of the association every year no inkling that the CIA itself was in any way involved. The unprofessionalism of the whole operation was compounded when the CIA set up a whole series of fronts— fake trusts and charitable institutions to provide subsidies— in such a way that when one front was blown they were all blown.

There is a wishful tendency in the intelligence business to suppose that because an operation has not been blown for a number of years, it will never be blown (the U-2 episode is also an example of this tendency). The Prudent Professionals of the Helms era CIA are thus vulnerable to criticism in the matter of the National Student Association and the other cover operations, not for having started them in the first place, but for having carried them on in the same way year after year. Resistance to change in the way things are done, if there is no immediate and crying need for change, is of course built into any bureaucracy, and it is no doubt this resistance which chiefly explains the unprofessionalism of the Prudent Professionals in the matter of the student operation.

Oddly enough, after the student association and other

front operations were blown sky-high, the man who was in charge of them all was promoted—another bureaucratic tendency. He is Cord Meyer, a liberal, and a wounded war veteran who, like Bundy, was also once a target of McCarthyite charges. Meyer, a bright but rebarbative man, with a certain genius for making enemies, is as this is written deputy to Karamessines, and his heir apparent as DDP.

Karamessines' predecessor as DDP was Desmond Fitz-Gerald. FitzGerald (St. Mark's, Harvard '32) was the last of the Bold Easterners at the top of the CIA hierarchy. He succeeded Helms as DDP in June, 1966, when the unhappy Admiral William Raborn, who had been appointed Director of Central Intelligency in April, 1965, was handed his hat by President Johnson. Raborn, an amiable sea dog wholly without experience in intelligence work, was a near-disaster as DCI. (The current joke was: "Dulles ran a happy ship, McCone ran a taut ship, and Raborn runs a sinking ship.") Helms moved up to the directorship—the first agency professional to go to the top from the inside—and FitzGerald took over as DDP.

As suggested by his remark to Secretary McNamara, that "you can't judge a war" by "facts and figures," FitzGerald was a markedly perceptive intelligence officer, with a real feel for the political nuances. Perhaps his greatest triumph occurred just before he died, at the time of the brief Arab-Israeli war in early June, 1967. The CIA, basing its estimates largely on the DDP's intelligence, reported to President Johnson not only when the war would break out, but how long it would last. The President, skeptical of the CIA estimate that the war would be over in a few days, sent the report back for reappraisal. But the CIA stuck to its guns, and when the war was won by Israel in six days, the prestige of the agency (which had needed a boost) climbed sharply. Tragically, a few weeks later FitzGerald was dead; he died suddenly one

Sunday morning, of a heart attack, on the tennis court of his Virginia farm, at the age of fifty-seven.

FitzGerald, like Helms, or Bissell, or Wisner, was what is known in the patois of Political Washington as a "generalist." Any one of them, if his career had taken a different turn, might have served with distinction as, say, one of the State Department's top policy-making officials. Karamessines is a different sort of CIA man.

He has been called by a colleague "a damned good seals and flaps man." No one, it is said, knows more about the business of opening and photographing documents in such a way that the closest examination fails to reveal that they have been tampered with. Karamessines is, in short, a technician, and a very good one. On such matters as letter-drops, cutouts, safe houses, two-time codes, "magic" and the other tricks and treats of the espionage trade, Karamessines is said to have no peer.

Like most of the upper hierarchy of CIA, Karamessines is a graduate of the wartime Office of Strategic Services, where he served in X-2, the counterespionage section. Since the war he has been a case officer (the man who handles the agents in an espionage net) or a station chief in various European capitals, including Vienna and Rome. Karamessines is, in short, like most of the top men in the CIA today, something new on the American scene—a genuine professional in the ancient trade of espionage.

It is in this sense that Karamessines is a different sort of man from his predecessors. Wisner and FitzGerald were lawyers by profession, and Bissell is an economist and former MIT professor. Even Helms was originally a newspaperman by profession, and a good one. (He scored an important news beat before the war when he interviewed Hitler.) Karamessines went to law school, and served for a couple of years in the District Attorney's office in New York in 1941, as a very young man. But he is essentially an espionage professional, and nothing else.

Until rather recently, there was no such thing in the United States. Before the war there was no serious intelligence agency in the government; the War and Navy Departments' intelligence sections were run by elderly ladies with a penchant for pince-nez glasses, who filed the gossipy reports amassed by the military and naval attachés on their social rounds. The appointment of Karamessines signals the fact that American espionage and intelligence—CIA's twenty-first birthday is in 1968—has come of age, for better or for worse.

His appointment was in part a result of simple bureaucratic seniority. In the pecking order, he was next in line for DDP when Helms took over as Director, but he was by-passed in favor of FitzGerald, the last of the Bold Easterners. To by-pass him again, besides being unfair, would have angered and frustrated his fellow technicians and career professionals, who now abound in the agency.

Karamessines' opposite number as DDI (Deputy Director, Intelligence) is R. Jack Smith, who replaced Ray Cline when Cline was exiled to Germany during the brief Raborn regime. (The admiral's innocence made for good stories, and Cline, who has a sense of humor, told one too many Raborn stories at Georgetown cocktail parties.) Especially in the period when Wisner was running the agency, the DDI always took a respectful back seat to the DDP, and the DDP still employs more men and spends more money. But under Amory, Cline (who was a dark-horse candidate to become DCI), and Smith, the reach and power of the DDI, especially outside the agency, have steadily expanded. Smith, an ex-history teacher who, like Helms, was in OSS during the war and made a postwar career of intelligence, is both prudent and professional, and he is accounted very able as well.

Smith, it has been said, is the publisher of "the most expensive newspaper with the smallest subscription list in the world." The newspaper in question is the daily Top Secret intelligence report to the President. Some years ago, it had a subscription list of one—the President. Now the Secretaries of State and Defense, as well, of course, as the DCI, are on the list. But it is still a rather expensive product per capita.

The whole "intelligence community" spends on the order of $3 billion a year, and employs about 160,000 people. Of this, the CIA's share is around a half-billion, and less than 16,000 people (other than agents and other foreigners). The code-breaking National Security Agency spends the most money—on the order of $1 billion—and employs, incredibly, over 100,000 people. The Pentagon's Defense Intelligence Agency spends around $300,000,000. The aerial reconnaissance effort, for which the Pentagon picks up most of the tab, costs close to $1 billion.

The President's intelligence report is the intelligence community's quintessential end product, the final distillation, of all this expenditure of money and manpower. Two filtered versions of the President's report are sent to the second level, and to the third or "working level," of the intelligence community. Editing the daily reports is a risky business, for while the customers of a newspaper or magazine can express their displeasure by canceling their subscriptions, the customer of the President's daily report can fire the editor. President Kennedy used to complain that the reports were too wordy, and that besides he had read it all in the newspapers. The reports were therefore edited to eliminate all except the genuinely secret information.

In those days, for purposes of ingratiation, occasional paragraphs intended to appeal to the Presidential sense of humor were added. For example: "The virility of the Imam of Yemen has been restored, after a seven-year lapse, thanks to the ministrations of an American physician." Nowadays such light touches are excluded, and the information is presented with extreme terseness, since President Johnson is more interested in information than style. An item might read, for example: "CYPRUS, *Quiet*."

The DDP, with its monopoly of espionage, is of course a main source for the DDI, but by no means the only source. Other sources include aerial photography, by planes or surveillance satellites (photographs from satellites at altitudes of more than a hundred miles are almost as detailed and clear as U-2 pictures, partly because above about seventy thousand feet there is very little obscuring atmosphere); reports from diplomats and military attachés; foreign broadcasts and publications; interrogation of U.S. experts in various recondite fields; and decoded electronic intercepts. This last is a subject which causes all members of the intelligence community to assume a tight-lipped, blank expression. But its importance can be judged by the fact that the National Security Agency spends far more money and employs far more people than the CIA.

Smith's empire almost certainly has a higher concentration of Ph.D.s—more than 60 percent in the higher ranks—than any other Washington fiefdom. It includes specialists in all sorts of recondite subjects, from the Naga tribesmen of the Vietnamese highlands to the state of health of Kosygin and Brezhnev. One lady Ph.D., for example, has been specializing in the study of Indonesia's Sukarno for more than fifteen years, collecting every scrap of information available about the man, from his extensive amatory adventures to his political triumphs and disasters. "If Sukarno made wind," one colleague has remarked, "she would be able to tell you the force, direction and chemical composition of the gust."

This extraordinary specialization and attention to detail involve a great deal of waste motion, of course, and some of the DDI's intellectual hired help unquestionably tend to collect information for its own sake, as a miser collects coins. But specialization can also pay off in a crisis.

In the Cuban missile crisis, for example, members of a recondite profession called "cratology"—the study of the shapes of crates—played a key role. After the Kennedy-Khrushchev settlement, the cratologists were able to assure the President that Khrushchev was keeping his side of the bargain. By studying aerial photographs, they came to the firm conclusion, from the shape of the crates being loaded aboard the Soviet vessels, that the Soviet missiles were in fact being removed.

Another empire which has been growing in recent years is that of the DDR—Deputy Director, Research. The current DDR is a technician called Carl E. Duckett (not Dr. Duckett, since this DDR, unlike all his predecessors, is not a Ph.D.). Duckett, whose job was created by John McCone, is chief of a new and growing branch of the intelligence business—technological espionage. Increasingly, and especially since the first U-2 took to the air over Russia, the Mata Haris and beautiful blonde spies of tradition have been replaced by sophisticated technological techniques.

After a rather bitter jurisdictional wrangle at the time of the Cuban missile dispute, operational control of most of "Dick Bissell's private air force" was transferred from the CIA to the Pentagon. The Pentagon also operates the surveillance satellites, and other, still-secret means of technological espionage. But the technical information which derives from the resulting photographs, electronic intercepts, and the like goes to the DDR to be collated and interpreted.

Some insiders credit the DDR with supplying more hard and valuable information to the U.S. Government than the DDP.

A fourth major figure in the CIA is the Chairman of the Board of National Estimates. The board was headed until recently by a tough-talking, tobacco-chewing intellectual called Sherman Kent, who is expected to be replaced, before this book is published, by his able deputy, Abbott Smith. The Chairman of the Board of Estimates ranks in the pecking order below the Deputy Directors, but his job is in one way the most important in the whole CIA empire. His job (and his board's) is to try to figure out, not just what the intelligence is but what it *means*. The results of this figuring take the form of "National Intelligence Estimates," or NIEs.

This is not at all an easy job, and inevitably the Board of Estimates has occasionally guessed wrong. For example, in the late nineteen-fifties, while shaving the grossly inflated Air Force estimates of Soviet missile production, Kent and his board accepted the basic theory of the missile gap, until the U-2s provided incontrovertible evidence to the contrary. (But the NIEs of Soviet bomber production were right on the nose.) Again, before the 1962 Cuban missile crisis, the board produced an NIE to the effect that the Soviets would not adopt the "high-risk" policy of placing nuclear-capable missiles in Cuba. At the height of the missile crisis the board produced a "crash" estimate, which happily also turned out to be wrong, to the effect that the Soviets might be prepared to risk nuclear war rather than back down in Cuba.

But by and large, the record of the board in reading the tea leaves provided by the intelligence has been good. The board's most spectacularly correct forecast occurred in the winter of 1953–54, when the Eisenhower administration asked for an estimate of when the Soviets were most likely to orbit an earth satellite. The board's answer—the second half of 1957—was scoffed at by the economy-minded policy-makers in the administration, who disliked the expensive implications of the estimate. The first Sputnik was duly orbited in October, 1957.

Most notably, the board has been continuously unoptimistic about the chances of quick success in Vietnam. This was true even in the days when it was fashionable in the Pentagon and elsewhere to suppose that the application of American air and ground power would quickly persuade Ho Chi Minh to cry uncle.

In the Dulles-Wisner-Bissell era the CIA stood very near the top in Washington's pecking order of power. Partly this was because Allen and John Foster Dulles were brothers, and very close brothers. The older brother often consulted the younger on policy matters, and Allen Dulles always had immediate access to both the Secretary of State and the President. Partly it was because the State Department had been weakened, by the McCarthy attacks, by Wristonization, and by John Foster Dulles' peculiar method of operating as though the department had ceased to exist. The weakness of the State Department caused a vacuum which the Bold Easterners rather gleefully filled—Dulles, Wisner, Bissell, and company had no compunctions about involving themselves in matters of high policy.

After the CIA's Bay of Pigs disaster John McCone revived the "sick dog," and made the agency a very powerful bureaucracy again. Like Allen Dulles, he was deeply involved in matters of high policy. He was a member of Ex Comm, the inner cold war cabinet at the time of the missile crisis and thereafter. In this capacity, when he took a position on policy matters, he was careful to remove his DCI hat—"I'm speaking now simply as John McCone," he would say. But whatever hat he wore, McCone was a powerful figure in the late Kennedy era. Senator Richard Russell once labeled him "the second most powerful man in the government," and he was in truth one of the half-dozen most powerful.

The CIA suffered a sad relapse, falling back several notches in the Washington pecking order, after Lyndon Johnson became President. John McCone ceased to be among the half-dozen most powerful men in the government, one reason why he decided to resign. The relapse was even more marked during the era of Admiral Raborn and his sinking ship.

McCone never did get on Lyndon Johnson's wave length, and this was one reason for the CIA relapse. Another was Raborn's inexperience. A more important reason was a difference in attitude between Johnson and Kennedy. Kennedy thoroughly enjoyed the whole intelligence business (Ian Fleming was one of his favorite authors), and he loved to pore over intelligence reports, absorbing even the smallest details. Kennedy's first order of business during his working day was the morning intelligence report, labeled "INTELLIGENCE CHECK LIST—FOR THE PRESIDENT—TOP SECRET." His military aide, Major General Chester Clifton, would put this fat daily booklet on his desk, and Kennedy would spend a half-hour or more leafing through it, asking questions, sometimes ordering action on the basis of one report or another.

For a while, Clifton would bring the "Check List" into Johnson's office in the morning. The President would glance at it, and turn to other matters. Finally, the daily report was simply included, in abbreviated form, in the President's "night reading." This made life easier for those in the DDI's office charged with compiling the President's report; in Kennedy's day they had to begin work at the CIA building in Langley at three in the morning or earlier, whereas they now have all day to prepare the report. But the President is the most essential of all customers in the big business of intelligence, and the comparative indifference of the most important customer reduced the CIA's standing in the pecking order.

In the era of Richard Helms and the Prudent Professionals, the CIA has been slowly but steadily climbing back up the pecking order, although it has not reached, and doubtless never will again, the heights it occupied in the Dulles-Wisner-Bissell era. One reason for this renaissance is that long before he resigned Secretary of Defense Robert McNamara (in contrast to the days when Desmond FitzGerald amazed him with his comment on "quantifications") had learned that he needed the CIA.

There was a time when McNamara did not think that he needed the CIA—or at least not very much. In the Kennedy era McNamara tended to rely primarily on his newly created Defense Intelligence Agency. CIA men were deeply perturbed by McNamara's answer at a hearing by a House committee in 1962, when he was asked, during questioning about Cuba, whether he was "operating on the intelligence you get from the CIA."

"No, sir," McNamara replied briskly. "I receive information directly from the Defense Intelligence Agency, and that information is screened by no one outside the Pentagon."

As this exchange suggests, the DIA looked at the time, through CIA eyes, like a dangerous bureaucratic rival, the more so because the Pentagon disposes of far more manpower and money than the CIA. Nowadays the CIA no longer considers the DIA dangerous. Partly this is because the DIA is simply no match for the CIA in terms of expertise and professionalism. To the military, intelligence has long been considered a useful provider of "slots" for senior officers without a command. Many military men are very able, and some know a good deal about intelligence, but a really first-rate intelligence professional is a rarity among the military.

The CIA was particularly fearful that the DIA would become a major rival in the operational field. In fact the military's previous experiments in operations had been marvelously inept, and the CIA soon realized that the DIA was not a serious rival. One military operation, for example, involved throwing masses of used whiskey bottles left over from officer's messes into the Danube. Anti-Communist messages would be inserted into the bottles, and when, carried on the Danube's broad bosom, they reached the Communist countries, the inhabitants, hopefully, would fish them out of the river, read the incendiary messages, and revolt against their Communist masters. This plan was finally abandoned after much debate—no doubt fortunately, since it is hard to imagine anything more likely to instill anti-American sentiments than the disappointment of finding thousands of whiskey bottles filled only with inept propaganda.

By the time of this country's deep involvement in Vietnam—around 1965—Secretary McNamara had come to realize that he needed the CIA; and that the National Estimates, flawed though they occasionally were, were far more reliable than the inherently parochial estimates of the military men in the DIA. It was largely the Vietnamese war, about which the military were for a long time consistently over-optimistic, that taught McNamara this lesson.

Clark Clifford seems likely to listen to the military estimates with more respect than McNamara. Indeed, he promised to do so at his confirmation hearing before the Senate Armed Services Committee. "These men are trained," he said. "They have made it their life study." But as the Kennedy-appointed chairman of the Foreign Intelligence

Advisory Board, he knows the whole intelligence community intimately, and he respects the CIA's professionalism. He therefore seems very unlikely to try to build up the DIA as a real rival of the CIA.

The fact is that the CIA has prevailed over the DIA and other potential rivals simply because it is a better, more professional, and more experienced intelligence agency. It is as simple as that. But it is never again likely to cut the great swath in Washington that it cut during the era of Allen Dulles and the Bold Easterners. No doubt this is as it should be.

The notion that the CIA is the "invisible" government of the United States is a myth. But it is more clearly a myth today than it was a decade or so ago, when the Bold Easterners had moved into the vacuum left by the State Department. After the Bay of Pigs, and again during the Raborn period, there was some danger that the pendulum would swing the other way, and that the CIA would indeed become a "sinking ship." Under the Helms-Karamessines-Smith triumvirate, the ship seems most unlikely to sink.

When John McCone left, he recommended Helms to the President as his successor. But his recommendation was decidedly tentative, no doubt one reason why the President tried the Raborn experiment instead. At the time there seemed to be sound reasons for McCone's doubts about Helms.

For as McCone pointed out, Helms had neither a private fortune nor a secure political base. McCone, of course, had both—he had "Kennedy kind of money" and a strong base with the Republican conservatives. Allen Dulles also had a fortune, though a far more modest one, and a political base as his brother's brother and as a solidly established Establishmentarian. Predecessors like Bedell Smith, Hillenkoetter, and Hoyt Vandenberg (who also had a useful connection with his Uncle Arthur, the Senator) had the powerful Pentagon base. As an apolitical civil servant without serious money of his own, Richard Helms—or so McCone and others thought—would stand naked to the winds that blow through Washington's corridors of power.

It has not worked out that way. Helms has had his troubles, to be sure. But his reputation as a nonpolitical professional has served him as a shield, and he has been at pains to maintain it. Unlike Dulles and McCone, he assiduously avoids involvement in policy matters. Whereas McCone used to say, "I'm speaking now simply as John McCone," Helms will say, "I'm sorry, Mr. President, but that's a policy matter, and policy is not in my field."

The line between policy and intelligence is blurred and sometimes invisible. Policy is, or ought to be, largely based on intelligence, which is why bitter rivalry and angry controversy have always swirled around the CIA. Moreover, Helms is by no means a political eunuch, without views of his own. Instinct as well as "facts and figures" have led him to a consistent bearishness about the likelihood of quick success in Vietnam—a bearishness which has proved an asset to the agency. Even so, Helms' insistence that policy is no business of his or of his agency's has protected the CIA both on Capitol Hill and in the downtown bureaucracy. The CIA may not be as powerful as it once was, but it is no longer the subject of such bitter animosity as it has been in the past. Its Congressional critics have been appeased, and the agency is even on reasonably friendly terms with both the State Department and the FBI, once bitter rivals and bureaucratic enemies.

The fact is that after more than two decades the CIA has moved into middle age, with "all passion spent." Veterans of the old days of the Bold Easterners regret the change, and tend to blame it largely on the CIA's huge building at

Langley. The building (which has been called "The Allen Dulles Memorial Mausoleum") was erected on the insistence of Allen Dulles, over the loud objections of Bissell and others of the Bold Easterners. It was dedicated shortly before Dulles and Bissell were replaced.

One of the Bold Easterners, who was also a veteran of OSS and Rosa Lewis' Cavendish Hotel in wartime London, had this to say about the building soon after the CIA had moved into it: "The real trouble with this new building is that it tends to make an honest woman of the old madam—you know, no spittoons, keep the antimacassars clean, and no champagne in the morning. We ought to be lurking in scrabby old hideouts, with the plaster peeling and stopped-up toilets. There's something about the atmosphere of this building that leads to too many memos, too many meetings, and not enough dirty work."

Even among the Prudent Professionals of the Helms era, there are those who privately agree that the CIA these days goes in for "too many memos, too many meetings, and not enough dirty work." The fact is that the CIA has now found its place within the enormous federal bureaucracy, and it has itself become, more than ever before, an enormous bureaucracy.

It still, to be sure, enjoys advantages over the bureaucracy of the State Department, or over the Pentagon bureaucracy, the most horrendous of all. With his unvouchered funds and his right to hire and fire without being hamstrung by Civil Service, the Director of CIA has a flexibility enjoyed by no official of Cabinet rank. The men who work for CIA begin to do important work when their State Department opposite numbers are still shuffling visas or opening doors for Madam Ambassadress. In later life they pay a price, to be sure—a price which is resented especially by their wives. For it is the paper-shuffling State Department men who inherit the embassies and the big flag-bedecked cars, and whose wives in their turn become Madam Ambassadress, while the CIA station chief—the highest CIA rank in an embassy—is still a junior officer, outranked in protocol by some often dim-witted military or naval attaché.

The frustrations of life in the CIA are many and various. But despite these frustrations, the CIA has never produced a defector—unlike the NSA—and as far as is known, it has never been penetrated by "the opposition." That opposition —the Soviet KGB—has been penetrated to a fare-thee-well, by Colonel Penkovskiy among others. British MI-6 has been so penetrated that it looks like a piece of Swiss cheese, the brilliant, infamous Kim Philby being the most important of the penetrators. The German intelligence service has also been thoroughly penetrated—not long ago, its opposite number to Karamessines turned out to be a Soviet agent— and French intelligence is even more cheeselike than MI-6. Penetration of the opposition is the equivalent of a grand slam in the intelligence business, and in this respect the CIA is clearly ahead on points.

There are too many people in CIA, and the agency spends too much money, but there is no department or agency in Washington (except perhaps for the Budget Bureau) of which the same could not be said. All in all, a sensible assessment of the CIA would give the agency a kind of solid, B-minus rating. The CIA is not really a very dramatic organization. It is not a "secret government" or a "Stadt in Stadt." Neither is it a brilliant nest of daring spies, in the James Bond manner. It is a prudently professional bureaucracy, run by prudent professionals—and as such, in times like these, it performs an often rather tedious and uninteresting, but nevertheless indispensable, function.

Vice President Hubert Humphrey attended the ceremonies marking the twentieth birthday of CIA in 1967. With his accustomed ebullient hyperbole, he remarked that "the American people are happier in their minds because of the CIA." They're not. But they probably ought to be.

9

THE INNER CABINETS

The top guys only.

....

It is interesting to list the twelve departments of the President's Cabinet in their pecking order, as judged by three criteria: money, people, and real political importance. Here is the pecking order in terms of numbers of employees in each department, according to the fiscal 1968 budget:

1.	Defense	4,819,000
2.	Post Office	701,368
3.	Health, Education, and Welfare	105,596
4.	Agriculture	92,449
5.	Treasury	89,129
6.	Transportation	88,164
7.	Interior	69,500
8.	Justice	33,788
9.	Commerce	30,559
10.	Housing and Urban Development	14,792
11.	State	13,248
12.	Labor	10,005

Here is the pecking order in terms of money, again using the 1968 budget, leveled off to the nearest million:

1. Defense	$76,044,000,000
2. Treasury	15,125,000,000
3. Health, Education, and Welfare	13,264,000,000
4. Agriculture	6,001,000,000
5. Transportation	5,430,000,000
6. Housing and Urban Development	3,179,000,000
7. Interior	1,859,000,000
8. Commerce	1,160,000,000
9. Post Office	651,000,000
10. Labor	650,000,000
11. Justice	467,000,000
12. State	415,000,000

Here is the pecking order in terms of real political power and impact:

1. Defense
2. State
3. Treasury
4. Justice
5. Interior
6. Health, Education, and Welfare
7. Labor
8. Agriculture
9. Commerce
10. Post Office
11. Housing and Urban Development
12. Transportation

This listing is arguable, of course. The State Department is the number one department in protocol, and ought to be number one in fact. But as a practical matter it isn't. The Defense Department has a great deal of impact on foreign policy, and State has very little impact on defense policy. Defense also has an enormous impact on the national economy, and State has none at all. Even so, State takes quite a jump, from number twelve in money and number eleven in people to number two in the pecking order. Despite all the horrors of working for the State Department, it is still a lot more prestigious in Political Washington to be a State man than an HUD man, say, or even an HEW man.

The other listings are arguable, too. Larry O'Brien, for example, plays an important role in Political Washington, as political adviser to the President, as the last Washington survivor of John F. Kennedy's Irish Mafia, and as one of the shrewdest political professionals in town. But his Post Office Department has very little political impact, even in its old role as a patronage disbursement center. Thanks to Civil Service, there is less and less patronage to disburse.

There is a difference, too, between the political importance and prestige of a department in Washington and outside Washington. The Western empire of the Department of the Interior, for example, is truly Roman in its reach. Interior administers 852,727 square miles of public lands, almost all in the West. If Alaska is included, the department runs 64.4 percent of all the land west of the foothills of the Rocky Mountains—48 percent without Alaska. (Alaska, more than 98 percent government-owned, is a fiefdom of Interior.) But the department's impact on Political Washington is wholly peripheral.

Interior only becomes clearly visible on the horizon of Political Washington when there is a row about the redwoods, or the Indiana dunes, or shale oil. And compared with the war, the rumors of war, and the threats of nationwide racial violence which preoccupy Political Washington, the sort of row which involves Interior is comfortingly familiar and dealable with.

In the New Deal days, Henry Wallace and his Department of Agriculture loomed large on the Washington political scene. Nowadays the Department of Agriculture, with a budget of over $6 billion, spends far more than even the free-handed Wallace ever dreamed of, and its 92,000 employees make the department Washington's fourth largest bureaucracy. But Political Washington is only intermittently and dimly aware of Secretary Orville Freeman—usually when he is booed by audiences of angry farmers. One reason is that the farmers, angry or otherwise, make up a smaller and smaller proportion of the U.S. population.

In 1937, in Henry Wallace's day, 24 percent of the population was on the land, and the farmers had decisive voting strength in many states. Nowadays the farmers constitute only 6 percent of the population; many of the marginal farmers who provided the bulk of the "farm vote" have been forced off the land and into the urban proletariat. Even in Iowa, the archetypical farm state, the proportion of farmers is down from 38 percent in 1937 to 25 percent. Obviously, that $6 billion is still important in Iowa and in other farm states. But in Washington the Secretary of Agriculture is that sad figure, a politician who is losing his constituency.

The constituency of HEW, number three both in spending and in number of employees, is a rapidly expanding one. Moreover, the social welfare programs operated by HEW have a more immediate impact on the lives of more Americans than the programs of all the other departments, except perhaps Defense. But the Washington end of HEW is a vast administrative bureaucracy, of which Political Washington is hardly aware. John Gardner, former Secretary of HEW, had great personal prestige, as the administration's philosopher-in-residence and one of its last remaining intellectuals. But his prestige was only remotely related to his job.

Secretary of Labor Willard Wirtz also has much personal prestige, and for somewhat similar reasons: he is a highly intelligent man and a good talker, fond of arguing from the particular to the general. But his Labor Department is hardly a major center of power these days. Neither is the Commerce Department, especially since Congress turned down an administration proposal to combine it ignominiously with the Labor Department. Commerce has an interesting oddity, in a small aquarium filled with American freshwater fish, including the lowly bluegill, in the basement. But as far as Political Washington is concerned it scarcely exists.

The Justice Department certainly exists, and if the nightmare of a race war becomes a reality, it could become again what it was in the Kennedy era—a major center of power. It was a major center of power then partly because it was deeply involved in the drive for civil rights in the South, then the focus of the whole civil rights movement, and partly because the Attorney General was Robert Francis Kennedy, who had a decisive voice in all matters of high national policy, however removed from the usual preserves of the Justice Department. The Attorney General is now a pleasant, rather taciturn young man, Ramsey Clark, son of former Supreme Court Justice and former Attorney General Tom Clark. Ramsey Clark shows signs of being well to the left of his Texas-conservative father, and he may become in time a major Washington figure. He is not that now.

As for the other two departments of the Cabinet—HUD and Transportation—they spend large sums of money (more than $8 billion) and they employ large numbers of people (over 100,000). But they hardly matter at all, in terms of their impact on Political Washington. In the journalist's trade, they are the exclusive domain of the specialists; to find a generalist, a Tom Wicker or a Joseph Kraft, wandering the halls of HUD would be as surprising as to come upon a reverend in a den of sin.

The fact is that the Cabinet, as a body, is one of Washington's large collections of vermiform appendices. The Cabinet still meets in the Cabinet Room with the President, but really only because Presidents have always met with their Cabinets. These meetings tend, according to those who have sat through them, to be fatuous affairs, in which the appearance of doing serious business is substituted for the reality. The main reason for the obsolescence of the Cabinet is the same as the main reason for the decay of Congress as an originator of legislation and a true maker of policy. The business of government has become too complex, compartmentalized, and specialized to be dealt with effectively by a body like the U.S. Cabinet.

An Alexander Hamilton or a Thomas Jefferson, as members of George Washington's Cabinet, could, and did, have strong (and usually conflicting) views about every aspect of government. Even in Franklin Roosevelt's day the Cabinet met regularly and argued and decided many aspects of policy.

Nowadays no one (except perhaps some such genetic mutation as Robert McNamara) is really equipped to discuss such matters as the production rate of combat helicopters for Vietnam; the optimum number of housing starts under the veterans' housing program; the desirable interest rate on short-term Treasury bonds; whether to go from a "thin" (anti-Chinese) to a "thick" (anti-Soviet) ABM system; whether limited intervention in the Congo is justified; and at what price to support wheat and cotton. Because of such diversity and specialization, Cabinet meetings, when they do occur, are often mere gassy exercises in bloviation.

The American Government does not run on gas, and as the Cabinet has become increasingly obsolete as a means of providing the President with the advice he so desperately needs, other means of fulfilling that function have had to be found. Each President since the last war ended has found his own means. President Johnson has, in effect, two inner Cabinets, one for managing the domestic economy, the other for helping him to decide the central issues of defense and foreign policy.

On national security issues, the inner Cabinet is a small but fluid group which meets for lunch with the President every Tuesday, and was originally known as the Awesome Foursome. In matters concerning the domestic economy, another Awesome Foursome, known as the Quadriad, is the real inner Cabinet.

Three of the four members of the Quadriad are not members of the Cabinet, but protocol aside, each member of the Quadriad has more real impact and authority in Political Washington than any but three, or perhaps four, Cabinet members. For the members of the Quadriad are the money managers—they are the men responsible for controlling, or attempting to control, the pace and direction of the national economy.

They are, as of this writing: Secretary of the Treasury Henry Fowler; Chairman of the Council of Economic Advisers Arthur Okun, who replaced Gardner Ackley early in 1968; Director of the Budget Bureau Charles Zwick, who replaced Charles Schultze at about the same time; and in a special category all his own, Chairman of the Federal Reserve Board William McChesney Martin.

President Kennedy once complained to his legal counsel, Theodore Sorensen, that he had trouble distinguishing between the meaning of the words "monetary" and "fiscal." Sorensen replied that it was easy to remember that "M" stood for both Monetary and Martin. Nowadays it would be easier still, for "F" stands for both Fowler and Fiscal.

According to the dictionary, "monetary" means "pertaining to money." William McChesney Martin is the Grand

Pooh-Bah of Monetary Policy. Martin and his six colleagues on the Federal Reserve Board (a majority of whom almost invariably go along with him) control, or deeply influence, both the total supply of money (in all its forms, of course, not just the stuff a man carries in his pocket, which is a very minor form of money) and the rate of interest at which money is lent.

How Martin and his Fed exercise this mysterious power is outside the scope of this book (largely because the author of the book, after several attempts, has failed really to understand it). It is enough to say that, one way or another, the Fed controls, largely independent of the rest of the government, the amount of reserves banks must hold, and thus the amount of credit they are able to extend; and that by setting the "rediscount rate"—the interest which the Fed itself charges for loans to member banks—the Fed can nudge interest rates in the whole economy up or down.

Again according to the dictionary, "fiscal" means "pertaining to the public treasury or revenue." Fiscal policy thus concerns the government's power to tax and spend. Fiscal policy is the area of responsibility of the Secretary of the Treasury, the Chairman of the Council of Economic Advisers, and the Budget Director. When they are operating exclusively in the fiscal area, without Martin, these three are known as the Troika.

As everybody knows by now, the theory of the New Economics holds that the monetary and fiscal powers of the government must together be used to control the national economy. If the economy begins to sag, an easy-money policy, or lower taxes, or both, can be used to propel it upward again. Thus the economy is kept growing steadily, and unemployment is kept within "tolerable" limits. "Tolerable" unemployment is currently defined as 4 percent of the labor force, and the desired rate of growth is at least 4 percent of GNP—the Gross National Product, or the sum total of all the goods and services produced by the economy in one year.

According to the New Economics, what is important is not a budget surplus or deficit, but the state of the whole economy. As Gardner Ackley put it: "We no longer regard deficits as important, *per se.*" If the economy is stagnant, then the money managers put their foot down heavily on the accelerator, deficit or no deficit.

This theory has received one major test. In 1962 John F. Kennedy became the first President explicitly to accept and attempt to apply the theory of the New Economics when he asked for a major tax cut, in the face of a big prospective deficit. In 1964 Congress gave Lyndon Johnson what Kennedy had asked for. The experiment worked like a charm. All the happy economic consequences predicted by Walter Heller and other proponents of the New Economics came to pass. GNP rose steadily and dramatically, tax revenues increased rapidly despite the tax cut, and prices held steady within a percentage point or so. The New Economics was, or seemed to be, triumphantly vindicated.

Whether the New Economics will continue to be triumphantly vindicated—whether the miracle of sustained growth and ever-increasing prosperity will become so permanent a feature of American life as to cease to seem miraculous—remains to be seen. On this score it is quite clear that the two older members of the Quadriad, Bill Martin and Joe Fowler (nobody ever calls them William or Henry), have been markedly less confident than the younger members.

The Troika meets once a week, usually for lunch in Joe Fowler's handsome dining room in the pre-Civil War Treasury Building next to the White House. When the Troika is joined by Martin, to become the more august Quadriad, it meets on an irregular basis—usually about ten times a year—

with the President in the Cabinet Room of the White House, and more frequently for lunch in the dining room of the Secretary of the Treasury.

As Secretary of the Treasury, Fowler is the senior member of the Quadriad in terms of protocol, though not necessarily in terms of real power. Both Fowler himself and the office which he occupies, in a corner of the Treasury Building overlooking the White House, exude a reassuring atmosphere of soundness and integrity.

You approach the office of the Secretary of the Treasury through wide halls, on floors covered with black and white marble in a checkerboard pattern. The halls are lined with slatted doors, like the doors on an old-fashioned liner, and with gilt pilasters topped by federal eagles. The office itself has a handsome fireplace, which works, a full-length portrait of Alexander Hamilton, and an air of restrained and traditional opulence.

Into this atmosphere "Joe" Fowler fits comfortably. At fifty-nine, Fowler has white hair, no eyebrows to speak of, a pleasant pink face, and the rather courtly manners of a Virginia gentleman. He is a prime example of that valuable Washington institution the in-and-outer, dividing his time between important work inside the government and a lucrative law practice outside it. Joe Fowler, who knows all Washington's chief movers and shakers, and is liked by all of them, has been in and out of the government since before World War II. By the time this book is published, he may well be out again. He faces a long-delayed gall bladder operation, and the operation may be the occasion of his leaving the Treasury.

Usually, he is mild-mannered almost to the point of deference. But sometimes he gets his dander up. Early in 1967 when various Senators accused him and his colleagues on the Troika of faulty judgment on taxes and bad economic forecasting in 1966 (which Senator William Proxmire called "the year of the big goof"), Fowler slammed back hard, calling his critics "herd-thinking, Monday-morning quarterbacks." Later in 1967, in a speech to the National Press Club he warned members of Congress that a vote against the administration-proposed 10 percent surtax would be a vote in favor of all sorts of unpleasant things, including "an economy in shambles."

Both Fowler's colleagues in the Troika work a block away, on the other side of the White House, in the flossy old State, War, and Navy Building, now officially known as the Executive Office Building. It is the job of the Chairman of the Council of Economic Advisers to keep the President constantly aware of what is happening to the economy, and what seems likely to happen. This job has made most of Arthur Okun's predecessors as Chairman of the Council major Washington figures. Leon Keyserling, way back in Harry Truman's day, *was* the Fair Deal—the basic Fair Deal domestic policies (most of which, like the Brannan farm plan and the Ewing health and welfare plan, were strangled at birth by Congress) were all vetted and in part originated by Keyserling. Similarly, Walter Heller and Gardner Ackley both had a very important impact on policy in the Kennedy-Johnson administrations. Whether Okun will emerge as a major mover and shaker remains to be seen.

It also remains to be seen whether Charles Zwick, who had been Charles Schultze's rather self-effacing deputy, will carry the same weight in Washington that Schultze and many of his predecessors carried. His is one of the most powerful and least-known jobs in the executive branch.

The Director of the Bureau of the Budget has never been one of Washington's public men—it is doubtful if more than 1 percent of the citizenry could give him a name. The Bureau employs only about three hundred people—the merest corporal's guard, by the standards of the Washington bureaucracy. Yet a very good case could be made for the proposition that the Budget Director ranks in terms of real power ahead of the Secretary of the Treasury and every other Cabinet officer except the Secretaries of Defense and State.

Congress, at least theoretically, has the last say on how much money each department and agency of the government will have to spend. But the Budget Bureau has the first say on how much the President will ask of Congress for each department and agency, and this in turn usually determines the ultimate amount, within a few percentage points. This is what makes the Budget Director so powerful within the executive branch; he is to the President what the Keeper of the Privy Purse was to England's early kings.

William McChesney Martin is also at least as powerful as the Secretary of the Treasury, and perhaps a bit more so. For Martin, at sixty-one, having served as Chairman of the Fed since 1951, occupies a position unique in Political Washington, and indeed throughout the whole world of international finance.

What makes Martin unique is the fact that his power to control monetary policy is an independent power; in no other major industrial country is monetary policy made independently of the national government. Martin can make major policy decisions against the wishes of both the President and Congress, and he has done precisely that.

Martin's independence is by no means total, of course. Martin and his board are appointed by the President, and this gives the President bargaining power. Congress created the board in the first place, and could, if sufficiently irked, clip its wings. Martin is quite aware of such limits on his independence. "We are independent *within* the government," he has said, "but not *of* the government."

Yet his independence within the government is real

enough. Late in 1965 Martin increased the rediscount rate, and thus put his foot down on the economic brakes, against the express wishes of all three members of the Troika and the President himself. Most economists and businessmen (and most members of the Troika, though they won't say so for the record) believe in retrospect that he was right.

As Martin has said, "We have no desire to be obstreperous," and on the whole he has worked well with the Troika and the White House, despite these past disagreements. This is fortunate, for given the independence of the Fed, the whole cumbersome and peculiar American governmental machinery for controlling the national economy could simply come apart, like the wonderful one-hoss shay, if the monetary and fiscal managers were consistently and fiercely at odds. Luckily, the members of the Troika are accommodating and unabrasive personalities, and so is Bill Martin.

Perhaps Martin works off his aggressive instincts during his daily game of tennis, which he plays on the Fed's private tennis court, directly across the street from the marble mausoleum, built in New Deal days, which houses the Fed. In any case, whether thanks to tennis or to his genes, Martin has a reassuring and disarming personal style; he is the sort of man from whom any sensible person would instantly buy a secondhand car.

He has his critics, including Leon Keyserling, the Truman era Chairman of the CEA, and Representative Wright Patman, the chief Congressional advocate of easy money. But his prestige among conservatives in Congress rivals that of J. Edgar Hoover (John Kennedy annoyed liberals and mollified conservatives by announcing immediately after his election in 1960 that he would reappoint both Martin and Hoover).

Martin is as much admired by the international bankers—those famous "gnomes of Zurich"—as by the Congressional conservatives. This admiration is said to be worth a billion dollars' worth of gold bars in Fort Knox. For the international banking community is happily confident that the United States will continue to buy and sell gold at $35 an ounce as long as the U.S. gold reserve holds out and Martin is Chairman of the Federal Reserve Board. This confidence in Martin has been a particularly important national asset since the devaluation of the British pound.

Martin himself has no mystical reverence for gold. It became a universal medium of exchange, he says, simply because "it's scarce, and it looks nice, and it doesn't corrode." But he does not agree with Russell Long, Senate Finance chairman, who says that "all the gold we need is what we have in our teeth." Over the centuries, Martin says, "a tradition of acceptance" of gold has grown up, and gold has become a necessary medium of international exchange.

Martin is a sound money man as well as a gold man; indeed, the two are inseparable, since a really serious inflation would melt the U.S. gold reserve like butter in August. "You can't have *perpetual* easy money and a *perpetual* deficit," he says, "without running into trouble." In 1966, alone of the Quadriad, he begged the President to push for a tax increase, because "I just disagree with the guns-and-butter idea." Again, most businessmen and economists, and, in private, most members of the Troika too, now think he was right.

His sound money views put Martin to the right of the other members of the Quadriad. But Martin is no doctrinaire conservative; he is by instinct an accommodator. Martin remembers telling Walter Heller, President Kennedy's first Chairman of the CEA: "I'll go along with you on an easy-money policy as long as there are high levels of unemployment and unused plant and equipment—if you promise to go along with me if the situation is reversed." This spirit of give-and-take helps to explain why the national economic machinery, seemingly so cumbersome, has worked well in recent years. For if you judge by results, it *has* worked well—quite miraculously well.

The *real* income, in constant dollars, of the average citizen is up fully 25 percent since 1961. Total business profits after taxes are up from 1961 by a whopping 71 percent. Such results have been accomplished with a lower proportion of government spending to national income, and a lower rate of inflation, than in any major non-Communist industrial nation.

The secret of this economic success story is growth. The Gross National Product went up between 1961 and 1968 by more than $250 billion, which is more than the *total* GNP of France, or West Germany, or England. Secretary Fowler quotes economic studies which forecast a GNP of one *trillion* dollars by the early nineteen-seventies. Asked how confident he is in predicting this forthcoming Age of the Trillion, Fowler hedges a bit.

"When I get into one of those big jets," he says, "I'm not worried about mechanical error. I know those machines are so good they're not going to just fall out of the sky. But I'm just a little bit worried about human error—a radar man who's not paying attention, a mechanic who's had a couple of drinks. That's the way I feel about this economy. We know what we need to do, but I'm not sure we're going to do what we need to do."

In 1965 Martin made a speech which briefly scared the liver and lights out of Wall Street. He listed twelve ways, ranging from high consumer debt to French avariciousness about gold, in which the economic picture resembled that which prevailed just before the 1929 crash. The similarities have since become, if possible, even more obvious, but as of this writing Martin still believes, as he did in 1965, that the

United States has "a good chance to avoid another disaster."

One senses that Martin and, to a lesser extent, Fowler go along with the theory of the New Economics rather the way the older generation of priests go along with ecumenicism: with certain private reservations. Having vivid personal memories of 1929 and what came after, they have not quite been able to shake the old notion that what comes up must come down.

Their doubts about the New Economics are shared by some younger experts. The evidence, not only in this country but abroad, suggests that one price that must be paid for continuous full employment and a long boom is inflation. Doubts have also been expressed about the doctrine that big deficits always stimulate the economy; a really big deficit, by forcing up interest rates, may have the opposite effect.

Moreover, the war in Vietnam, which has distorted so much else, has dangerously distorted the national economy. Secretary Fowler rather wistfully shows visitors a series of charts marked "WITHOUT VIETNAM." The charts show a nice, comfortable Treasury surplus for fiscal 1969 instead of a huge deficit, with the implied promise of another tax cut in the offing. But perhaps the most serious doubts about the New Economics derive from the nature of the American political system. Congress took two years to give Lyndon Johnson, in 1964, the tax cut which John Kennedy had asked for in 1962. A tax increase is politically painful, while a tax cut is politically agreeable. How do you "fine-tune" an economy if Congress takes months or years before permitting the executive branch to change the tune?

Despite such caveats, the optimism of the younger economic experts is markedly less guarded than Fowler's and Martin's. Before they left, both Ackley and Schultze predicted a "very strong economy" through 1968, and neither, unlike some Wall Street seers, foresaw a "1929 in 1969." These views are shared by their successors.

At any rate, it is clear that the four money managers who make up the Quadriad have, as a group, more real power over basic domestic policies than the Cabinet, the Office of Economic Opportunity, and all the other domestic agencies combined. Within the executive branch, the Quadriad has— subject to the White House, of course—the real power of the purse, and that power is in the nature of things decisive.

William McChesney Martin first began to meet with the Secretary of the Treasury, the Chairman of the Council of Economic Advisers, and the Budget Director in the second Eisenhower administration. The initiative came from Robert Anderson, Eisenhower's second Secretary of the Treasury, and at first the meetings were wholly informal and casual. No one seems to remember who first invented a name for the four money managers—"The Quadriad"—but in any case the meetings have now been institutionalized, as is the way of Washington, and the Quadriad is recognized throughout the government as a Presidential inner Cabinet for the domestic economy.

The bureaucratic history of the President's inner Cabinet for defense and foreign policy is more complicated. The story starts with the once-august National Security Council, created in 1947, and known only a few years ago in a journalistic cliché as "the nation's highest policy-making body." The National Security Council is now (like the Cabinet itself, but more so) a bureaucratic vermiform appendix.

The full story of the birth, life, and slow death of the NSC would make an interesting monograph for a political scientist. For the story tells a lot about how high policy is—and is not—made. It also tells a lot about how each President, almost unconsciously, shapes the policy-making mechanism to his own particular personal and political style, whatever may be written into law or shown on the organization charts.

Moreover, the life and death of the NSC perfectly exemplify the curious blooming-and-withering process which goes on constantly within the Washington bureaucracy. A new agency or organization will become bureaucratically and journalistically fashionable, blooming luxuriantly, putting out shoots in the form of subagencies and subordinate committees and committees-within-committees. It will then begin to die of its own weight, withering away into near-nothingness. But because government organisms, like old soldiers, never die, it will continue to exist indefinitely, in theory and on paper, wholly shorn of its former glory, a bureaucratic ghost.

The whole process recalls the brief existence of Solomon Grundy:

> Born on a Monday,
> Christened on Tuesday,
> Married on Wednesday,
> Took ill on Thursday,
> Worse on Friday,
> Died on Saturday,
> Buried on Sunday.
> This is the end
> Of Solomon Grundy.

The National Security Council was born in 1947, flourished until 1952, took ill with bureaucratic elephantiasis in 1952–60, got worse in 1960–62, died in 1963–68, but remains unburied.

The NSC was chiefly the brain child of the first Secretary of Defense, James Forrestal. Its mission, as defined by Congress in the National Security Act of 1947, was to "advise the President" on all matters "relating to national security."

Since every foreign policy decision above the level of how to decorate the consul's living room in Ougadougou relates to national security, this put the NSC right at the top of the bureaucratic heap. This was as Forrestal intended. He wanted foreign and defense policy to be made in an orderly, sensible way, for already in 1947 the tendency of each department and agency of the U.S. Government to have its own private foreign policy was becoming evident. Forrestal also wanted to make sure that the Defense Department and the military men had at least as decisive a say in major foreign policy decisions as the State Department and its professional Foreign Service Officers.

Thus in its original form the NSC was heavily weighted in favor of the Pentagon. The Secretary of State was a statutory member, so designated by Congress, but he was greatly outnumbered by denizens of the Defense Department—the Secretary of Defense and the Secretaries of each of the three services were statutory members of the NSC, while the Joint Chiefs of Staff were given access to the President as "advisers." Another Congressionally designated member of the NSC was the Chairman of the National Security Resources Board, a postwar collateral descendant of the War Resources Board.

In 1949 the balance was righted somewhat when Congress amended the National Security Act, and eliminated the three service Secretaries. That left the Secretary of State and the Secretary of Defense as coequal members of the NSC. And this in turn automatically made the NSC the supreme arbiter of policy, beneath the President himself. For as Bromley Smith, a self-effacing but highly perceptive long-time Secretary of the NSC, has said: "The relationship between State and Defense—that's the guts of the power equation in Washington. Everything else is subsidiary."

But, rather oddly, the Chairman of the NSRB also remained a statutory member of the NSC, in theory coequal with the Secretaries of State and Defense, as his bureaucratic descendant does to this day. As will be seen, this is one reason why "the nation's highest policy-making body" is no longer the nation's highest policy-making body.

That is what it was in the Truman era. Except for a rather brief period of semiparalysis, when Secretary of State Dean Acheson and Secretary of Defense Louis Johnson were scarcely on speaking terms, the NSC functioned remarkably well as the essential instrument of decision-making. There was one area—Israel, with its sensitive domestic political implications—which Truman ruled out of bounds for the NSC. Otherwise, all the great key decisions of the Truman era, so remarkably productive in retrospect, were debated and shaped in the NSC. The Berlin blockade (the NSC's baptism of fire), the H-Bomb, the Korean War, and the NATO alliance were probably the four most important issues with which the NSC was "seized" in that period.

The NSC also produced in the Truman era the basic policy paper which for many years formed—and still forms in part—the philosophical basis of American foreign and defense policy. This was the famous "NSC-68"—the sixty-eighth NSC paper to be approved by President Truman. NSC-68 was the joint product of Acheson and Paul Nitze, currently Deputy Secretary of Defense, then chief of the State Department's Policy Planning Staff (immensely influential at the time, now still another bureaucratic vermiform appendix). NSC-68 called for a great and costly American effort to create Western "positions of strength" in order to right the world-power balance with the then monolithic Communist bloc. It was during this period also that the basic structure of the Western alliance, which remained intact until Charles de Gaulle wrecked it more than a decade later, was put together.

There were several reasons why the National Security Council was in those days so effective an instrument of decision-making. President Truman firmly kept the NSC in its place. Forrestal had originally planned to put the staff and the conference room in the Pentagon, but Truman would have none of this; room was found for the staff in the Executive Office Building next to the White House, and the meetings took place in the Cabinet Room. Truman also made it abundantly clear that the function of the NSC was strictly to "advise." The responsibility for final decision was his and his alone. "The buck stops here," read the plaque on his desk.

Even so, Truman believed strongly in the NSC and used it regularly. "I don't know how all the other Presidents got on without the NSC," he remarked toward the end of his Presidency.

In those days, moreover, a lot of very able men were involved in the making of foreign policy. After the Korean aggression proved Louis Johnson's policy of unilateral disarmament in the name of economy disastrously wrong, Johnson was fired, and Acheson worked well together with Robert Lovett, who replaced Johnson as Secretary of Defense. Aside from Acheson and Lovett, Truman benefited from the brilliant talents of such men as Forrestal, George Marshall, John McCloy, Averell Harriman, George Kennan, Charles Bohlen, Paul Nitze, and Richard Bissell. Never since —not even in the Kennedy era—have so many men of superlative ability advised the President on foreign and defense policy.

There was another reason as well why the NSC in those days worked well: the fact that its Executive Secretary was a now forgotten Missourian called Sidney Souers. Souers, a pleasant, very shrewd man with an anonymous sort of face and a wispy mustache, was very close to Truman, whom he in many ways resembled, and whom he briefed every morning on the affairs of the world and the NSC. He was that *rara avis*, a perfect staff man, uninterested in building empires or making decisions of high policy, but capable of seeing that the necessary decisions were made, and made intelligently.

Souers grasped the essential fact about a mechanism like the NSC, the fact that the more it expands the less useful it becomes. In the early fifties he returned to work after a brief absence to find that Truman had virtually ceased to go to NSC meetings, because more and more people were attending the meetings. There were twenty-nine people in attendance on one recent occasion, the President complained—the NSC had become "nothing but a town meeting."

Souers persuaded the President to issue an order limiting the attendance to "the top guys only"—the heads of agencies and departments invited to attend, and no one else. "Unless you keep just the top guys who really make policy," Souers told Truman, "the thing will fall apart." Truman issued the order, and the NSC ceased to be "nothing but a town meeting."

During the eight Eisenhower years, the NSC bloomed luxuriantly, and it was also during those years that it began to die of bureaucratic elephantiasis. President Eisenhower, like Truman, was a believer in staff systems, but his kind of staff was the top-heavy kind produced by the U.S. Army, whose staff system is the most elaborate and the most over-populated of any army's in the world.

The NSC in the Eisenhower years became a sort of American Politburo, to be whispered about with awe. This was partly because the President used the NSC machinery in arriving at virtually all major policy decisions, so that the NSC really was "the nation's highest policy-making body." It was also during this period that the cult of secrecy-for-the-sake-of-secrecy reached its finest flower. The secrecy cult was fostered particularly by Robert Cutler, Executive Secretary of the NSC. Cutler, an amiable Bostonian, adored Eisenhower and also adored secrecy the way small boys do. Secrecy combined with real power exerts a magnetic attraction on the bureaucracy, and attendance at NSC meetings became the essential status symbol for the rising bureaucrat.

At some meetings in the late Eisenhower period, as many as sixty officials from a dozen agencies would be stuffed like ambitious sardines into the Cabinet Room of the White House. Inevitably, the NSC spawned offshoots in the form of parallel interdepartmental committees, down into the lower reaches of the bureaucracy. The two most important of these offshoots were the Planning Board, which was supposed to draft decisions for NSC approval, and the Operations Coordinating Board, which was supposed to "implement" the decisions of the NSC, once they were taken.

Thus the NSC apparatus grew—and grew. The Souers rule—"the top guys only"—was long forgotten. When President Kennedy inherited the NSC machinery, Eisenhower version, he was appalled by what seemed to him a monstrously cumbersome way of arriving at decisions. The overpopulation of the NSC meetings was a continual irritant.

"What does that fellow come to NSC meetings for?" he would ask of some middle-level bureaucrat who attended all the meetings but never opened his mouth. Curiously, Kennedy never fully understood the magnetic attraction which surrounds the Presidency like the "divinity that doth hedge a king"; or the crucial importance to a rising bureaucrat of being able to remark casually to his envious lesser colleagues: "As the President said at the NSC meeting last Thursday . . ."

Kennedy dispensed with the Planning Board and the Operations Coordinating Board, and he installed in Souers' old job McGeorge Bundy, a brilliant and aggressive man who had none of Souers' reluctance to involve himself in the substance of high policy. Kennedy and Bundy, in the first months of Kennedy's administration, began to by-pass the whole NSC machinery, relying on direct contacts with the men involved in whatever area of decision concerned them at the time.

Thus the NSC machinery was not involved in the planning for the Bay of Pigs invasion. (Neither was the State Department bureaucracy—no Foreign Service Officer was seriously consulted in the decision to go ahead with the Bay of Pigs.) The fiasco which resulted had a chastening effect on Kennedy and his overconfident staff, and as a result the NSC machinery was in part revived, and NSC meetings were again scheduled, although more rarely than in the Eisenhower years.

But Kennedy was never happy with the cumbersome bureaucratic machinery for making policy, and his instinct always was to by-pass it if possible. He was particularly irked by the bureaucratic sludge in the State Department. Arthur Schlesinger writes: "The President used to divert himself with the dream of establishing a secret office of thirty people or so to run foreign policy while maintaining the State Department as a façade in which people might contentedly carry papers from bureau to bureau."

In the greatest crisis which confronted him in his brief years in office—the Cuban missile confrontation in October, 1962—that is, in essence, precisely what Kennedy did. In the process, the NSC, already moribund, was dealt its death blow, and for a curious reason.

Back in 1949, when a vacancy had occurred, President Truman had nominated an old political crony, Mon C. Wallgren, a former Governor of the State of Washington, as Chairman of the National Security Resources Board. Wallgren was said to be a first-class pool player. But the Senate

Armed Services Committee, discerning in him no special qualifications to make high national policy as a statutory member of the NSC, tabled his nomination.

Thereafter, the NSRB went through a series of transmutations, progressively losing all serious reason for being, especially after it was divested of responsibility for civil defense. Yet the agency, under its various titles—it is now the Office of Emergency Planning—lingered palely on, and its Chairman, as directed by Congress back in 1947, remained a member of "the nation's highest policy-making body."

Meanwhile, the custom grew up of using the chairmanship of the NSRB, in all its succeeding transmogrifications, as a sinecure for deserving ex-governors and other party faithful. At this writing, for example, the Chairman of OEP is Price Daniel, an ex-Governor of Texas, an amiable politician whose chief mission is to be political liaison man for President Johnson with the Democratic governors. As Chairman of the moribund OEP, Daniel remains a statutory member of the moribund NSC.

At the time of the great Cuban missile crisis, the Chairman of the OEP was Edward McDermott, an Iowa lawyer, who had been counsel of a House committee. McDermott was, and doubtless still is, a pleasant fellow, but somewhat inclined to garrulity, a characteristic which always irritated Kennedy, and with no visible qualifications for advising the President in the greatest of all postwar crises.

Partly in order to exclude McDermott, Kennedy created "the Executive Committee of the NSC," which came to be known as "Ex Comm." (Arthur Schlesinger and others have written that "Ex Comm" was a journalistic invention. In fact, the word first appears in an official joint State-Defense briefing paper.) Ex Comm simply consisted of those people whose advice Kennedy wanted during the crisis and excluded those whose advice he didn't want. Thus Kennedy in fact created a "secret office . . . to run foreign policy while maintaining the State Department as a façade." But he found he didn't need as many as thirty people for this purpose—there were nineteen members of Ex Comm.

Ex Comm, by making the by-passing of the NSC official, made the NSC a terminal case. To be sure, NSC has been a long time a-dying, and it is not—officially—dead even yet. But its lingering demise, well started under Kennedy, has continued under President Johnson.

Johnson hates being bored even more than Kennedy, and in his first few NSC meetings he was very visibly bored. The NSC no longer meets on any regular basis, although, *pro forma*, a meeting is occasionally called to consider such large, meaningless subjects as "how to encourage democratic processes in the underdeveloped areas." But no one now ever calls the NSC "the nation's highest policy-making body." The NSC machinery has not really been used in any of the key decisions which President Johnson has taken, like his decision to intervene with force in the Dominican Republic, to bomb North Vietnam, and to commit U.S. combat troops to South Vietnam. Like so many bits and pieces of the government, the NSC machinery is rusting and disused.

The machinery has been replaced, in effect, by the President's Tuesday lunches. The "Awesome Foursome" attending these lunches consisted originally of the President, Secretary of State Rusk, Secretary of Defense McNamara, and McGeorge Bundy. Clark Clifford has replaced McNamara, and White House foreign policy aide Walt Rostow has replaced Bundy. Meanwhile, the Tuesday luncheons have become a major Washington institution, and what happens at them is almost as much gossiped about and wondered at as the Thursday meetings of the NSC used to be. These luncheons became an institution in a typically Washingtonian way.

Soon after his 1964 electoral triumph, the President asked Rusk, McNamara, and Bundy to lunch on a Tuesday, and a useful discussion of Vietnam and other matters ensued. The President suggested that they lunch again a week thence. After this second luncheon, which was also useful, the secretary of Rusk or McNamara (no one now remembers which) called a White House secretary to ask whether "the President's regular Tuesday luncheon" would be held. The query was put up to the President, who scheduled the luncheon, and thus the weekly meeting of the Awesome Foursome over the lunch table became an institution.

Nowadays there is an agenda, with advance clearances of topics to be discussed, so that no one will be caught unprepared. Rostow takes care of the agenda, and also distributes minutes of the meeting. Before he left, Bill Moyers used to attend these luncheon meetings, and one or two other staff men, including George Christian, Moyers' successor as press secretary, have joined the Awesome Foursome from time to time. So have a few others—the Chairman of the Joint Chiefs, currently General Earle Wheeler, for example, regularly attends, and CIA Director Richard Helms is often invited. But—so far at least—the Tuesday lunches have shown no signs of becoming the mass gatherings which NSC meetings were in the days when the NSC bloomed and then began to wither and die.

These Tuesday lunches of course *are* the National Security Council, Johnson style. They achieve precisely the purpose for which Forrestal designed the NSC machinery. Moreover, they adhere, even more closely than in Truman's day, to Sidney Souers' wise rule—"the top guys only"—for the Secretaries are accompanied by no retinue. Walt Rostow performs essentially the same function that Souers performed, and performs it well. Those who attend the Tuesday luncheons are in effect the inner Cabinet, concerned with the great affairs of foreign and defense policy, which the NSC was originally supposed to be—and which, for a time, it actually was.

Thus the bureaucracy, which works in a mysterious way its wonders to perform, has come full circle. And thus President Johnson, like Presidents Truman, Eisenhower, and Kennedy before him, has devised a way of arriving at decisions which has nothing whatever to do with legislation or organizational charts, and a great deal to do with the kind of man he is.

10

THE SINKING HILL

Only ninety-nine other people in the world have
as good a job, and no one has a better one.

....

There are three interesting questions about the Congress
of the United States. They are:

a. How crooked is Congress?

b. Who really runs Congress?

c. How much power does Congress have in the American
governmental system?

It is possible to give a short and roughly accurate answer
to these three questions, as follows:

a. Not very.

b. The chairmen of the key standing committees of both
houses.

c. Less and less.

Like all short answers to complex questions, these are only
very roughly accurate. Moreover, all three are interrelated.

Thus the most important fact about Congress is (c)—the
fact that its share of power in the American Government has
been steadily dwindling. And (c) is directly related to both

281

(a) and (b). The fact that many people suspect that Congress is crooked has eroded the prestige of Congress, and in Political Washington power and prestige go hand in hand. Moreover, the people who really run Congress—the committee chairmen and other members of the Congressional hierarchy—are well to the right of both Congress and the country. And this fact, too, is related to the dwindling power of Congress, for the Congressional system assigns to Congress an increasingly negative, or nay-saying, function.

It is surprising how many citizens believe that Congress is very crooked indeed. As Senator Thruston Morton of Kentucky has observed, "All of us are under some sort of suspicion." To be a member of either house is automatically to be suspect at least of low crimes and misdemeanors. This is not a new phenomenon—Mark Twain described Congress as of a "distinctly American criminal class." But the prestige of Congress has not in modern times been lower than it is now, except perhaps during the brief McCarthy era. As Senator Morton says, "The public has lost confidence in Congress. . . . There has never been a time in my memory when Congress has been at such a low ebb in the judgment of the American people."

Three names suggest why so many people believe that a great many members of Congress are little better than crooks: Bobby Baker, Adam Clayton Powell, and Thomas Dodd. In fact, there is a sharp difference between the three.

Bobby Baker and Adam Clayton Powell are familiar figures in American politics, back to the time when Wicked Sam Ward served lobster tails stewed in champagne at his parties, and bought a Senator or two between courses. They are gay deceivers, honest rogues. They were entirely aware that they were cutting a few corners and entirely happy to do so as long as they could get away with it.

Senator Dodd, a sad old man with a sad old face, is quite

different. Dodd, according to the findings of the Senate Ethics Committee, undisputed by him, collected close to half a million dollars from seven fund-raising dinners, and used a big chunk of the money for such purposes as paying his income tax, fixing up his house in Connecticut, club expenses, vacations, meals at luxury restaurants, and even buying a girdle for his wife. While this was going on, Dodd collected another $160,000 in legal and lecture fees, on top of his $33,000 a year as Senator.

This reporter went to see Dodd while the Senate was considering his case. He had done "nothing immoral or illegal," Dodd said. His "friends," who contributed to his testimonial dinners, were quite aware that they were making "gifts" to him for his personal use—not one of them had asked for his money back. And his "legal advisers" had told him that he did not have to pay income tax on these "gifts."

"It never occurred to me that there was anything wrong with what I did," he said sadly. "Never even occurred to me."

His tone carried conviction. It was quite clear that it really never *had* occurred to the Senator that there was anything wrong with what he did. This is the difference between the case of Tom Dodd and the cases of Bobby Baker and Adam Clayton Powell. Obviously, if there was "nothing immoral or illegal" about what Dodd did, the young man who aspires to a fortune should give up thoughts of oil or real estate and go into politics. For if it is both moral and legal for a Senator to collect large sums from interested citizens, pocket those sums, and pay no income tax on them, a seat in the Senate is potentially worth more than several oil wells. A really enterprising and influential Senator should be able to collect at least six million tax-free dollars in his six years in office, and even a Representative should be able to pile up a modest competence.

Thus the case of Tom Dodd is far more significant than the traditional shenanigans of a Bobby Baker or an Adam Clayton Powell. Almost all prominent politicians collect very large sums of money from interested constituents. They have to if they want to survive as politicians, unless they are very rich indeed in their own right. Moreover, the whole money-collecting process is a shadowy business, in which deception must be practiced in order to stay within the law. A lot of politicians have something like the "Nixon fund"—a fund provided by friends and admirers to support the politician's political career. As the Dodd case illustrated, the line between using this money for "political" and for "personal" purposes is not clear at all, and a politician with the limited perceptions of a Tom Dodd cannot be much blamed for crossing it.

There has, in fact, been a gradual but basic change in the way a man gets elected to high political office. The American mythos holds that any American boy can aspire to any office, up to and including the Presidency. That is still more or less true—especially if the boy is white, comes from a big state, and is not Jewish or a member of one of the other smaller racial or religious minorities. But there is now a further condition: he must be either very rich himself or willing to be beholden to very rich men.

The change is vividly illustrated by the sad case of Senator Truman Handy Newberry. Senator Newberry was a Michigan capitalist who had served as Teddy Roosevelt's Secretary of the Navy, and who was elected to the Senate in 1919. He spent what was regarded in those days as a vast sum of money on his nomination and election, and he was therefore tried and convicted in the Michigan courts on charges of corruption. The case was thrown out by the Supreme Court, and Newberry was exonerated by a sympathetic Senate committee. But the public outcry was such that he resigned from the Senate in 1922. Before resigning, he tearfully confessed on the Senate floor that he had been "astonished and amazed" when told by his employees that he had spent $195,000 on his election. The vastness of this sum brought gasps of disbelief.

Now the notion that a man could be elected Senator from a big industrial state like Michigan for so small a sum—or even double that sum, to allow for inflation—would still bring gasps of disbelief, but for the opposite reason. Expenditures on the order of $750,000 to $1 million are considered rather modest for a major political post. Television alone would eat up Truman Newberry's $195,000 before his campaign got off the ground. Television, in fact, which is responsible for so much else that is obnoxious in American life, is largely responsible for the immense cost of modern political campaigning.

More and more with every election, television has become the essential instrument of political persuasion. It is a very expensive instrument. Even in the smaller states television budgets in six figures have become standard for state-wide campaigns. Other instruments of persuasion have also greatly risen in cost.

The old notion that a man could run for office with the help of a few friends, getting his views known by making speeches here and there across the state, is long dead. Instead, the institution of the professional campaign manager, invented in California, has spread fast, and most campaigns these days are carefully prepackaged, with the aid of computer analysts, media specialists, and all the other paraphernalia of modern salesmanship.

Thus, while poor old Truman Newberry was chivied out of public life for his miserable $195,000 investment in his political future, nobody is a bit shocked when a Rockefeller or a Kennedy spends a million or so of his own or his family's money on a campaign; or when Ronald Reagan's rich friends raise a cool $5 million—more than $1.50 a voter—to make him Governor of California.

This kind of spending is illegal, of course, according to the plain English of the Corrupt Practices Act, passed by Congress in 1925 partly in reaction to the Newberry scandal. The act limits the spending of a candidate for the Senate to $25,000, and a candidate for the House to $5,000, such spending to include "each expenditure made by him or by any person for him with his knowledge and consent." If these words were taken at face value, a large majority of the members of Congress would have to be bundled off to jail; only a few members with safe seats would remain at liberty.

As this is written, efforts are being made to rewrite the rules to bring them into line with reality. Meanwhile, a way around the plain meaning of the act has of course been found: in any serious campaign, numerous committees are established, and these committees ostensibly collect and spend their hundreds of thousands, or even their millions, without the "knowledge and consent" of the candidate. This faintly ludicrous device has served to keep Congress out of jail, but it has also made liars out of most of the members of that body.

There are many techniques for extracting money from the citizenry for political purposes, but for a man not rich enough to finance his own campaigns the most painless and widely accepted method of money-grubbing is the "testimonial dinner," like the affairs that got Tom Dodd into trouble. These expensive repasts range upward from modest $25-a-plate affairs. For a major political dinner, $250-a-plate has become more or less standard.

The final flowering of this system is found in the $1,000-per-member "President's Clubs," to which many rich men, mostly important executives of corporations doing business with the government, belong. In 1967 members of these not very exclusive clubs contributed more than $1 million to the coffers of the Democratic National Committee, ostensibly for the exquisite pleasure of mingling socially or breaking bread with the President. Such purposes are, of course, ostensible only. The dinner lists even of rather modest "plate dinners" in Washington are always studded with the names of lobbyists and others with a financial stake in the big business of big government. At some such affairs, the compliant lobbyists are even assigned a given number of plates to buy; a major lobbyist, for example, may be expected to buy a whole table, say, eight plates at $2,000.

"Who will buy a $250 plate?" Senator Albert Gore asked rhetorically on the Senate floor, of a routine Democratic fund-raising affair. "We know—and we are ashamed of it— the lobbyists and special interests, seeking favors of the Congress or this government, will buy those plates and tables."

In another speech, Senator Gore charged that "there is a degree of accepted and tolerated corruption inherent in our system of private subsidy of political campaigns. . . . The area of corruption is rapidly spreading." In fact, and rather surprisingly, the area of corruption has not really spread very far—at least not yet. It has not, for example, spread far enough for Senator Dodd's version of what is moral and legal to be widely accepted in the Senate.

In his passionate if somewhat irrational defense of Dodd, Senator Russell Long of Louisiana repeatedly said or implied that most of his colleagues regularly did what Dodd had done. He did not thereby endear himself to the Senate. And according to most close observers of the workings of Congress, what he said is, fortunately, simply not true.

Most of the Capitol Hill reporters agree that there are not more than two or three men really "on the take" in the

Senate, and not many more in the House. There are corner-cutters, too, of course—men who profit from their political position via law partnerships or in other legal ways. And there are a few who, though less candidly, take the same position as the late Robert Kerr, the immensely rich Senator from Oklahoma who dominated the Senate between Lyndon Johnson's departure in 1960 and his own death in 1963. Kerr frequently and flatly stated that he was in the Senate to look after his own financial interests—mostly oil and banking—and the interests of his constituents similarly situated.

But such men are in the minority. Thruston Morton does not greatly exaggerate when he says that "99 percent of the members are thoroughly honest and reputable," by their own lights. Very few pocket the money given them as political contributions, or spend it to fix their houses or buy girdles for their wives. What most of those who are heavily dependent on such contributions do—what they almost have to do—is to listen with close and sympathetic attention to major contributors who are "seeking favors of the Congress or this government."

Indeed, most Capitol Hill reporters agree that it is rather surprising that the "lobbyists and special interests," who are in the market not only for "those plates and tables," do not own outright more Senators and Representatives. At the turn of the century, many influential Senators were known to be in the pay of the "trusts"—a Senator was known as "an oil man" or a "railroad man" or a "sugar man."

Nowadays a Texan, for example, is as unlikely to oppose the oil depletion allowance as an Iowan, say, is to be inimical to corn-fed hogs. But although members of Congress are —and in most cases ought to be—responsive to the major economic interests of their state, they are not directly in the pay of those interests. One reason is very simple. At present pay scales, although a member of Congress may badly need money for his election campaigns, he does not really have to have money to keep his wife in girdles—not unless he has especially extravagant tastes and a passionate desire to impress others with his importance.

In simple dollars-and-cents terms, the members of both houses are much better off than they have ever been before. They are thus *personally*—though not *politically*—more independent than they used to be. They are under no desperate compulsion to line their pockets with what Daniel Webster (one of the ablest and one of the most corrupt men ever to sit in Congress) used to call "the usual retainers." In money terms, being a member of Congress is not a bad job, and it has steadily gotten better in recent years.

A hundred years ago, Senators and Representatives received a measly allowance of $8 a day, and that only while Congress was in session. As recently as the early nineteen-fifties the pay was a mere $12,500, and as late as 1960 it was $22,500. Now all members are paid $30,000 a year. Even allowing for inflation, they have never had it so good. And there are hidden perquisites, which mean that they have it even better than they seem to.

Until 1946, for example, there were no pensions for Congressmen; a defeated Congressman was expected to shift for himself. The first, very modest pensions were voted in that year, despite considerable public outcry. Since then Congressional pensions have been quietly but steadily rising—the cost of pensions for more than two hundred former members of the House or Senate now comes to nearly $2 million a year. Former members with long service draw $2,000 a month in pensions, and even those with relatively short service draw useful sums, especially if they have been in the armed services—every year in uniform is counted as the equivalent of a year in Congress. A man with, say, three terms in the House, plus a couple of years in uniform, has a pleasant additional income of $6,000 in pension rights until he dies.

A wife or son on the payroll also adds usefully to the family income, and nepotism is so common a practice that it is hardly noticed any more. Then there are also small perks and gimmicks which rarely come to public notice.

Perhaps the oddest gimmick is the cash rebate on the stationery allowance. In 1966, for example, $441,000 which was appropriated for stationery went unspent, and those who had underspent their $2,400 stationery allowance drew the balance in cash—often more than $1,000. Despite the surplus, the House in 1967 voted to increase the allowance to $3,000—the equivalent of a useful increase in salary for most members.

A few Senators and Representatives have objected to this gimmickry—notably Senator John Williams of Delaware, who actually let the unused portion of his stationery allowance revert to the Treasury. But there was no general outcry; this kind of corner-cutting has come to seem the way the game is played.

One reason why such lagniappe as the extra stationery allowance is welcome is that a member of Congress—especially a Senator—is expected by his constituents and his fellow politicians to behave like a Big Shot. He is expected to pick up checks, dispense food and drink, ride in a large, new car, dress well, live in a good house, and display all the other status symbols of the modern American Big Shot. The cost of living like a Big Shot is not measured in the cost-of-living index, but there is no doubt that it has risen vertiginously.

In the earlier days of the Republic, when Washington was "scarce any better than a swamp," and when communications were slow and difficult, life was simpler for a member of Congress. Even in the early years of this century most members would leave their wives at home, and eat and sleep throughout the sessions (then mercifully much shorter) in boardinghouses, sometimes four to a room.

Some of the older members, especially from the South, still live simply in apartment hotels when in Washington. But Senators especially now find it politically rewarding—and rewarding also to their self-esteem—to maintain a Washington establishment in which important persons from back home and the denizens of Political Washington can be entertained. The really rich congregate in Georgetown. But Georgetown real estate prices—it is difficult to find a reasonably comfortable house there for less than $75,000—has a filtering effect, and as a result only twenty-two members of Congress have Georgetown addresses, as of this writing. But even a Cleveland Park or Chevy Chase address runs into money.

The money it costs to live like a Big Shot contributed to the downfall of poor Tom Dodd, whose chief defense was, in effect, the plea that living like a Big Shot was part of a Senator's job. It is also one reason (the cost of campaigns is another and more important reason) why the number of poor men in Congress is constantly decreasing, by a process of natural selection, and the number of rich men constantly increasing.

In the Senate, there are at least half a dozen multimillionaires (the richest are probably the two Kennedys and Joseph Clark, all three liberal Democrats) and many more with capital in the high hundred thousands. (It is an interesting commentary on the money-politics equation that of all the men currently being seriously discussed as potential future Presidents, only one—Hubert Humphrey—is not a millionaire, Richard Nixon having almost certainly achieved that enviable status, thanks to his lucrative law practice. Largely because of television, the United States has probably seen its last poor President, and its last ugly President.)

For a man who is reasonably well off, being a member of Congress—and being a Senator especially—is an agreeable and rewarding life. "This is the most wonderful job in the world," Senator Claiborne Pell (who has no money worries) remarked exultantly soon after his first election. "Only ninety-nine other people in the world have as good a job, and no one has a better one."

Senators have always enjoyed being Senators. When he was urged to seek the Republican Presidential nomination, Warren Gamaliel Harding expostulated: "Why should I? . . . If I don't run for the Presidency I can stay in the Senate all my life. It is a very pleasant place." He would have died a happier man if he had stayed in that pleasant place.

There have, of course, been exceptions. Elihu Root, a contemporary of Harding's, Theodore Roosevelt's Secretary of State, and a brilliant, ambitious man, hated the Senate. It was galling to find himself, as a mere junior Senator, stripped of all real power. "I am tired of it," he said. "The Senate is doing such little things in such little ways."

John F. Kennedy in his Senate years also became visibly tired of doing little things in little ways. I once asked him an obvious question: why did he want to be President? He gestured with his right index finger in the direction of the White House. "Because that's where the real power is," he said. This clearly seemed to him an entirely adequate answer.

But most members of Congress like being members of Congress all the same. Unless he is very sick, or very old, or very unelectable, a member hardly ever vacates his seat of his own accord. The fact that members of Congress, and Senators especially, very much like their jobs is a very important fact about Congress. It explains two otherwise mysterious things about Congress: why there are so many able men in the place, despite the "low ebb" referred to by Senator Morton; and why the peculiar system under which Congress works continues, after a fashion, to operate.

One reason most Congressmen like being Congressmen is the fact that Capitol Hill is, for a member of Congress, a curiously pleasant place to work. It has a special atmosphere of its own, cozy, clublike, and at the same time, thanks to its smell of the past, faintly and pleasantly awe-inspiring. The pictures, most of them awful and a few very good, the statuary, the Brumidi frescoes, the little cubbyholes and hideaways and subterranean passages, the almost palpable ghosts of those who have gone before—Calhoun and Clay and Randolph, Webster and Benton and Sumner, Vandenberg and Taft and Rayburn—all this gives a member a feeling of belonging, of being on the inside, which is to many men as pleasant a feeling as there is.

The general air of camaraderie among the members—most politicians are almost by definition jovial fellows—reinforces this sense of belonging. So does the endless parade of gawking tourists and awed constituents, the outsiders who don't know where the hideaways are, who aren't admitted to the members' restaurants or the lobbies with their overstuffed black-leather chairs, and who don't know Mike or Ev or Carl or Jerry or Mel.

Representatives, to be sure, tend to have more mixed feelings about their jobs than Senators, and almost any Representative who is not a committee chairman or high in the House hierarchy will willingly risk his seniority and his seat for a chance to go to "the other place." Freshmen Representatives tend to be lost in the crowd, and to feel, for a while at least, rather like new boys at school. As a freshman Representative, the reaction of George Bush of Texas is typical. He has described the experience as "fascinating but

frustrating"—frustrating because it is so difficult for a freshman to get anything done, fascinating in large part because
of the human relationships.

"Usually, a man makes his close friends in school or
college, or in a war," says Bush, "and after that he just has
acquaintances. But I think I may have made some real
friends by the time I leave this place."

The experience of being a member of Congress in a
certain session of a certain Congress is an experience both
shared and unique, like the experience of going to a certain
school in a certain year, or fighting a certain war in a certain
unit. As in a school or a war, the members of Congress get
caught up in the particular world in which they find themselves—the world of Capitol Hill. They want to shine in that
world, for the same reason that they wanted to get that
promotion or that medal in their war days, or to become a
BMOC in their college days.

The desire to shine in the world of Capitol Hill is one of
the intangible human factors which make the peculiar Congressional system work. The best way to shine in the world
of Capitol Hill is to get on a good committee (or an important subcommittee), and stay on it until you head the
committee itself. The committee system *is* the Congressional
system.

For old habitués of the Senate galleries, it is always a bit
amusing, and a bit sad too, to look at the faces of the tourists
as they take their turn in the galleries. They invariably
register, first surprise, then disappointment. Expecting to see
something like the Webster-Hayne debate, they see instead
a handful of elderly men, dozing or chatting, while another
elderly man drones on inaudibly. The fact is, of course, that
the real work of Congress is hardly ever done on the floor of
either house. It is done in committee. In committee is where
reputations are made and unmade.

To get on a good committee, to make a good reputation on it, and thus to shine in the world of Capitol Hill, it is important—indeed, it is essential—to get along well with the people who really run Congress. These people are collectively known as the Establishment (Senator Joseph Clark's designation) or the Inner Club (columnist William White's phrase). Their power over the rest of Congress is directly dependent on their desire to shine.

A man who defies or alienates the Establishment does not shine; or at least he shines, if at all, not within the world of Capitol Hill, but outside that world. This is why the members of the Inner Club have something of the same power over the other members of the Senate or House—although all are theoretically equal—as, say, the prefects in a boarding school, or the field-grade officers in a regiment, have over their juniors. The way that power is exercised and maintained makes an interesting study in the interrelationship between people and power.

Simple human likability has a lot to do with the maintenance of the Congressional power structure. Take, for example, Representative Wilbur Mills of Arkansas, chairman of the House Ways and Means Committee, and a leading member of the House Establishment—some would say *the* leading member.

The House has the constitutional responsibility for raising revenue, and the Ways and Means Committee is, of course, the tax committee, so Wilbur Mills would be a powerful man in any case. But what makes his power all but legendary is his ability to swing, first his committee, then the whole House, behind whatever position he may take on taxes. This ability derives in part from hard work, careful calculation, and a sensitive smell for the mood of the House. But Mills is also a notably courteous, fair-minded, and pleasant man, almost universally liked in the House, and especially on his own committee. Nobody wants to tangle with good old Wilbur, so Mills almost always has the last say on tax measures, which makes him one of the dozen or so most powerful men in Washington.

Most of the members of the Club are likable people; since most of them are Southerners, their charm often has the special Southern accent. They are also, without exception, Capitol Hill careerists—their lives and their ambitions are tied to the Senate or the House. This is why John F. Kennedy was never even a candidate member of the Club (neither is his brother Robert, though the youngest Kennedy of all, Edward, is considered a candidate in good standing). John Kennedy was resented by some of the members of the Club, as Robert Kennedy is today—the very essence of Clubmanship is that those who are not members must dearly wish they were, and John Kennedy quite obviously had no hankering at all to join the Club.

There is and always has been room for argument about who is in the Club and who isn't. But in general the Club consists of the official hierarchy of both parties in both houses; the chairmen of the important standing committees; plus most of the ranking minority members of the standing committees. There are also one or two, notably in the Senate —like Senator Edmund Muskie of Maine or Senator John Stennis of Mississippi or Senator John Pastore of Rhode Island—who have no exalted standing in the hierarchy or key committee chairmanships, but who are members of the Congressional ruling class for reasons of personality, intelligence, energy, or absorption in the affairs of Congress.

At the top of the hierarchy, of course, are the Majority Leader of the Senate and the Speaker of the House. When Lyndon Johnson and Sam Rayburn held those positions, the Congressional Establishment in both houses was wholly dominated by the two Texans. Nothing like the same degree of power is exercised by their successors, Mike Mansfield of Montana and John McCormack of Massachusetts.

The sharp decline in the power of both the Majority Leader and the Speaker has contributed to the decline of the power and prestige of Congress itself. For a semivacuum of power at the top has created an impression of aimlessness, of talk without action. The impression accords with the reality, especially in the Ninetieth Congress.

Mike Mansfield is a living demonstration of the fact that, although likability is a useful adjunct to power in Congress, it is not the same thing as power. For Mansfield is a very likable man—certainly more likable than his predecessor, Lyndon Johnson. He looks like an amiable, exhausted monk (John McCormack looks like an older and even more exhausted monk), and he is rarely without a stubby, leather-covered pipe. Once he was asked by this reporter whether his critics might be right when they said he wasn't tough enough to be a really good Majority Leader. He removed the pipe from his mouth and replied in a characteristic monosyllable: "Yes."

Since the days of the revolt against Speaker Joseph Cannon, the Speaker's power under the rules has been severely limited, and the Majority Leader's powers have been even less—before Lyndon Johnson, many Majority Leaders were nonentities. "The leadership," as Mike Mansfield has said, "has no special powers to lead." This is true enough. Rayburn and Johnson simply created their own "special powers to lead."

Lyndon Johnson used every carrot, no matter how small and seemingly unappetizing, and every stick, no matter how thin and seemingly fragile, to create his own "special powers." Any instrument of persuasion that came to hand—the offer of a broom-closet-sized office in the Capitol, a tip, an invitation, a traded vote, even a genial slap on the back or a sudden chilly snub—was put to use. But Johnson's control of the Democratic Steering Committee, which in turn controlled committee assignments, was one of his two great instruments of power. The other was his personality. His engulfing character enabled him to absorb the entire Democratic Party staff on the Senate side, so that the staffers, from Bobby Baker on down, became *his* men. The Johnson personality also enabled him to outtalk, cozen, or frighten his colleagues.

"Lyndon had two smiles," recalls one Senator from the days when Johnson dominated the Senate. "He'd give me one kind of smile and in a day or so something good would happen. He'd give me another kind of smile, a little puckery one, and in a day or so I'd be walking around with a knife in my back."

Rayburn's style was different from that of his young friend, Johnson. His power was a compound of his vast seniority and experience, the authority of his personality, his love of the House (which was wife and mistress to the lonely bachelor), and the economy with which he employed his power. When Rayburn wanted to exert his authority, he would step down from the House rostrum and make a personal plea from the floor. But he was careful to do so very rarely.

"Rayburn's personal power and prestige," Representative Richard Bolling has said, "made the institution *seem* to work. When Rayburn died, the whole thing just fell apart."

Bolling (who once had ambitions, now dashed, to be Speaker himself) was certainly exaggerating; the institution still seems to work, and indeed does work, after a fashion. But it is true that John McCormack, increasingly old and frail, has little of Rayburn's personal power and prestige, while amiable Mike Mansfield is both unable and unwilling to put a knife into anybody's back. He does not have, and he does not want, anything like the power Lyndon Johnson exercised. Power in both houses is thus increasingly atomized.

McCormack's two chief lieutenants, Carl Albert and Hale Boggs, have a far larger share of the Speaker's power than in the Rayburn period. Both aspire to the speakership, with Carl Albert, a very able man with a real feel for the mood of the House, the odds-on favorite if his health holds out (in 1966 he had a severe heart attack). Wilbur Mills would also be a serious candidate if he decided he wanted the job, and in any case a major intraparty bloodletting may occur when McCormack steps down. (He may do so before this book is published.) On the Senate side, some blood has already been drawn; a muted and intermittent battle has been going on between Mike Mansfield and his erratic, ambitious deputy, Russell Long of Louisiana, the Senate Whip.

Another result of the atomization of leadership is that the minority leadership is more powerful than the lopsided division of the Ninetieth Congress—64 Democrats to 36 Republicans in the Senate, and 247 to 186 in the House—might suggest. There are, of course, actually two parties in both houses, and they are not, in terms of the political realities, the Democratic and Republican parties. They are the Congressional-Conservative and the Presidential-Liberal parties. The Congressional-Conservative Party is the normal majority party.

In the Eighty-ninth Congress, for the first time since the New Deal, the Presidential-Liberal Party had a thin but fairly solid majority. The result was a remarkable record of legislation, which completed the process begun more than thirty years before—the process which made the federal government, for the first time, centrally responsible for "the General Welfare" (the Constitution's phrase) of the American citizenry. The 1966 election returned the Congressional-Conservative Party to its normal majority position. The House, for example, has about 170 Democrats, plus 10 or 15 Republicans, who normally vote the Presidential-Liberal line. This is, of course, far short of a majority.

Thus in both houses the Republican Minority Leaders are very much part of what is in fact, though not in name, the majority party in Congress. Senator Everett Dirksen, the Senate Minority Leader, House Minority Leader Gerald Ford, and Republican Whip Melvin Laird are certainly among the people who really run Congress, and they are thus part of the Congressional Establishment.

Everett Dirksen's reputation is at least in part a tribute to the unsatisfied American hunger for the colorful, the eccentric, the amusing, and the different in politics. In the pretelevision era there were plenty of odd and idiosyncratic personalities on Capitol Hill—such figures from the very recent past as the red-bearded and wildly eccentric Jim Ham Lewis; or Tom Connally of Texas, with his string tie, his Simon Legree-style planter's costumes, and his savage wit; or Tom-Tom Heflin, Theodore (The Man) Bilbo, Huey Long, and many others from an earlier period. Television is the principal reason why the great majority of American politicians these days have a bland, homogenized quality. Oddness is rarely telegenic.

But Dirksen is both telegenic and unabashedly odd. Until rather recently, Dirksen had little prestige on Capitol Hill. He was regarded as a trimmer, too eagerly responsive to the whims of the Chicago *Tribune*'s late publisher, Colonel Robert McCormick, and thus not a politician to be taken seriously.

Curiously enough, while Dirksen has increasingly achieved the status of a national Comic Character, he has also become a politician to be taken seriously. His aging-Shakespeareanham act guarantees his views an audience, because it is entertaining. Dirksen can be genuinely funny. Some years ago, I happened to be in the Senate press gallery when Dirksen showed up, sat cross-legged on a table, and did a very funny imitation of Everett McKinley Dirksen, out-hamming his own haminess. But he is also a shrewd and effective political leader, who carefully husbands his power. It is even said that Dirksen has developed genuine convictions—in respect to the need to support the President during the Vietnamese war, for example—and a sense of the responsibility of power. Even so, his "image," which is both eccentric and superannuated, is regarded by a good many younger Republicans as disastrous in an election year, and rumblings of revolt against him are increasingly heard.

Representative Gerald (he prefers "Jerry," understandably) Ford, Dirksen's opposite number in the House, is by contrast a rather typical television-age politician—a square-jawed, handsome, ex-athlete from Grand Rapids, Michigan. Ford has his critics in the Republican ranks. "We wanted a TV personality instead of a floor leader," says one such, "and that is what we got."

Ford's number two, Republican Whip Melvin (he, also understandably, prefers "Mel") Laird of Wisconsin, is more of a floor leader and less of a TV personality—he has a roundish, jut-jawed face and watchful eyes. By most House-watchers he is considered shrewder than Ford. Both are able men, with a taste for power and rather typical middle-right Republican views. There have been frequent predictions that at some point there will be a struggle for primacy between them. That could happen if a Republican majority ever takes over the House and thus controls the speakership, but it has not happened yet.

A list of other Republican Establishmentarians in the House would include, at a minimum, John Byrnes of Wisconsin and William McCulloch of Ohio. In the Senate, the list would include Bourke Hickenlooper of Iowa, who plans to retire, Roman Hruska of Nebraska, and Thruston Morton of Kentucky. It might stretch to Thomas Kuchel of California, the liberal Senate Whip; conservative Peter Dominick of Colorado; John Cooper of Kentucky (an atypical, nonclubbish Senator whose views especially on foreign affairs are nevertheless listened to with great respect); and perhaps Charles Percy of Illinois, even though he is a freshman. Percy is well liked by the conservative Establishmentarians such as Hruska, and he is the only fairly serious Presidential possibility among Capitol Hill Republicans.

On the Democratic side, in contrast to the Johnson-Rayburn era, Mike Mansfield and John McCormack both play the role of French kings when the king was mere *primus inter pares*—and not all that *primus* either—among ambitious and fiercely competing dukes and barons. The dukes and barons are the chairmen of the twenty standing committees in the House and the sixteen standing committees in the Senate. The dukes are the chairmen of the key committees. Again, there is room for argument about just which are the key committees, and which chairmen are dukes and which mere barons.

But most Congress-watchers would agree that the most powerful and prestigious committees of the Senate are Armed Services, Appropriations, Finance, Foreign Relations, and Judiciary; and of the House, Appropriations, Armed Services, Foreign Affairs, Judiciary, and Ways and Means. Thus the dukes of Congress, on the Democratic side, are the chairmen of these committees. They are, in the Senate: Richard Russell of Georgia (Armed Services); Carl Hayden of Arizona (Appropriations), ninety years old, a member of Congress since 1912; Democratic Whip Russell Long of Louisiana (Finance); William Fulbright of Arkansas (Foreign Relations), much admired by liberals because of his dovelike stand on Vietnam, but in fact on his voting record a Southern conservative; and James Eastland of Mississippi (Judiciary), more Southern and more conservative.

The Democratic dukes of the House are: George H. Mahon of Texas (Appropriations); the petulant L. Mendel Rivers of South Carolina (Armed Services), who has delivered so many rich contracts, installations, and other good things from the Pentagon to his Charleston district that he is locally known as "Rivers Delivers"; Thomas E. Morgan of Pennsylvania (Foreign Affairs); Emanuel Celler of New York (Judiciary); and Wilbur Mills of Arkansas (Ways and Means).

Some of the ducal figures are to the manner born. Richard Russell in the Senate and George Mahon and Wilbur Mills in the House are all extremely able legislators. Russell is the closest thing there is to being the president of the Inner Club. He was the original patron of Lyndon B. Johnson—Johnson became Majority Leader because of his backing.

Others, like old Carl Hayden and Mendel Rivers, have reached ducal estate thanks to longevity and the seniority system; they are not born leaders. Fulbright is a personally charming man who likes to go his own way. Being a loner can require courage, and Fulbright displayed more courage in opposing Joseph McCarthy, when McCarthy was intimidating the Senate, than many Northern liberals. His opposition to the Vietnamese war has become almost obsessive, and on occasion it has degenerated into mere peevish opposition for the sake of opposing. Fulbright does not have much influence in the Senate, even on his own committee; his influence is all away from Capitol Hill. In this sense he is not at all a typical Establishment man.

Russell Long is a special case. He idolizes his father, the murdered demagogue, Huey Long, the exuberant, undisciplined, unpredictable, and unscrupulous "Kingfish." In his early days in the Senate, Huey's boy Russell seemed to be cut from a different cloth; he seemed a rather quiet and humorous chap, well liked by his colleagues, who elected him party Whip when Hubert Humphrey moved up to the Vice Presidency. (Mike Mansfield, who would have preferred Muskie of Maine, characteristically held aloof.) A man who is both the Senate Whip and the chairman of the powerful Finance Committee is in the nature of things one of the Senate's great powers, and a leading candidate for the majority leadership. There is no doubt that Russell Long very much wanted—and no doubt still wants—to be Majority Leader. But in the first session of the Ninetieth Congress Russell Long suddenly began acting like a "Kingfish" himself.

For five long weeks he tied up the whole Senate, delaying action on important legislation, because the Senate wanted to repeal his Presidential Campaign Financing Act. His wordy, arm-flailing defense of Tom Dodd further alienated many Senators, and so did his cavalier treatment of popular Mike Mansfield. No one knows why Russell Long so suddenly changed—perhaps it was simple *folie de grandeur*, the pride that precedes a fall. In any case, although he retains ducal status because of his committee chairmanship and his standing in the hierarchy, he almost certainly has lost his chance to wear the uneasy crown of the leadership.

Any listing of the Congressional aristocracy points up the extent to which the Congressional machinery is in the hands of the Southerners especially, and in general of WASPs (white Anglo-Saxon Protestants) who are politically well to the right of the Democratic Party as a whole.

Four of the five chairmen of the key committees in the Senate are from the Old Confederacy, and Arizona, Carl Hayden's state and also Barry Goldwater's, is a kind of

honorary Southern state. In the House, two Northerners
—Morgan of Pennsylvania and Celler of New York—have
graduated to the chairmanship of key committees. But the
majority of the committees in both houses are in the hands of
Southerners. Texas actually boasts five House committee
chairmanships. Four Senators usually characterized as liberal
—Anderson of New Mexico (Agriculture), Monroney of
Oklahoma (Post Office), Jackson of Washington (Interior),
and Magnuson of Washington (Commerce)—chair relatively
minor Senate committees. But these men are liberal in a
Western, border-state, tentative sort of way. In the Senate
the big-city liberalism which accounts for most of the Democratic Party's national voting strength has no representation
at all among committee chairmen, and it has very little in the
House.

Especially in the Senate, the hold of the Southerners on
the key committees is not as firm as it once was. This is
partly because the liberal Democrats elected in the big
Democratic off-year victories of the Eisenhower era are
edging up in seniority. And it is partly because especially in
1966 the electorate has sent a batch of modern-minded,
relatively liberal Republicans to the Senate—men like Percy
of Illinois, Hatfield of Oregon, Brooke of Massachusetts,
Baker of Tennessee. Eastland, for example, is easily outvoted
on the Judiciary Committee, and other Southern conservatives control their committees tenuously or not at all.

But by and large, the Congressional-Conservative Party
prevails, when it wants to prevail, over the Presidential-
Liberal Party, partly because a big majority of the men who
really run Congress belong to the Congressional-Conservative Party. The chief reason, of course, is the seniority
system, which operates with the force of law, and which
guarantees that the men in the key positions will come from
the safe seats. This in turn guarantees that at least two-

thirds of the committee chairmen will be relatively conservative WASPs from the South or from the smaller Western and border states.

The result is that, especially when the Congressional-Conservative Party is in its normal majority position, Congress is catatonic. (Catatonia is defined in the dictionary as "a syndrome . . . with muscular rigidity and mental stupor, sometimes alternating with great excitement and confusion.") The periods of muscular rigidity and mental stupor prevail far more often than those of excitement and confusion. As a consequence, Congress, most of the time, is a bore. The boringness of Congress has hurt Congressional prestige far more than the Bakers and Powells and Dodds. Congress is a bore because Congress nowadays has the power to delay, or to emasculate, or to deny, but it almost wholly lacks the power to originate.

There was a time, not very long ago, when a Senator or even a lowly Representative could aspire to leave behind him a personal legislative monument—Representative Carter Glass's Banking Act, Senator Robert Wagner's labor law, Senator George Norris' TVA. Since World War II only one piece of major legislation was originated, debated, shaped, and passed by Congress wholly independent of the executive branch—Robert A. Taft's Taft-Hartley law. It may be the last such legislation Congress will ever originate.

Nowadays the role of Congress is to pass, or to refuse to pass, legislation originating in the executive branch—and sometimes, by not permitting an administration proposal to come to a vote, to do neither. This nay-saying power is still important, of course. But as the Congressional power becomes increasingly negative, Congress' slice of the whole pie of governmental power steadily becomes smaller.

The Constitution grants to Congress "the power to provide for the Common Defence and . . . to Declare War."

The most obvious example of the withering of Congressional power is the fact that, since World War II ended, the country has fought two rather large wars without the formality of a declaration of war by Congress. The Congressional power to "provide for the Common Defence" has also been similarly eroded.

All the basic strategic decisions involving the "Common Defence" are now made in the executive branch. True, such Congressional grandees as Richard Russell and George Mahon are listened to with respect and attention. They can influence the major decisions. But they do not *make* the major decisions, and neither does Congress as a whole.

Consider two examples. With strong support from both Armed Services Committees, Congress in the early sixties began appropriating money to build a "follow-on manned bomber"—the B-70—to replace the obsolescent B-52. Secretary of Defense McNamara thereafter curtly reported to Senator Russell that "the President chooses not to implement that section of the program." In short, the executive branch vetoed the clear intention of the Congress in "providing for the Common Defence," and the veto stuck.

Again, the Congressional grandees in the Armed Services Committees of both houses almost unanimously favored a "thick," or anti-Soviet, antiballistic-missile system, and in the mid-sixties money to start such an ABM system was twice voted. McNamara, with the backing of the President, simply refused to use the money—until, in September, 1967, he gave a reluctant yellow light to a "thin," or anti-Chinese, ABM system, which was not what the Armed Services Committees wanted.

In both cases—especially in the case of the B-70—McNamara was almost certainly right. The plain fact is that "providing for the Common Defence" has become a matter so complex and technical that Congress cannot really do the job any more. In simpler days, Congress could intelligently debate whether the United States needed a standing army of ten or fifteen divisions; whether the United States fleet should match the British fleet; or whether there should be conscription. But a body of 535 men from all walks of life is not qualified to decide such arcane matters as the proportion of the national budget that should be devoted to the multiple-warhead ICBM as against the Nike-X; or even such relatively simple questions as the comparative merits of the nuclear-powered frigate as against the cheaper conventional-powered frigate. A few genuine experts in Congress, men like Russell and Mahon, may have intelligent opinions in such matters, but the final decision has to be taken after an infinitely complex process of technical analysis in the executive branch.

Even many areas of domestic policy have become so complex, as the power of the federal government has inexorably expanded, that Congress retains only a sort of vague watching brief over the activities of the executive branch. Consider, for example, a large volume published by Sargent Shriver's Office of Economic Opportunity, which is to be found in almost all Congressional offices. Its title is *Catalog of Federal Assistance Programs*, and it is about the size of a Sears Roebuck catalogue.

It lists all the ways in which Uncle Sam is ready to help his eager nephews and nieces, from such major programs as Medicare and the U.S. Employment Services to "Captioned Films for the Deaf" and "Farm Fish Pond Management." A total of 459 separate and distinct programs are listed, administered by 34 separate and distinct agencies. The "authorizing legislation" for each program is duly noted in the catalogue. But in virtually every case the program was actually originated in the executive branch, almost always in the agency charged with administering it. No Congressman (and nobody else) can hope to master the whole complex of "federal assistance programs." Most members of Congress use the catalogue to help them act as intermediaries, or tipsters, for interested parties back home who want to get their share (or perhaps a bit more) of the federal gravy.

Moreover, both the executive and judicial branches have been invading, more than ever before, the lawmaking prerogative of Congress. Not only does almost all really important legislation now originate in the executive branch; a great body of "administrative law" has also been created by the administrative decisions of the regulatory agencies. These decisions have the force of law, and there are highly paid Washington lawyers who specialize in this kind of law and nothing else.

The Supreme Court has also created an increasingly large area of judicial law, or "judge-made law," as the Court's critics call it. The law on school integration, or the rights of criminal suspects, or legislative apportionment may be "judge-made." But it is the law of the land, all the same, to be obeyed by Congressmen like everybody else, and in certain areas this judge-made law affects the structure of American society more directly than legislation duly debated and passed by Congress. These are the areas, like school integration or voting rights, where Congress feared to tread; the Supreme Court, by boldly rushing into them, has seized a share of the power of Congress, as many anti-Court members of Congress are sulkily aware.

The loss of power by Congress should not be exaggerated. The power to delay, emasculate, and deny is a very great power, however negative. And the watching brief that Congress holds is also important. A major speech by a major Senator—Robert Kennedy's call in 1966 for incorporation of the National Liberation Front in a future Vietnamese government, for example; or Thruston Morton's hawk-to-dove speech on Vietnam in 1967—remains an Event, to be covered on the front pages, and therefore capable of influencing national opinion.

The will of Congress, even when the legislative process is not involved, can still importantly affect national policy. It is most unlikely that Robert McNamara would have given even a yellow light to the "thin" ABM system, which he himself described as of "marginal" value, if he and the President had not been under heavy Congressional pressure. When Establishmentarians Richard Russell and John Stennis of Mississippi joined William Fulbright in denouncing the despatch of three cargo planes to the Congo's Mobutu during the creeping civil war there, all thoughts of further intervention in the Congo were hastily abandoned.

Incredible numbers of man-hours are wasted by the top appointed officials of the executive branch in testifying on the same subject before four or more Congressional committees. Sargent Shriver, for example, has estimated that he spends about 90 percent of his time defending his antipoverty program on Capitol Hill, and about 10 percent actually administering it. And yet the knowledge that they will have to answer a lot of questions—even stupid, repetitious, and irrelevant questions—is not necessarily an unhealthy knowledge for the presidential appointees and the powerful upper bureaucrats to labor under.

Moreover, most Capitol Hill reporters would agree not only that there are very few real crooks in Congress, but that there are a surprising number of surprisingly able men, especially in the Senate. Most reporters, asked to give a rough guess at the number of men of real ability in the Senate, come up with some such estimate as a quarter or a third. But when they go through the hundred-man list name by name, they find themselves checking off a much higher proportion. Recently I collaborated with a reporter who has covered the Senate full time for several years (and who therefore knows the place far better than I do) in producing the following list:

ABLE

Clinton Anderson, N.M.
Wallace Bennett, Utah
Edward Brooke, Mass.
Robert Byrd, W.Va.
Frank Carlson, Kan.
Clifford Case, N.J.
Frank Church, Idaho
Joseph Clark, Pa.
Norris Cotton, N.H.
Peter Dominick, Colo.
Howard Baker, Jr., Tenn.
Philip Hart, Mich.
Mark Hatfield, Ore.
Roman Hruska, Neb.
Jacob Javits, N.Y.
Thomas Kuchel, Calif.
John McClellan, Ark.
Gale McGee, Wyo.
Warren Magnuson, Wash.
Lee Metcalf, Mont.
Mike Monroney, Okla.
Joseph Montoya, N.M.

Wayne Morse, Ore.
Thruston Morton, Ky.
Gaylord Nelson, Wis.
John Pastore, R.I.
James Pearson, Kan.
Claiborne Pell, R.I.
Winston Prouty, Vt.
Abraham Ribicoff, Conn.
Hugh Scott, Pa.
George Smathers, Fla.
Margaret Smith, Me.
John Sparkman, Ala.
John Stennis, Miss.
Stuart Symington, Mo.
Herman Talmadge, Ga.
John Tower, Tex.
Joseph Tydings, Md.
John Williams, Del.
Ralph Yarborough, Tex.
Milton Young, N.D.
Stephen Young, Ohio

VERY ABLE

George Aiken, Vt.
Birch Bayh, Ind.
John Cooper, Ky.
Everett Dirksen, Ill.
J. W. Fulbright, Ark.
Albert Gore, Tenn.

Ernest Gruening, Alaska
Fred Harris, Okla.
Carl Hayden, Ariz.
Bourke Hickenlooper, Iowa
Daniel Inouye, Hawaii
Henry Jackson, Wash.

Edward Kennedy, Mass.	Walter Mondale, Minn.
Robert Kennedy, N.Y.	Edmund Muskie, Me.
Russell Long, La.	Charles Percy, Ill.
George McGovern, S.D.	William Proxmire, Wis.
Mike Mansfield, Mont.	Richard Russell, Ga.

My reporter-friend (who does not want to be named, since he has to live with the unlisted Senators) was surprised when we counted the list and found we had named, not a third of the Senate, but two-thirds. And as he pointed out, the list is weighted against the Senate, partly because neither of us knew several Senators well enough to judge their ability. Personally, I was surprised by several of his choices, but deferred to his more intimate knowledge of the Senate.

Here again, the fact that members of Congress like their jobs, and Senators especially love being Senators, is an important fact. A lot of intelligent and ambitious men scramble over each other to get into Congress, with the result that the Hill boasts so high a proportion of able men, along with a share, of course, of trimmers and pompous fools. This is one reason why the voters, who are, as pointed out earlier in this book, by and large a remarkably ignorant and prejudiced lot, get better than they deserve.

And yet the fact is that the Congress of the United States has been rather steadily losing power and prestige. This is a process which has been going on elsewhere in the world—both the British and French Parliaments have also lost power and prestige, the latter more rapidly than the former. The conventional response to this loss of power and prestige is to express hand-wringing fears for the future of democracy.

If the process went too far—as it has in France, for example—it could indeed endanger the democratic system. But Congress is still capable of exercising the important nay-saying and watchdog functions. And it may be that those functions are, in fact, the only ones which a body of 535 men is capable of usefully exercising.

The periods of Congressional dominance, as after the Civil War, or in the nineteen-twenties, or in the early McCarthy period, have not been proud chapters in American political history. Especially in such times as these, the facts of life at home and abroad seem to dictate that the real policy-making power should rest increasingly with the executive branch, and that the power of Congress should become increasingly negative. In any case, that is what is happening.

11

THE COURT:
MYSTIQUE AND REALITY

Poverty is no longer to be regarded, like syphilis,
as prima facie evidence of sin.

The Supreme Court of the United States has a historical rhythm of its own. It has long periods of hibernation, when it is scarcely visible at all on the national political scene. During these periods it is rather vaguely revered, much as the Constitution which the Court is supposed to interpret is revered, but most people are not much aware of it. The Court entered several periods of hibernation in the nineteenth century, again in the nineteen-twenties, and again in the period between 1937, when Franklin Roosevelt's Court-packing plan was defeated, and 1954.

Then there are other periods, when the Court awakes from its long slumber and becomes as visible as a large, energetic, and rather angry bear. Such periods of high visibility include the era when "the Great Chief" (as he is still respectfully referred to on the Court), Chief Justice John Marshall, made the Court in fact as well as in name one of the three coequal branches of the American Government by

314

insisting on the Court's power of judicial review; or the pre-Civil War period which produced the Dred Scott decision; or in the nineteen-thirties when the Court and its supporters in the Senate won their Pyrrhic victory over Roosevelt. Since the school integration decision of 1954, the Court has entered another of its periods of high visibility.

There are indications that a period of hibernation may ensue in the rather near future. But meanwhile, the Court's visibility in the last decade or so could hardly have been higher. It is even visible on roadside signs and bumper stickers, reading "IMPEACH EARL WARREN," or "OUTLAW COMMUNISTS NOT PRAYERS," or even "SUPPORT YOUR LOCAL POLICE." The Court, in short, has again become one of the American Government's great storm centers.

A case could even be made that since Earl Warren became Chief Justice in 1954, the decisions of the Court have had a deeper impact on the life of the American citizenry than all the legislation passed by Congress since that year, with the possible exception of Medicare. Yet curiously enough, despite its high visibility in recent years, most people really know very little about the Court.

There are veteran Washington reporters (including, until rather recently, this one) who have never set foot inside the pompous marble mausoleum which houses the Court. And except rarely, on the occasion of some great and controversial decision, the Court goes about its business almost unnoticed, and its nine Justices, in comparison with Washington's other major movers and shakers, remain rather pale and distant figures. Yet the Court is an interesting place, and its nine inhabitants are interesting people, once the tangled thickets of legal verbiage and ancient myth which surround the Court are cleared away.

One ancient myth is carved in huge marble letters on the portico of the Supreme Court Building: "EQUAL JUSTICE

UNDER THE LAW." The plain fact is that the nine Justices hardly ever agree about what the law is, or what equal justice under it consists of. Everything about the Court, from the ancient traditions in which it is wrapped to the prevalence of marble in the building in which it is housed, tends to belie this fact. But it is a fact all the same.

The Court is by tradition reconvened on the first Monday in October, after the summer recess, and by tradition, reaching back now for close to two centuries, the Court crier proclaims in a loud voice: "Oyez! Oyez! Oyez! All persons having business before the Honorable, the Supreme Court of the United States, are admonished to draw near and give attention. . . ."

In order to "draw near" the Supreme Court, you climb forty-two marble steps, pass through a forest of Corinthian pillars, and go through a pair of sculptured brass doors which weigh six and a half tons apiece. Just inside the doors, in the front and center of an imposing marble corridor, the first object to catch the eye is a sign, standing on a wooden pedestal. The sign bears an imperious, one-word command, painted in gilt letters: "SILENCE."

The sign is obeyed. In the echoing marble halls, and in the pillared, curtain-draped courtroom itself, the tourists in their shorts and halters stand in reverent silence, or walk on tiptoe, whispering to each other, as in a cathedral. They have been transformed into worshipers at a shrine.

The transformation is the result of a shrewdly calculated exercise in atmospherics. The Supreme Court Building was designed in the late nineteen-twenties under the direct supervision of William Howard Taft, the only American who has been both President and Chief Justice. Taft did not much like being President, but he loved the Court; the Court, he once wrote, "next to my wife and children, is the nearest thing to my heart in life." Taft knew what he wanted: a building that would impress the humble citizenry with the power and majesty of his beloved Court. And that is what he got.

Everything about the Court—the marble building, the black robes of the Justices, the crier with his "Oyez! Oyez!," the sculptured bas-reliefs of ancient lawgivers—is designed to promote the carefully cultivated mystique of the Court. The mystique is one of the Court's most important attributes.

Alexander Hamilton said of the Court that it had the power of "neither purse nor sword." But the mystique serves as a useful substitute for both. It endows the Court with an air of Solomonic wisdom above mundane political struggle, and this in turn serves as a shield for the Court in the fierce political struggle in which it has been intermittently engaged since it came into existence in 1790. This is the ancient struggle between the three branches of the American Government for a bigger share of the pie of power.

Because the Court in recent years has been steadily extending its reach and authority, thus getting a bigger share of the power pie, the struggle has rarely been fiercer, and the shield of the Court has been wearing rather thin. The Court has never been under more bitter attack, not even when the Dred Scott decision made the Civil War inevitable, or when the "nine old men" were ruling the New Deal unconstitutional.

The Supreme Court is assailed everywhere, not only on those signs and bumper stickers, but in the halls of Congress, where the Justices have been called an "unpredictable group of uncontrolled despots," and their decisions described as "malicious, atheistic, and sacrilegious." Barry Goldwater invented an expressive word—"jackassian"—to describe the Court's decisions, and the late Herbert Hoover, after the famous prayer decision, accused the Court of causing "a disintegration of one of the most sacred American heritages."

The Court has been fiercely criticized by such important bodies as the American Bar Association, the Governors' Conference, and the National Association of Attorneys General. The Court has also alienated by its decisions large and important segments of the American body politic—church groups, police and law enforcement officials, conservatives everywhere in the country, and virtually the entire white South. No wonder the mystique is wearing a bit thin.

The Court has made its large collection of powerful enemies by its rulings in three chief areas: Negro rights in general and school integration in particular; voting rights, starting with the one-man-one-vote ruling in 1962; and crime-detection and police methods. In a number of other areas— Communist subversion, religion, censorship of obscenity— the Court's rulings have provided added enemies, as well as large numbers of friends and admirers.

The Court's major decisions are, of course, duly reported in the press. Yet the curious fact is that the much-damned and much-admired "Warren Court" has received far less press coverage than its theoretically coequal branches, the Congress and the executive branch. The Court is, in fact, the only underreported branch of the overreported American Government.

One reason is an aloofness toward the press which is part of the Court's mystique. The Justices, while they attack each other very caustically indeed in their written and oral opinions, frequently accusing each other of irrelevance, faulty logic, bad history, and ignorance of constitutional law, are polite and circumspect in public. "It is our proudest boast," says one Justice, "that no member of this Court has ever fought his battles in the press."

One result of this calculated aloofness is that covering the

Court is a reportorial nightmare. In their decisions, the Justices refer to each other as "my brother so-and-so" and "my brethren," and however bitterly they disagree on the issues, the Justices behave to outsiders like members of a secret fraternal society. Future decisions are simply not discussed, and no Justice will publicly take issue with one of his "brethren."

Covering the Court, one reporter has remarked, "is like trying to cover Skull and Bones or the Delphic Oracle." "We have no sources at all," says Fred Graham of the *New York Times,* one of the ablest of the handful of reporters who cover the Court full time. "Even the law clerks will hardly give us the time of day. And Decision Monday is really hell."

Most decisions are handed down on a Monday. To avoid the undignified spectacle of reporters rushing in and out of the Court, the working press is assigned small cubicles in the basement of the building, and decisions are sent down to the reporters through pneumatic tubes. The reporters grab desperately for the decisions as they pop out of the tubes, and write their stories in fierce competition with other reporters in other cubicles. Once the text of an important decision got stuck in the UPI man's pneumatic tube, and he almost had a nervous breakdown.

In the early nineteen-fifties, a lady reporter covering the Court found out that all her colleagues, without exception, suffered from nervous stomach on Decision Mondays. She reported her discovery to Fred M. Vinson, then Chief Justice, and with womanly charm pleaded with him to do something to ease the reportorial burden.

"But, my dear," the Chief Justice replied, "I have always understood that a little cleaning out never hurt anyone."

The Chief Justice may have been medically correct, but the Court pays a price for its aloofness. When the Court's decision outlawing state-ordered prayers was bitterly at-

tacked, Justice William Brennan complained that the attack-
ers had obviously not read the decision, and said that this
made him "a bit sad." It *is* a bit sad that the Court's
decisions are so rarely read; they are often interesting, and
sometimes even moving. But the Court's habit of handing
down several decisions at once, and its refusal to permit
press briefings or any public explanations or elaborations,
make it inevitable that the Court's decisions will be largely
unread, misinterpreted, or misunderstood.

To begin to understand the Court, another ancient myth
needs clearing away first. This is the notion, promulgated by
the first John Adams, that the American Government is a
"government of laws, not men," a phrase often cited by
worshipers at the Supreme Court shrine. In an indiscreet
moment before he joined the Court, Chief Justice Charles
Evans Hughes demolished this myth in one famous sentence: "We are under a Constitution, but the Constitution is
what the Judges say it is." The nine men who say what the
Constitution is are most interesting men.

A wit has likened the black-robed Justices to "nine black
beetles in the Temple of Karnak." In their majesty on the
bench, or in their official photographs, they do look rather
like nine more or less identical black beetles. But seen at
closer range, they look a lot more like nine self-opinionated
and highly idiosyncratic human beings.

They are a variegated lot. There are two men on the Court
who may be responsible for the fact that Lyndon Johnson is
President today; two men who might have been the President themselves; the Negro son of a Pullman car waiter; a
Jew; a Catholic; a former member of the Ku Klux Klan; a
once-great athlete who is on the court partly because he
went on a toot with John F. Kennedy when they both were
scarcely out of knee pants; nine lawyers of far-above aver-

age competence; and nine men who are often in bitter and profound disagreement on basic constitutional issues. These men live for most of the year more or less in each other's pockets. It is natural that, in their personal relations with each other, they experience what Justice Brennan has called "quite agonizing tensions at times."

One of the men who might have been President is, of course, the Chief Justice, Earl Warren, former Governor of California. Warren was a Presidential contender in 1948 and again in 1952. He was rewarded for throwing his support to Dwight Eisenhower in the 1952 convention with a promise of a seat on the Court when the first vacancy occurred.

The first vacancy occurred when Chief Justice Vinson died in 1954. An attempt was made to fob off Warren with a promise of a seat when the *next* vacancy occurred, but Warren stubbornly insisted that a promise was a promise, and he became Chief Justice. According to his conservative critics, he has been a disastrous Chief Justice. According to such liberal admirers as Yale Law Professor Fred Rodell, he has been the greatest Chief Justice in American history.

A constantly smiling, grandfatherly sort of man, Earl Warren is a living example of the curious chameleon effect which the highest bench produces on many of those who sit on it. It has happened again and again: a liberal President will appoint a liberal Justice, and the new Justice becomes increasingly conservative over the years; or vice versa.

As a young politician—he was District Attorney of Alameda County in California before the Second World War—Earl Warren was known as "an L.A. *Times* Republican," which meant in those days a down-the-line right-winger. New Dealer Carey McWilliams went further and called Warren "the personification of reaction." During the war, as Attorney General of California, Warren played a leading part in one of the most disgraceful chapters of American history, when the state's citizens of Japanese ancestry were bundled off to concentration camps.

Thereafter, in his three terms as Governor, Warren moved steadily toward the political center. But Eisenhower certainly thought he was getting a fellow middle-of-the-road conservative as his Chief Justice. He got nothing of the sort.

There is at least one point on which every Justice is wholly in accord with his "brethren." They all hate to be labeled, whether as "liberals," "conservatives," "activists," "judicial restrainers," or whatever. But a Justice who uses—and in fact stretches—the power of the Court to protect and extend the rights and prerogatives of the poor in general and Negroes in particular is, by any sensible definition, a liberal. By that definition, the Chief Justice is far and away the most liberal Chief Justice in American history. By the same token, the Court over which he presides is the most liberal in our history—and steadily growing more so. If it grows very much more so, a direct power confrontation with an essentially conservative Congress may be inevitable.

The story of the Warren Court starts, of course, with the unanimous decision in 1954 ruling segregation in the public schools unconstitutional—one of the half-dozen most important decisions in the Court's history. The school decision was the prelude to a whole series of decisions almost as important and controversial.

The direction which the Warren Court has taken was undoubtedly much influenced by a struggle for the heart and mind of Earl Warren, in the years immediately following the school decision. This spiritual wrestling match was between Justice Hugo Black, the Court's senior Associate Justice, and Justice Felix Frankfurter. The brilliant, peppery little Frankfurter was another example of the Court's chameleon effect. When he was appointed to the Court by Franklin Roosevelt, he was viewed by conservatives as little better than a Bolshevik. But on the Court he became the chief defender of the conservative doctrine of "judicial restraint," and by the time he died in 1962 he had become a minor deity in the conservative pantheon. But he had also lost his struggle with Hugo Black, and he knew it. In his first term Warren differed frequently with Black, but as the years passed Warren and Black were increasingly on the same side, while Frankfurter found himself more and more often in the minority.

This is not to suggest that Hugo Black has played Svengali to Warren's Trilby—Warren has a mind of his own. But it is certainly true that Hugo Black is a most determined man. (At eighty-one he was operated on twice for cataracts, but he had his tennis court resurfaced, so that it would be ready when he could see again.) His convictions are deeply held, and his sometimes acidulous tongue is persuasive. There is no doubt that he has greatly influenced the thinking of the Chief Justice and other Justices too. In fact, today's Supreme Court is as much a Black Court as a Warren Court.

Black is another in the Supreme Court's collection of human anomalies. One of the most fearful rows in the Court's history broke out when it became known, after Black's appointment by Roosevelt, that Black as a young politician had been a member of the Ku Klux Klan. In his thirty years on the high bench, Black's positions have been consistently precisely the opposite of what might have been expected from an ex-Klansman.

Second in seniority to Black is another Roosevelt appointee, William O. Douglas, still rugged at sixty-nine. In the pre-Warren era, Black and Douglas were the Damon and Pythias of liberal dissent; in decision after decision, "Justices Black and Douglas dissenting" became routine. Both felt so frustrated that they seriously considered resigning from the Court. Now, in their old age, their hour of triumph has come: they are no longer a beleaguered minority on the Court, but the chief architects of an almost-sure majority.

Triumph seems to have strained the Damon-and-Pythias relationship. In 1966 they began to differ sharply in certain areas. When Black wrote the majority opinion upholding the conviction of Negro civil rights workers who had invaded state-held property in Florida, Douglas remarked acidly: "We now have set into the record a great and wonderful police-state doctrine." The remark was scarcely calculated to endear him to his old ally, and it seems very likely that there have been some "quite agonizing tensions" in their recent relationship.

Douglas is the other Justice who might have been President. Franklin Roosevelt at first fully intended to offer him the Vice Presidential nomination in 1944. If he had done so, Douglas would have become President in 1945, and the history of the world would have been changed. In those days Douglas was considered a much bigger man than Harry Truman. In recent years—perhaps unfairly, and certainly in part because of his April-and-November marriages—his reputation has dwindled, and in Political Washington he is not taken as seriously as he once was.

After Douglas in seniority is John M. Harlan, an able, elderly, quiet-spoken man who looks more like a Supreme Court Justice than any of his colleagues. He was President Eisenhower's second appointee, and this time Eisenhower got a conservative Justice who stayed conservative. Harlan is the last consistent apostle of Frankfurter's doctrine of "judicial restraint." He has been labeled "a Frankfurter without the mustard."

Eisenhower's third appointee, William J. Brennan, occupies the Court's "Catholic seat." He has a pleasant, map-of-

Ireland face which conceals a sharp intelligence. From the first, Brennan joined the Warren-Black-Douglas liberals—again, no doubt, to Eisenhower's surprise, and certainly much to Felix Frankfurter's chagrin. Brennan had been a student of Frankfurter's at the Harvard Law School, and he smilingly recalls a remark Frankfurter made about him: "I like my students to be independent-minded, but Bill Brennan carries independence too damn far."

Potter Stewart, the fourth Eisenhower appointee, is an able big-city lawyer whose opinions are particularly well written and pithy. He usually sides with the dwindling conservative bloc. So does Byron White, the only Kennedy appointee still on the Court since the departure of Arthur Goldberg for the UN. A former all-American football player, White has the rugged, he-man look Kennedys prefer. He first got to know John Kennedy well when they spent a few gay days in Munich together before the war. They got to know each other better in the Navy during the war, so that by the time Kennedy became President White was one of the small band of honorary Kennedys. White was appointed to the Court by Kennedy in 1962.

Abe Fortas was the first Justice appointed by Lyndon Johnson, and he may well be the next Chief Justice. If so, he will be the first Jewish Chief Justice—he occupies the "Jewish seat" once occupied by such brilliant men as Frankfurter and Brandeis.

Fortas, soft-spoken, with a long, intelligent face, is another brilliant man. He reluctantly gave up a highly lucrative law practice to go on the bench when Lyndon Johnson, who is a powerful insister, insisted. He remains what he was before he went on the Court—one of Lyndon Johnson's closest advisers. He still often moonlights from his job on the Court to do special confidential chores for the President.

A very good case could be made for the thesis that

Lyndon Johnson is President thanks to Abe Fortas and old Hugo Black. In 1948 Johnson was threatened with political oblivion when a Texas judge issued an injunction against his name appearing on the ballot as the Democratic candidate for the Senate, on the grounds that his tiny primary margin of eighty-seven votes came mostly from the graveyard. Johnson sent an SOS to Abe Fortas in Washington. Fortas persuaded Hugo Black to issue a Supreme Court order staying the injunction, and thus Johnson's political career was saved.

If it had not been, it is unlikely that Johnson would be President today, or that Fortas would be on the Court. As things stand, if Warren dies or retires while Johnson is President, the betting is good that Abe Fortas will take his place. Most of his fellow lawyers believe that Fortas, who is a rare combination of political pragmatist and idealistic philosopher, would make a good, and perhaps a great, Chief Justice. But Fortas has his critics, too. Some lawyers charge that the political implications of a decision concern him more than its legal and constitutional implications.

The newest member of the Court is Thurgood Marshall, the big easygoing former Solicitor General who is the first Negro to sit on the highest bench. Marshall is no stranger to the Court. As counsel to the NAACP, he argued thirty-two cases before the Court, winning twenty-nine, including the 1954 school case. The chameleon effect may work on him, too. But his record clearly indicates that on all issues involving race, and on most other issues too, Marshall will side with the liberal-activists, giving them a safe majority of six.

Thus the Court has been wholly transformed in the thirteen years since Warren became Chief Justice; a two-out-of-nine minority has become on many issues a six-out-of-nine majority, and on some issues Justice Harlan, the only consistently faithful apostle of judicial restraint, may be a lonely minority of one. But what does this change really *mean,* in terms of the balance of power within the American Government, and in terms of the relationship of the American citizen to his government? What have the Justices, in their unending argument with each other, really been arguing about?

Instead of trying to answer that question in generalities, consider a specific case—the case of *Ernesto A. Miranda, Petitioner,* v. *State of Arizona.* The Miranda case was one of the major cases decided by the Court in 1966, in a typical five-to-four split decision.

Recently, Abe Fortas, musing on his new role, remarked that "the job of being a judge is much, much more taxing than an advocate's job. . . . There's no such thing as perfect justice, assessed in the abstract." Reading a case like the Miranda case, and trying to put yourself in the shoes of a judge who must decide one way or the other, you can see what Fortas means. You can also see how deep are the legal and philosophical (and, one suspects, personal) differences among the nine men on the Court.

The Miranda case was not only a famous Supreme Court decision. It was also an agonizing human experience which involved a young girl who was raped on a lonely road; a mentally ill Mexican-American who confessed to the rape; and beyond those two, in the words of Justice Byron White, "the next victims . . . uncertain, unnamed, and unrepresented in this case."

The Miranda case divided the Court deeply and bitterly. Both sides agreed on the essential facts in the case. They are these:

On March 3, 1963, an eighteen-year-old girl (unnamed, of course, in the records) was raped near Phoenix, Arizona. Ten days later, Ernesto Miranda, a twenty-three-year-old school dropout, was arrested on suspicion of the crime. The girl was summoned to the police station, and picked Miranda out of the police line-up as her attacker.

Thereafter, at about eleven-thirty on the morning of March 13, two policemen conducted Miranda into "Interrogation Room No. 2" of the Phoenix detective bureau. Miranda at first denied his guilt, but within two hours he orally confessed to the rape, and he then wrote out in his own handwriting a full confession admitting and describing the crime. He also signed a typewritten statement—presumably one of the policemen was the typist—to the effect that he had confessed voluntarily, without threats or promises, and "with full knowledge of my legal rights, understanding any statement I make may be used against me."

Miranda, according to a doctor who subsequently examined him, indulged in frequent sexual fantasies and had schizophrenic tendencies. But he was legally sane and competent to stand trial. Both sides on the Court agreed that the confession was not the result of physical force or the threat of force—there had been no third degree. Both sides also agreed that the policemen did not specifically inform Miranda that he had a right to have a lawyer present during the questioning.

An Arizona jury convicted Miranda, and he was sentenced to twenty to thirty years in prison. The sentence was appealed, and with the disgraceful slowness which characterizes the judicial process in the United States, the case made its way to the Supreme Court. Oral argument was heard by the Court on February 28, 1966, and again on March 1 and 2. The appeal was based on the Fifth Amendment to the Constitution: "No person . . . shall be compelled in any criminal case to be a witness against himself."

Was Ernesto Miranda, in those two hours in Interrogation Room 2, compelled to be a witness against himself?

That was the question which confronted the nine Justices when they met, on Friday, March 4, for one of their regular day-long conferences. Every Friday during the term, the Justices spend all day discussing the business before the Court. The conferences last from ten in the morning until five or six, with a half-hour break for lunch. The long, concentrated, often argumentative meetings are exhausting —Justice Potter Stewart, who dines out more than his brethren, has given orders to his wife not to accept Friday dinner invitations, and the other Justices are hardly ever seen on the Washington social circuit on Friday evenings.

The Justices meet in a handsome oak-paneled room, with a fireplace at one end. Over the fireplace hangs the only picture in the room—a Rembrandt Peale portrait of John Marshall. Only the Justices themselves are present at the Friday conferences. There are no law clerks, no secretaries, no stenographers. Thus each Justice is strictly on his own, and the Supreme Court is therefore the only segment of the American Government which has defied Parkinson's Law. This is one reason why the proceedings in the paneled conference room, though they foreshadow decisions which may have a profound impact on the American social or political system, are hardly known about, or written about, at all.

On this occasion, as always, the Justices were summoned to the conference room by a buzzer which rang in their chambers five minutes in advance. As always, each Justice shook the hands of all his brethren—an ancient custom. They called each other by their first names, except for Warren, whom they called "Chief" or "the Chief Justice"— another ancient custom.

The Chief Justice took his accustomed place at the south end of the long conference table, facing the Marshall portrait, and the senior Associate Justice, Hugo Black, sat opposite him. The other Justices ranged themselves in order of seniority around the table, with Abe Fortas, then the junior Justice, nearest the door. (It is the junior Justice's duty to take and deliver messages at the door. During the World Series he is kept busy taking the latest baseball scores—the Chief Justice is a passionate baseball fan.)

Warren opened the discussion on the Miranda case. He talked for about twenty minutes, giving a number of reasons to support his conclusion that Miranda's conviction should be reversed. Black spoke next, saying simply that he "agreed with the Chief," and Douglas concurred with equal brevity. So did Brennan and Fortas, when their turns came, thus providing a majority of five to reverse Miranda's conviction. One or two of the four Justices in the minority argued with some heat against reversing the conviction, but the minds of the five men in the majority, who had almost certainly concerted their collective opinion in advance, were clearly not going to be easy to change.

There was much writing and revising of opinions before the decision was handed down, and much talk and argument between the Justices. But the five-man majority for reversal held firm. On June 13, 1966, Warren delivered the opinion, which, because it represented a majority, thereupon became "the opinion of the Court."

The "opinion of the Court" was that Ernesto Miranda had indeed been "compelled" to testify against himself, even though the two policemen had used no force, and no threat of force, to obtain his confession.

In the Chief Justice's opinion there is certainly something of the past of former District Attorney Earl Warren, who knew a lot about how cops get confessions from suspects. There is even, one suspects, in the aging Chief Justice of the Miranda decision a sort of expiatory mirror image of the rising young politician who took the lead in hounding California's Japanese-American citizens into concentration camps, in flagrant disregard for their constitutional rights. At any rate, as his opinion makes very clear, Earl Warren, at the age of seventy-six, at the pinnacle of prestige and power, remains quite capable of imagining what it must be like to be a frightened, semiliterate young man, held in a bleak interrogation room and questioned about a terrible crime.

The heart of the majority's opinion, as expressed by Warren, can be summed up very simply. Modern police practice has replaced the third degree and other physical means of obtaining confessions with "interrogation [which] is psychologically rather than physically oriented." In other words, the cops, instead of beating a suspect like Miranda half to death, scare him half to death. A suspect subjected to "incommunicado interrogation in a police-dominated atmosphere" is in the very nature of things being "compelled to bear witness against himself," even if the police never threaten him and never touch him physically.

Having reached this conclusion, Warren and his four concurring brethren proceeded to lay down certain rules for police behavior based upon their conclusion. A suspect who has been "taken into custody or deprived of his freedom in any significant way" must be "warned that he has a right to remain silent, that any statement he makes may be used as evidence against him, and that he has a right to the presence of an attorney, either retained or appointed." If at any point the suspect says, or "indicates in any way," that he doesn't want to answer any more questions, that's that—the police must instantly stop questioning him.

These rules were not mere recommendations or guidelines. Since they represented "the opinion of the Court," even if only by a five-to-four majority, they instantly became the law of the land, to be obeyed by law enforcement officers anywhere in the United States. Any policeman violating them is guilty of violating the Constitution of the United States, as interpreted by "the Honorable, the Supreme Court of the United States."

Of the four dissenting Justices, only one, Potter Stewart, simply concurred in the main dissenting opinion, written by Justice Byron White. The others, Justice Tom Clark (since retired) and Justice Harlan, felt so strongly that they wrote dissenting opinions of their own.

Justice Clark, a former Attorney General, wrote tartly that "such a constitutional specific inserted at the nerve center of crime detection may well kill the patient." Justice Harlan wrote that "the thrust of the new rules is to . . . discourage any confession at all." Miranda's confessions, he wrote, "were obtained during brief, daytime questioning, unmarked . . . by any of the traditional indicia of coercion." In sum, he concluded, "One is entitled to feel astonished that the Constitution can be read to produce this result."

John Kennedy's boyhood friend Byron White, who has a reputation for caution, was most caustic of all. Like the other dissenters, he saw "no significant support" for the decision in the Constitution. But what worried him much more was the effect of the decision in discouraging convictions of guilty criminals.

As a result, White wrote, "in some unknown number of cases the Court's rule will return a killer, a rapist, or other criminal to the environment which produced him, to repeat his crime whenever he pleases. As a consequence there will not be a gain, but a loss, in human dignity." It is nonsense, White wrote angrily, to suppose that punishment has no deterrent effect on crime. "The easier it is to get away with rape and murder, the less deterrent effect on those who attempt it. This is still good common sense. If it were not, we should posthaste liquidate the whole law enforcement establishment as a useless, misguided effort to control human conduct."

White predicted that the chief impact of the new rules would be "on those who rely on public authority for protection, and who without it can only engage in violent self-help with guns, knives, and the help of neighbors similarly inclined." In short, the rule of law would be replaced by the rule of the vigilante.

Strong words. Equally strong words can be found in many other dissents. In fact, by far the most cogent and informed criticism of the "activist" majority on the Court has come from the Court itself. It may be a "bit sad" that so few people read the Court's opinions. But it may also be just as well, as far the mystique of the Court is concerned. Central to the Court's mystique is the notion that the Court is the dispassionate interpreter of the Constitution. Read a few divided opinions, and it becomes obvious that this is nonsense.

The Court's opinions, both majority and dissenting, are always heavily larded with learned references to previous decisions, reaching back to the earliest days of the Court. But these legal references (most of which are supplied by the law clerks) are little more than genuflections. In fact, the opinions of the nine men on the Court obviously derive from no mystical contemplation of the Delphic mysteries of the Constitution, which only they (according to the mystique) are qualified to interpret. They derive, instead, from their own attitudes, preconceptions, and experience, both as lawyers and as men.

In the Miranda case, the five men in the majority were really asking Earl Warren's favorite question, which he often asks in open court: "Is it *fair?*" Their answer was that Ernesto Miranda was not treated fairly in Interrogation

Room No. 2; and that therefore rules must be laid down to make sure that poor and ignorant men like Miranda are treated fairly in the future. The four men in the minority were also asking the same question. Their answer was that Miranda *was* treated fairly, and that the majority's rules limiting the powers of the police would *not* be fair to "the next victims . . . uncertain, unnamed, and unrepresented in this case."

Despite all the learned legal genuflections, it is quite clear that any reasonably fair-minded and well-informed person has just as much right to give his own answer to Earl Warren's question as any of the black-robed Justices. It is just as clear that the answers given by the Justices, on both sides, have at most a tenuous connection with the words written into the Constitution.

The framers of the Fifth Amendment certainly did not intend it to be applied to out-of-court interrogation by the police. They could not have so intended, if only because, when the Amendment was written, there was nothing in existence remotely resembling a modern police force.

For that matter, the men who wrote the Fifth Amendment and the other nine Amendments in the Bill of Rights intended only to limit the powers of the *federal* government in its dealings with the citizenry and the several states, as the first words of the First Amendment—"Congress shall make no law"—clearly indicate. The Court itself, under the great federalist, John Marshall, ruled that the Bill of Rights did *not* extend to the relationship between the citizen and the state government. How does it happen, then, that the Supreme Court has applied the Fifth Amendment to the relationship between a criminal suspect and the local cops?

The answer tells a lot about what lawyers can do with words. For the answer is to be found in fifty-two words, the most important of all the millions of words which have been written into laws of the United States since the Union was founded:

No State shall make or enforce any law which shall abridge the privileges or immunities of citizens of the United States; nor shall any State deprive any person of life, liberty, or property, without due process of law; nor deny to any person within its jurisdiction the equal protection of the laws.

The words are, of course, from the Fourteenth Amendment, written into the Constitution in 1868. Learned tomes have been written on the intent of those who wrote those fifty-two words; Justice Black once devoted two years to studying the matter. But their primary purpose was quite clear: to protect the newly freed slaves.

In the century since it was passed the Fourteenth Amendment has been used for quite different purposes. Between the Civil War and the second New Deal, the Court was a bulwark of conservatism—a good many of the Justices sympathized with the dictum of the first Chief Justice, John Jay: "Those who own the country ought to govern it." Corporations were ruled to be "persons" under the Fourteenth Amendment, and all sorts of legislation, state and federal, designed to regulate these "persons" was outlawed. The final upshot was the great Court crisis of 1937, which ended in a Pyrrhic victory for the conservatives. Franklin Roosevelt's "Court-packing bill" was defeated, but the Court has never since used the Fourteenth Amendment to veto progressive legislation.

It has been used instead, by the Warren Court, to protect those who *don't* "own the country"—the Negroes, the poor, and the people Justice Abe Fortas calls "constitutional unpersons." The Fourteenth Amendment was first used by the Warren Court to outlaw school segregation. But the Fourteenth Amendment has also played a key role in virtually all the Warren Court's landmark decisions. It has been used as a sort of bridge, to extend the Bill of Rights to the states.

The process began, to be sure, long before the Warren Court. Back in 1925, for example, the Court first ruled that by reason of the Fourteenth Amendment a citizen was protected from any breach of the First Amendment—the free-speech Amendment—by a state government. But under the Warren Court the process of extending the Bill of Rights to the states has been going forward with a rush. According to Justice Brennan, the Bill of Rights contains twenty-five "specific guarantees" of the rights of the American citizen. By this time, seventeen of the twenty-five, Brennan says, have been ruled by the Court to be "fundamental rights binding upon the states," and he makes clear that there are more to come.

To the layman, all this may smack of legalistic quibbling. In fact, by using the Fourteenth Amendment boldly to extend the reach and power of the Bill of Rights, the Warren Court has deeply altered the whole delicate relationship between the federal government, the states, and the individual citizen. At the same time, not entirely by coincidence, it has greatly extended the reach and power of the Supreme Court. Pre-Warren, it was thought to be no business of the Court, or indeed of the federal government, what went on in the schoolrooms, or local police stations, or boardinghouses, or houses of juvenile correction, or the like. Now, in these and many other areas, what the Court says—at least theoretically—goes.

The result, critics of the Court are fond of saying, is "judge-made law." The activists cheerfully agree. "Judges have *always* made law," says Justice Brennan, emphasizing that making law is not the same thing as making laws.

Justice Fortas is the most articulate exponent of the doctrine that the Constitution not only is, but *ought to be,* "what the Judges say it is." "The Bill of Rights and the Fourteenth Amendment are great statements of fundamental principles, like the Ten Commandments," Fortas says. "The problem is not to determine precisely what their framers meant, but to interpret their moral thrust in the light of the problems of today. . . . Events have so changed conditions as to require a different interpretation of the Constitution to meet those changed conditions."

The direction of this "moral thrust" is suggested by a remark Fortas recently made to this reporter: "Poverty is no longer to be regarded, like syphilis, as prima facie evidence of sin." The underlying philosophy of the Warren Court—or rather of the Warren majority on the Court—is profoundly egalitarian.

"In our nation the progress toward freedom for all and equality of status has not been in a straight line," Fortas wrote in a recent article for a law review.

We are now again involved in a gigantic thrust forward toward this magnificent objective. In the past years . . . we have declared the doors to the schoolhouse are open to all; the doors to the voting booths; to libraries and parks, to jobs and training and opportunity. . . . Now we are involved in the formidable, revolutionary task of implementing these declarations—of investing them with reality.

This "formidable, revolutionary task" may, in the end, bring the Court into a direct power confrontation with the Congress, and thus bring on a major constitutional crisis. Andrew Jackson once said grimly of a Court decision he disliked: "John Marshall has made his decision. Now let him enforce it." In the Congress there are many powerful men who have a similarly grim attitude toward the decisions of the Warren Court. And many of those decisions have a long way to go before they are "invested with reality."

Take, for example, *Brown* v. *Board of Education*, the school integration decision. The Brown in the case was a Negro minister in Topeka, Kansas, who wanted his little girl, Linda, to go to the all-white Sumner School, instead of the all-black Monroe School. The Court shook the nation by ruling that little Linda should go to the Sumner School, thus in theory outlawing segregation by race. But the Monroe School today, thirteen years after that nation-shaking decision, is still overwhelmingly black, while the Sumner School has less than 5 percent Negroes.

The same pattern holds nationwide—only more so. There has been some token desegregation in the South, to be sure. But Harold Howe, U.S. Commissioner of Education, is the authority for the statement that there is today *more* racial segregation in the schools than in 1954, the year when the Supreme Court sent little Linda to the Sumner School.

"Separate educational facilities," the Court ruled in 1954, are "inherently unequal," and thus unconstitutional under the Fourteenth Amendment. But because of the growth of *de facto* segregation, reflecting the flight of the whites from the cities, "educational facilities" are more separate than in 1954, and as a practical matter *de facto* segregation is just as "inherently unequal" as *de jure* segregation.

If the Court follows its 1954 reasoning to its logical conclusion, and moves in some way against *de facto* segregation—approving, for example, some such ruling as the 1967 lower court decision in the District of Columbia, which requires the bussing of Negro children to the few remaining predominantly white schools—an enormous national uproar will certainly ensue. For the name of the Supreme Court will then instantly become a hissing and byword, not only in the South as in 1954, but in white neighborhoods all over the nation. Those neighborhoods house a large majority of the nation's voters, and Congress would surely respond to the uproar by reacting in some rude fashion against the Court.

There are other issues which may one day soon face the Court, and which could cause the Congress to react rudely. For example, Hugo Black and William Douglas, bellwethers of the liberal majority, are both "absolutists" where the guarantees of the First Amendment are concerned. Justice Black, for example, holds that "our nation cannot be imperiled by mere talk," and he therefore believes that the American system "leaves the way wide open for people to favor, discuss, advocate, or incite causes and doctrines however obnoxious and antagonistic to the rest of us."

The big-city riots of recent years have made the doctrine of Black Power exceedingly "obnoxious and antagonistic" to the white majority, and although "mere talk" may not imperil the nation, in the current mood of the Negro ghettos it can imperil large parts of the nation's big cities. Negro militant H. Rap Brown was indicted in 1967 for incitement to insurrection in Maryland, and the words of Stokely Carmichael and other black militants have been as inflammatory as Brown's. Is the First Amendment's guarantee of freedom of speech so "absolute" that it extends to the right of a Negro leader to tell his followers to "burn America down"? If the Court were so to rule, the reaction of the Congress might be very rude indeed.

There are other ways in which the racial crisis, the most serious domestic crisis since the Great Depression, could bring the Court and the Congress to an angry showdown. The Miranda case was one of a series of Supreme Court decisions progressively restricting the procedures the police can use in arresting suspects or getting convictions. With every new decision, the law enforcement professionals have become angrier. For example, former New York Police Commissioner Michael Murphy had this to say: "What the Court is doing is akin to requiring one boxer to fight by Marquis of Queensberry rules while permitting the other to butt, gouge, and bite."

As a practical matter, the law enforcement authorities have not always played by the Marquis of Queensberry rules laid down by the Court. In the Newark riots in 1967, 1,397 people were arrested, and 7,207 were arrested in the Detroit riots. Were all these people told all about their rights, as laid down by Chief Justice Warren? The question answers itself. And it is by no means only when riots occur that the police do not religiously abide by the Warren rules. Again, if the Court moves too far and too fast in its "formidable, revolutionary task" of investing decisions like the Miranda decision with reality, the country, and the Congress, could become very angry indeed with the Court.

Already, of course, the Court has infuriated a lot of people, and this widespread fury is reflected in Congress. Every year new measures are introduced in Congress to curb the powers of the Court or to reverse its decisions. So far, a showdown between the Court and the Congress has been averted, and the annoyance of Congress has been expressed in such picayune ways as denying to the Court the extra law clerks the Justices badly need to help them carry their case load. But a showdown could come.

Article III of the Constitution, which creates the Supreme Court, also gives—or seems to give—the Congress the right to curb the powers of the Court by a simple majority vote. Article III gives the Court "appellate Jurisdiction, both as to Law and Fact," but it adds ominously, "with such exceptions, and under such regulations as the Congress shall make."

If these words mean what they seem to mean, a majority of Congress could in effect castrate the Supreme Court, by denying it jurisdiction in any area the Congress chose. The matter has been tested only once, in the post-Civil War period, when Congress forbade the Court to hear appeals in habeas corpus cases. On that occasion the Court complied, but the test was inconclusive.

There could have been a decisive test—and a showdown between the Court and Congress—in 1964. The one-man-one-vote rulings of the Court, starting in 1962, infuriated many powerful members of Congress. Previously the Court has sedulously avoided the "political thicket" (Frankfurter's phrase) of legislative reapportionment. It had been the exclusive province of the state legislatures to determine their own composition. But in 1962 the Court leaped into the thicket. Thereafter, in a series of split decisions, the Court ordered that both houses of a state legislature must be apportioned according to population. In 1964 the Court also ordered that the U.S. House of Representatives itself must more accurately reflect the population balance within the states, thus adding insult to injury. This series of decisions was widely interpreted as a direct challenge by the judiciary to the legislative branch of government.

The decisions were based on the "equal-protection" clause of the Fourteenth Amendment. Outraged critics pointed out that, if the Court's reasoning was correct, the United States Senate itself did not offer the citizenry "equal protection." In 1964 the U.S. House of Representatives voted, 218 to 175, to order the Court to keep hands off legislative apportionment. If the Senate had voted the same way, a conclusive test of Article III, and a showdown between Congress and the Court, would have been inevitable. The showdown was avoided, thanks in part to Senator Everett Dirksen, one of the Court's bitterest critics. Dirksen sponsored a constitutional amendment to reverse the Court's one-man-one-vote ruling. When the amendment fell seven votes short of the required two-thirds in the Senate, the issue became a dead letter, with the net effect that the Court's one-man-one-vote decision stands unchallenged.

It may be that there never will be a conclusive test. A majority of the members of both houses of Congress are lawyers, and though many lawyers are critical of the Court, there is in the legal profession an inbred respect for the Court's prestige and authority, rather like a priest's inbred respect for the Holy See. Congress would have to be very angry indeed to attempt to castrate the Court, and thus invite a direct test of power. Such a test of power would certainly result in a major constitutional crisis. For the Court would have to decide whether the action of Congress to deny the Court "appellate jurisdiction," as provided by the Constitution, was constitutional. The Court would thus be required to sit in judgment on itself.

Aside from the reluctance of Congress to challenge the Court directly, there is another reason for hoping that a constitutional crisis will be avoided. The Court, as Mr. Dooley pointed out, is in the healthy habit of reading the election returns. In other words, there are pragmatic men on the Court—the Chief Justice is one, and Abe Fortas is another—who are capable of sensing and responding to the political climate in which the Court operates.

The Court can always duck the really hot issues by refusing to review appeals, and by other techniques of masterly cunctation, and it often has done just that. The school desegregation decision was ducked and delayed for years before 1954, for example. It seems a good bet that for the immediate future a majority of the Justices will try to avoid making Congress and the country any angrier at the Supreme Court than they are already. This is why another period of hibernation may be in the offing.

It is easy to see why so many people are, and almost

always have been, angry at the Supreme Court. Great political, social, and financial issues are at stake in Supreme Court decisions, of course, and somebody's ox is always getting gored. But quite aside from that, there is always something infuriating about the assumption of superior wisdom.

Judge Learned Hand once said that a judge "must preserve his authority by cloaking himself in the majesty of an overshadowing past." The Supreme Court has learned that lesson well. The rather phony grandeur of the Court's physical setting—all that marble, all those frescoes of ancient lawmakers—is so obviously designed to awe the simple peasants that it invites a healthy iconoclasm.

A certain air of infallibility is at the heart of the Court's mystique. The Court's own record is the best proof of fallibility. According to the count of one Justice, the Court has reversed itself on major issues no less than 115 times—a record in mind-changing the most capricious lady might envy. Thus it is tempting at first blush to dismiss the Supreme Court as a pack of overage politicians and legal eagles masquerading as lawgivers and Delphic oracles.

And yet there *is* a certain grandeur about the Supreme Court of the United States all the same. There is something about the Supreme Court which, like the Presidency, seems to add a cubit to a man's stature, in defiance of the Biblical maxim. Anyone who (like this reporter) has talked seriously for the first time to a number of the Justices comes away impressed in spite of himself.

For here are nine men, for the most part men of real distinction and great attainments, who do really concern themselves deeply about such matters as whether Linda Brown should have the right to go to the Sumner School, or whether Ernesto Miranda got a fair shake from the Phoenix cops. The process of deciding such matters, Justice Brennan says, "can be a lonely, troubling experience for fallible human beings." Repeatedly, the result of the process is that the Justices reach diametrically opposite conclusions. But at least they really do care about the answer to Chief Justice Warren's favorite question—"Is it *fair?*"—and they do try hard to find the right answer to that question.

They also really do care about the Fourteenth Amendment and the Bill of Rights—those "stately admonitions," as Judge Hand called them, "the more imperious because inscrutable," which are the bulwarks of the American citizen's personal freedom.

In a time of riot, rebellion, violence, and war, it is good that there are nine powerful men, who, however they may differ in detail about their meaning, care deeply about these "stately admonitions," and mean to see that they are observed.

12

THE ERA OF THE INSOLUBLE

Perhaps we'd better learn to run a little faster.

....

Jean Monnet once remarked to my brother, Joseph Alsop, that Dwight Eisenhower had the one indispensable attribute of a President. Asked what that was, Monnet replied in a word: "Luck."

It may be that Lyndon Johnson lacks this necessary attribute. For a time, he seemed to have it. He was lucky in the caliber of the advisers he inherited from his predecessor; lucky in his opponent in 1964; lucky in the makeup of the Eighty-ninth Congress, which gave him the first sure Presidential majority in a generation. For a year and a half after President Kennedy's murder, Johnson seemed to have a political Midas touch—everything seemed to go right for him. Then, suddenly, everything began to go wrong for him.

Everything began to go wrong in the late spring and early summer of 1965, when the President made his fateful decision to commit American combat troops to Vietnam. With that decision, Lyndon Johnson, like the Ancient Mariner, shot his Albatross. But it may be that the President's worst piece of luck lay in becoming President at precisely the moment when the problems confronting the United States became insoluble.

The idol of Lyndon Johnson's young manhood, Franklin Roosevelt, faced very great problems—mass unemployment at home, Fascist aggression abroad. Both problems were solved in the end. They were solved by two instruments —money and power. The United States now disposes of more money, and more power, than ever before in its history, or the history of any other nation. But money and power no longer seem to be enough.

The Ancient Mariner, after he shot his Albatross, was plagued by fiends. There are two fiends that plague Lyndon Johnson—and the rest of us. They are the war in Vietnam and the threat of race war at home. Beside these two problems all the others which trouble the United States fade into insignificance. It ought to be possible to deal effectively with both of them, by using the familiar instruments of money and power. But it doesn't seem to be possible.

"You white liberals always think you can buy us off," Dan Watts, editor of *The Liberator*, organ of the Black Power movement, said to me after the Newark and Detroit riots in 1967. "You think you can toss us a bit of bread—money for schools and housing and like that—and then we'll be nice little Toms. You know something? Those cats in the streets in Newark and Detroit—they weren't lacking for bread. What they wanted was power, baby, black power, and you better believe it."

"Bread," of course, is Negro slang for money, and if anything is clear by now, it is that the racial crisis will be resolved, if it can be resolved at all, not by bread alone. No sensible man can any longer doubt that money, and lots of it, is going to have to be spent by the white majority to improve the situation of the Negro minority. But great sums have already been spent, on education, and housing, and the problems of poverty which are supposed to lie at the root of the racial crisis. And all the while the racial crisis has grown steadily more malignant. The riots in the ghettos have become more ferocious, and the chasm of misunderstanding, fear, and hatred between the races has grown deeper. Money is not the answer any more—certainly not the whole answer.

Power does not seem to be the answer either. The immense weight of American power has been brought to bear in Vietnam—half a million men, unlimited air power and fire power, tens of billions of dollars—and still an acceptable settlement, not to mention the victory which Americans have been taught to regard as their due, eludes us.

Perhaps American power will ultimately impose something like peace on Vietnam, rather the way a Japanese Sumo wrestler defeats a smaller opponent by crushing him by sheer weight. The sheer weight of American power may exhaust the Communists in the end. But that end is not in sight as these words are written. And what happens when American power is withdrawn?

The time could come when the race crisis could tear Washington apart, in the most literal sense. As this is written, Washington has thankfully escaped a full-scale riot, although in recent years there have been at least three near-riots. Meanwhile, in the psychological and political sense, it is Vietnam that is tearing Washington apart.

It is Vietnam that has poisoned personal relationships and destroyed old friendships. Above all, it is Vietnam that has eroded the basic self-confidence of the Washington political community. That self-confidence used to mark Washington off from other world capitals.

Perhaps London had the same sort of self-confidence in the era of Pax Britannica. Even in postwar London there were sunset glimmerings of the old self-assurance, but they faded fast. In Paris the arrogance of de Gaulle, like the over-assertiveness of a child, is a mark, not of confidence, but of confidence lost in the defeat of 1940. In Moscow, faith in the eventual achievement of the "great goal of Communism on earth" has become long since a *pro forma* ideological genuflection, like the religious faith of the more cynical medieval popes. Only in Washington was it possible to find, in the postwar years, a genuine conviction, unquestioned, unconscious, that the country of which Washington is the capital could do, and would do, whatever really needed to be done.

That conviction underlay the early postwar period of policy-making, the era of the Truman Doctrine, the Marshall Plan, the beginnings of NATO—the era which may yet see the ex-haberdasher from Independence listed by the historians among the great Presidents. In that period it never really occurred even to Truman's most vociferous opponents to doubt that, if the United States decided to revive the economy of all Western Europe, for example, or to defend Europe in case of war, the thing could and would be done.

This self-confidence has been deeply eroded. And this erosion of confidence is what chiefly distinguishes the Washington of today from the Washington of twenty years ago, or ten years ago, or even five years ago.

In a great many ways—a rather surprising number of ways—the Washington of today is very much like those other Washingtons of the recent and less recent past. Because of the nature of the single industry which supports the town, Washington has in the nature of things a shifting population. Presidents come and go, and so do Senators, Representatives, department heads, and others dependent, directly or indirectly, on the whims of the electorate.

But in its substructure, in the permanent government Establishment, among the in-and-outers of the legal profession, and in the press, Political Washington has a surprisingly stable population. Even among those ostensibly returned to their native heaths by the electorate, a surprising number remain stubbornly in Washington, as lobbyists, or in patronage jobs in the executive branch, or living on pensions or private incomes.

"All, all are gone, the old familiar faces," Charles Lamb lamented. If Lamb had lived in Washington, he could have dropped in at the Metropolitan Club at lunchtime (or perhaps in his case the more intellectual Cosmos Club) and he would have found plenty of old familiar faces.

In this and in other ways, the private life of the citizen of Political Washington is much as it has always been. But it is different in one way. Exuberant, loud-shouting political argument used to be a chief entertainment in Washington. That is no longer so, for the war in Vietnam, as soon as it is, inevitably, mentioned, inevitably produces bitter rows and recriminations which are anything but entertaining. This is a symptom of the way in which the old, carefree self-confidence which used to distinguish Washington from other capitals has been replaced by uneasiness, bitterness, and self-doubt, which hang over the city like a noxious fug. Old friends, groping through the fug, suddenly find that they have become enemies. Washington, in short, is an unhappy place.

Washington has been uneasy and unhappy before, of course. There have been at least four times since the last war ended when serious and sensible men feared that a war which would destroy Washington along with most of the rest of the world might be about to begin. That fear was real when Stalin blockaded Berlin; when the North Koreans attacked; when Khrushchev threatened to throw the Western powers out of Berlin; when the Soviets placed nuclear-capable missiles in Cuba. But those other times of crisis had a unifying effect—after all, the bombs would drop on everybody.

Washington was unhappy, deeply unhappy, in the days and weeks after the murder of President Kennedy. But that simple human grief, which was universally shared, also had a unifying effect.

Washington was also unhappy during the period when Joe McCarthy—rather mysteriously in retrospect—succeeded in terrorizing Political Washington. But curiously enough, the McCarthy terror also had a unifying effect. For after a few months of McCarthy, no one in Political Washington—or no one a sensible man would care to break bread with—had any real doubt that McCarthy was a totally irresponsible demagogue and a compulsive (if oddly compelling) liar. To sensible and self-respecting Washingtonians, McCarthy was the common enemy.

There is nothing at all unifying about the twin evils that plague the United States in this election year. Many Americans, no doubt, are only dimly aware of the race crisis and the war, but the political emotions of the country are concentrated on Political Washington as the rays of the sun are concentrated on a central point by a magnifying glass. As a result, The Center has rarely been a more unhappy place—certainly not since the last war ended, probably not since the Hoover days, perhaps never.

The erosion of confidence and the sense of disintegration which have characterized Washington increasingly since 1965 were accentuated by the departure of McNamara. After seven years, McNamara, even to his critics, had come to seem a permanent and reassuring symbol of intelligent and dedicated public service. McNamara himself certainly partook of Washington's general erosion of confidence and sense of disintegration. One of his favorite poems, to which he returned increasingly in the last years of his Pentagon reign, was by W. B. Yeats:

> Turning and turning in the widening gyre
> The falcon cannot hear the falconer;
> Things fall apart; the centre cannot hold;
> Mere anarchy is loosed upon the world,
> The blood-dimmed tide is loosed, and everywhere
> The ceremony of innocence is drowned;
> The best lack all conviction, while the worst
> Are full of passionate intensity.

"The centre cannot hold"—the words well express Washington's deep sense of anxiety, the sick feeling of having lost control, at home and abroad. But perhaps there is something usefully corrective in the Washington sickness, as there is in many illnesses. Perhaps The Center needed a corrective reminder that, although it is undoubtedly the political center of the United States, it is not the center of the universe.

The self-confidence of postwar Washington—the feeling that the United States could do whatever needed to be done—was exhilarating, but no doubt it was also dangerously deluded. Perhaps this country, in its new role as the world's greatest power, had to be taught two lessons: that the exercise of great power is accompanied by agony, and that the power of even a very powerful nation is limited.

Despite its unhappiness, moreover, Washington still remains in many ways a reassuring place. The war in Vietnam has torn the city apart, and produced much disingenuousness and even downright dishonesty on both sides in the process. But at least it has produced no new McCarthy, and the debate, however bitter, has been generally conducted within the ground rules of the American political system.

That system is peculiar, irrational, monstrously complex and cumbersome. Yet it is also remarkably adaptable and flexible. It responds, slowly but inevitably, to the realities of the national situation. President Johnson's decision to "watch the Pedernales roll by" after his current term is a tribute to the system's mysterious adaptability.

The President could almost certainly have bulled and beaten his way to the nomination, and he might very probably have been re-elected. But the price in what he calls "divisiveness" would have been very high. The horror of failure which is so deep a part of his nature certainly influenced his decision to pull out. But so far, to be fair to the man, did that rather old-fashioned patriotism which is also deeply part of him. Lyndon Johnson knew that his candidacy might tear the country apart, and could not bear that prospect.

Lyndon Johnson's withdrawal makes it possible for the system somehow to produce the men and means to deal with those fiends that plague us, race and the war. Those twin evils have served to obscure certain great and real achievements.

For all our troubles, the fact remains that the average American is better off by more than 25 per cent than he was as recently as 1960. To the young and idealistic, that statistic may seem to reflect America's crass materialism. To anyone who remembers the Great Depression, with its mass unemployment and misery, it is an immensely reassuring statistic. The American Government now has the will to prevent a recurrence of economic misery and if the prophets of the New Economics are right, it also has the means. Surely that is a great good to be weighed against such great evils as the race crisis and the war.

Meanwhile, to revert to Frank Kent's peculiar tale about the Baltimore judge, the sons-of-bitches haven't quite caught up with us yet. But they do seem to be gaining on us. Perhaps we'd better learn to run a little faster.

INDEX